Robustness Tests for Quantitat

The uncertainty researchers face in specifying tens the validity of their inferences. In regression analyses of observational data the "true model" remains unknown and researchers face a choice between plausible alternative specifications. Robustness testing allows researchers to explore the stability of their main estimates to plausible variations in model specifications. This highly accessible book presents the logic of robustness testing, provides an operational definition of robustness that can be applied in all quantitative research and introduces readers to diverse types of robustness tests. Focusing on each dimension of model uncertainty in separate chapters, the authors provide a systematic overview of existing tests and develop many new ones. Whether it be uncertainty about the population or sample, measurement, the set of explanatory variables and their functional form, causal or temporal heterogeneity, effect dynamics or spatial dependence, this book provides guidance and offers tests that researchers from across the social sciences can employ in their own research.

ERIC NEUMAYER is Professor of Environment and Development and Pro-Director Faculty Development at the London School of Economics and Political Science (LSE).

THOMAS PLÜMPER is Professor of Quantitative Social Research at the Vienna University of Economics and Business.

Both authors have published in highly ranked journals including the *American Journal of Public Health, Annals of the American Association of Geographers, International Organization, Political Analysis* and *World Development*.

Methodological Tools in the Social Sciences

EDITORS
Paul M. Kellstedt, Texas A&M University
Guy D. Whitten, Texas A&M University

The Methodological Tools in the Social Sciences series is comprised of accessible, stand-alone treatments of methodological topics encountered by social science researchers. The focus is on practical instruction for applying methods, for getting the methods right. The authors are leading researchers able to provide extensive examples of applications of the methods covered in each book. The books in the series strike a balance between the underlying theory and the implementation of the methods. They are accessible and discursive, and make technical code and data available to aid in replication and extension of the results, as well as enabling scholars to apply these methods to their own substantive problems. They also provide accessible advice on how to present results obtained from using the relevant methods.

Robustness Tests for Quantitative Research

Eric Neumayer
London School of Economics and Political Science

Thomas Plümper
Vienna University of Economics and Business

CAMBRIDGE
UNIVERSITY PRESS

CAMBRIDGE
UNIVERSITY PRESS

University Printing House, Cambridge CB2 8BS, United Kingdom

One Liberty Plaza, 20th Floor, New York, NY 10006, USA

477 Williamstown Road, Port Melbourne, VIC 3207, Australia

4843/24, 2nd Floor, Ansari Road, Daryaganj, Delhi – 110002, India

79 Anson Road, #06–04/06, Singapore 079906

Cambridge University Press is part of the University of Cambridge.

It furthers the University's mission by disseminating knowledge in the pursuit of education, learning, and research at the highest international levels of excellence.

www.cambridge.org
Information on this title: www.cambridge.org/9781108415392
DOI: 10.1017/9781108233590

© Eric Neumayer and Thomas Plümper 2017

First published 2017

Printed in the United Kingdom by Clays, St Ives plc

A catalogue record for this publication is available from the British Library.

Library of Congress Cataloging-in-Publication Data
Names: Neumayer, Eric, 1970– author. | Plümper, Thomas, author.
Title: Robustness tests : causal inference with observational data / Eric Neumayer, London School of Economics and Political Science, Thomas Plümper.
Description: Cambridge, United Kingdom ; New York, NY, USA : University Printing House, [2017] | Includes bibliographical references and index.
Identifiers: LCCN 2017012398| ISBN 9781108415392 (hardback : alk. paper) | ISBN 9781108401388 (paperback : alk. paper)
Subjects: LCSH: Robust statistics. | Social sciences – Methodology.
Classification: LCC HA31.5 .N48 2017 | DDC 519.5/4–dc23
LC record available at https://lccn.loc.gov/2017012398

ISBN 978-1-108-41539-2 Hardback
ISBN 978-1-108-40138-8 Paperback

Contents

Figures

Tables

Robustness Tests

Population Definition and Sample Tests		
Name	**Action**	**Pages**
Population boundary test	a) Includes observations that may not belong to population	94
	b) Excludes observations that may belong to population	
	c) Structured permutation variants	
Bootstrap test	Resamples with replacement	95
Jackknife test	Drops one or more observations at a time	95
Core group test	Includes only cases known to be in the population	97
Outlier elimination test	Drops "outliers"	97
Cross-validation test	Draws new sample	100
Selection test	Assumes cases are selected	101
Stratification test	a) Over-samples under-represented cases robustness limit variant	103
	b) Under-samples over-represented cases robustness limit variant	
Interpolation test	Replaces missings by interpolated values	105
Out-of-sample prediction test	Replaces missings by theory-based out of sample predictions	106
Multiple imputation test	Replaces missings by multiply imputed values	106

Concept Validity and Measurement Tests		
Name	**Action**	**Pages**
Alternative proxy test	Replaces one proxy variable with another	118
Principal component test	Combines multiple proxies into single principal component	118
Randomized components test	Randomizes weights of components of composite variable	119
Principal component jitter test	Adds "jitter" to weights of principal component	120
Rescaling test	Changes the scale of a variable	124
Measurement error injection test	Adds "artificial" measurement error	124
	Robustness limit variant	
Re-categorization test	Changes the assigned categories of categorical variables	127

Explanatory and Omitted Variables Tests		
Name	**Action**	**Pages**
Explanatory variables test	Adds and/or removes right-hand-side variables	133
Between-variation test	Stepwise reduces the between-variation in the data	136
Groupwise fixed-effects test	Reduces the between-variation by including group dummies for similar cases	138
	Robustness limit variant	
Correlated artificial variable test	Adds artificial variable with defined properties	140
Spatial-error test	Adds spatial-error variable	141

Functional Form Tests		
Name	**Action**	**Pages**
Higher degree polynomial test	Relaxes the functional form by estimating a higher-degree polynomial model	149
Semi-parametric test	Relaxes the functional form by estimating a semi-parametric model	154
Functional form break test	Allows for different effect strength at break point	155

Causal Heterogeneity and Context Conditionality Tests		
Name	**Action**	**Pages**
Bootstrap test	Tests the homogeneity assumption by resampling with replacement	162
Sample split test	Tests the homogeneity assumption by splitting the sample	162
Groupwise jackknife test	Tests the homogeneity assumption by groupwise dropping cases	163
Unit-specific effect test	Relaxes the homogeneity assumption by estimating case-specific effects	163
Group-specific effect test	Relaxes the homogeneity assumption by estimating group-specific effects	163
Random coefficients test	Allows random variation in effects	165
Multilevel test	Allows clustered variation in effects	165
Chow test of group heterogeneity	Relaxes the homogeneity assumption by interacting variables with group dummies	165
	Randomized permutation variant	
Conditionality test	Relaxes the homogeneity assumption by estimating an interaction effects model	168
Non-linear conditionality test	Relaxes the linear-symmetry assumption of interaction effects model	170

Temporal Heterogeneity Tests		
Name	**Action**	**Pages**
Trended effect test	Interacts variables with measure of time	182
Period fixed-effects test	Allows for unobserved time-varying heterogeneity	183
Temporal splines test	Allows for unobserved time-varying heterogeneity	183
Chow test of temporal heterogeneity	Interacts variables with dummies for shock or break periods	185
	Structured permutation variant	

Effect Dynamics Tests		
Name	**Action**	**Pages**
Temporal aggregation test	Changes the definition of periods	196
Dynamic specification test	Replaces static baseline with dynamic specification	197
Dynamic constraints test	Relaxes dynamic constraints	198
Alternative dynamic specification test	Replaces baseline dynamic specification	198
Effect onset test	Changes the assumption on lags and leads	199
Effect duration test	Changes the assumption on the duration of an effect	199
Temporal function form test	Changes the evolution of effect strength over periods	199
Random coefficients dynamics test	Allows for random variation in dynamics across units	203
Unit-specific dynamics test	Allows for unit-specific dynamics	203
Group-specific dynamics test	Allows for group-specific dynamics	203
Dynamic interaction effect test	Models conditional dynamics	203

Spatial Correlation and Dependence Tests		
Name	**Action**	**Pages**
Spatial specification test	Allows for spatial correlation	214
Spatial-error test	Controls for spatially correlated error processes	220
Alternative connectivity test	Varies the assumed mechanism causing spatial dependence	221
Connectivity functional form test	Varies the functional form of the connectivity variable	223
Heterogeneous exposure test	Allows for heterogeneity in exposure to spatial stimulus	223
Heterogeneous responsiveness test	Allows for heterogeneity in response to spatial stimulus	226
Spatial placebo variable test	Includes a placebo spatial-effect variable with randomized weights	226

Acknowledgments

This book provides a systematic foundation and justification for robustness testing as a way to improve the validity of causal inferences based on regression analysis of observational data. We define and operationalize robustness, and we make it measureable on a scale that ranges from 0 to 1. Not every social scientist will like the fact that we institutionalize a term, and many will disagree with our definition of robustness. This is very much intended. Definitions are not correct, they can only be useful. We believe in the usefulness of our definition. The same goes for the large number of robustness tests that we propose in part 2 of the book.

We have come a long way since we began the robustness project in 2012. We were helped along by the fact that the UK's Economic and Social Research Council (ESRC) did not have a program of funding risky but potentially transformative research agendas and that corresponding research proposals were not likely to be accepted by the ESRC's standard review process. As a consequence, the ESRC established a funding scheme for potentially "transformative research" and invented a fundamentally different refereeing process in which UK universities were only allowed to submit up to two proposals. Our project was successfully submitted through the University of Essex, for which we thank its then Pro-Vice Chancellor Research, Professor David Sanders.

We presented parts and preliminary findings of the project on various occasions: the annual conferences of the European Political Science Association in 2012 (Berlin), 2013 (Barcelona), 2014 (Edinburgh), 2015 (Vienna), and 2016 (Brussels), the annual meetings of the American Political Science Association in 2014 (Washington D.C.) and 2015 (San Francisco), the PSA Quantitative Network Conference at the University of Oxford in 2015 (thanks to Steve Fisher and Andreas Murr for organizing the meeting and inviting our presentation). Our incredible friends in Texas were so kind as to give us the opportunity to present central concepts of the book at the University of Texas at Austin's Research Methodology Conference organized and hosted by Chris Wlezien. We thank Harold Clarke, Guy Whitten, Stephen Jessee, Bob Luskin, Tse-Min Lin, Chris Wlezien, Marianne Stewart, Zach Elkins, Mike Findley, Randy Stephenson, and Robert Moser for comments and stimulating discussions. We also thank Guy Whitten for organizing the annual "come to Texas when it's cold in Europe" workshop at Texas A&M. Guy gave us the opportunity to present central aspects of the book in a special workshop.

The ESRC transformative research grant gave us the opportunity to organize a workshop on robustness testing at the University of Cologne. Many thanks to Andre Kaiser for hosting the conference, and to Adel Daoud, Alexander Schmidt-Catran, Andre Kaiser, Cameron Wimpy, Daniel Stegmüller, Guy Whitten, Holger Döring, Katja Möhring, Laron Williams, Luke Keele, Mark Kayser, Ole Ostendorf, Philip Manow, Ray Duch, Richard Traunmüller, Simon Hug, Thomas Gschwend, Rene Lindstädt, and Thomas König for presenting papers at the conference and for stimulating debates. Finally, we wish to thank John Haslam and Stephanie Taylor at Cambridge University Press for their support.

Numerous colleagues have read and commented on various parts at various stages of the project. In alphabetical order we want to mention: Dominik Hangartner, Dirk Junge, Bob Luskin, Alex Quiroz, Tom Scotto, Daniel Stegmüller, and Richard Traunmüller. Special thanks to Dirk Junge who helped in programming some of the tests proposed in this book.

1 Introduction

Regression analysis of observational data has always been and, we predict, will remain at the heart of the social sciences methodological toolkit. The major problem with regression analysis of observational data, broadly defined,[1] is that in order to produce unbiased and generalizable estimates, the estimation model must be correctly specified, the estimator must be unbiased given the data at hand, and the estimation sample must be randomly drawn from a well-specified population.

Social scientists know this ideal is unachievable. Empirical models of real world phenomena are hardly ever – we would say: never – correctly specified. Better theory, diagnostic econometric tests, other methodological advice, thoughtful sampling, experience, and even common sense can all help in the art of specifying an estimation model and creating a sample of observations for analysis. However, the world of interest to social scientists, human nature and the interaction of human beings at all levels, is too complex for social scientists ever to achieve the ideal of a correct model specification – a specification that closely matches the true data-generating process. We argue that given the limited information in data typically available to social scientists, social scientists should not even aspire to develop a model that closely matches the true data-generating process. Instead, based on the principle of parsimony, the optimal model specification trades off simplicity against generality, thereby ignoring many complexities. Empirical models cannot, at the same time, simplify and capture the true data-generating process. Rather, for each research question, there will be an optimal simplification of the true data-generating process and social scientists should use the entire theoretical and methodological toolkit to specify their baseline model as well as they can. Yet, there is no guarantee that the optimal baseline model is sufficiently similar to the "true" model to allow valid inferences with great certainty.

---

1 By regression analysis we mean all kinds of generalized linear and non-linear estimation techniques like logit, probit, Poisson, negative binomial regression, survival analysis, and so on, including semi-parametric techniques.

Robustness testing offers one and perhaps *the* answer to model uncertainty – the uncertainty researchers face as to which model specification provides the optimal trade-off between simplicity and generality. In multiple dimensions and in a quasi-infinite number of ways in each of these dimensions, a model requires choices to be made – specification choices that, even if well justified, could have plausibly been made differently.

Robustness testing allows researchers to explore the stability of their estimates to alternative plausible model specifications. In other words: robustness tests analyze the variation in estimates resulting from model uncertainty. To be sure, model uncertainty is but one source potentially leading to wrong inferences. Other important inferential threats result from sampling variation and from lack of perfect fit between the assumptions an estimator makes and the true data-generating process. In our view, model uncertainty has the highest potential to invalidate inferences, which makes robustness testing the most important way in which empirical researchers can improve the validity of their inferences.

Robustness testing reduces the effect of model uncertainty on inferences. Robustness testing does not miraculously transform uncertain and potentially invalid inferences into inferences that are valid with certainty. Rather, it reveals the true uncertainty of point estimates – the dependence of estimates on model specification. Importantly, robustness testing challenges the established logic of social science methodology: instead of trying to achieve the unachievable – to perfectly fit the model onto the data-generating process – the logic of robustness testing accepts the uncertainty of model specification and asks to what degree estimated estimates and ultimately inferences depend on model specifications.

Analyzing the influence of model specification on estimates is not the only way in which robustness testing can improve the validity of inferences, however. Even when estimates are not robust, researchers can analyze the causes for the lack of robustness. In this way, robustness testing can result in estimation models that have a higher chance of providing valid inferences. All tests can help in the individual and collective process of learning even if, and sometimes particularly if, estimates are found to be non-robust, as this opens up the challenge and opportunity of new research. Research agendas profit from identifying the robustness limits of empirical findings.

But not all is good. Unfortunately, the current practice of robustness testing does not live up to its full potential. Social scientists like to include robustness tests to improve their chances of getting their papers past reviewers and accepted by editors, not because they intend to explore the consequences of uncertainty about their model specification and learn about the robustness limits of their analysis. Practically all reported tests conclude that findings are indeed robust to changes in model specification even if few authors communicate to their readers what they mean by robustness. Yet, if we do not know what robustness means we cannot know what it means that results are robust.

1.1 CONTRIBUTION

This book contributes to the emerging field of robustness test methodology in three important ways. Firstly, we show that causal complexity of the phenomena that social scientists study imposes severe limits on inferential validity. We explain why all models need to simplify and therefore cannot closely capture the extremely complex true data-generating process. This generates uncertainty as to which model specification provides the optimal simplification and consequently uncertainty about the validity of inferences based on a preferred model or baseline model, as we call it.

As a second contribution, we develop the logic of robustness testing as the key way in which empirical researchers can tackle model uncertainty and thereby improve the validity of their inferences. We offer an operational definition of robustness and a typology of robustness tests. While a majority of social scientists seems to understand robustness in terms of statistical significance, we propose a definition of robustness that draws on effect size stability. As we discuss in chapter 4, our definition has a number of useful properties. It can be flexibly applied not just to frequentist analyses but also to Bayesian techniques. Having said this, all our examples use frequentist estimation methods. Still, robustness testing is all about model specification and not about a particular way of estimation. As we argue in chapter 6, no single methodology permits the formulation of perfectly valid inferences. Every design, procedure or estimation technique warrants subjecting its results to plausible alternative specifications to explore whether these generate sufficiently similar (robust) estimates. Exploring robustness tests for alternatives to regression analysis of observational data is beyond the scope of this book. We leave this important aspect of robustness testing to future research.

As a third contribution, for each dimension of model specification we show what the main uncertainties and therefore inferential threats are. We collect and systematize existing robustness tests that address these uncertainties but we also develop many new tests – or at least tests that we have not seen in the literature before. In this respect, this book seeks to demonstrate that the world of robustness tests is rich and diverse – much richer indeed than the limited number of tests that social scientists have used in the past suggests.

In sum, this book seeks to increase the take-up of robustness tests and improve the practice of robustness testing in the social sciences. It aspires to

overcome the narrow focus of most empirical researchers on model variation tests and open their eyes to the great potential that other types of
robustness tests offer. If it fulfils these two objectives, it will significantly
improve the validity of regression analyses of observational data.

1.2 OVERVIEW

We divide the book into two main parts. The first part discusses the theoretical and methodological foundations of robustness testing. In chapter 2, we
clarify why causal complexity of the social world renders the quest to specify
the correct model futile and requires all estimation models to simplify the
complex data-generating process. Causal inferences will always remain
uncertain and robustness tests explore the impact of model uncertainty on
the validity of inferences, which can improve if it can be shown that results
are robust independently of certain model specification choices taken.

Chapter 3 proposes a systematic approach to robustness testing in four
steps – specify a baseline model that in the eye of the researcher optimally
balances simplicity versus generality; identify potentially arbitrary model
specification choices; specify robustness test models based on alternative
plausible specification choices; and estimate the degree of robustness of the
baseline model's estimate with respect to the robustness test model. With
multiple dimensions of model uncertainty and multiple specification choices
in each dimension, robustness is also multidimensional. We argue that
robustness is best explored for each test separately instead of averaged
over all robustness test models. We suggest three main goals and aims of
robustness testing. Beyond its central focus of exploring the robustness of
estimates, these tests allow identifying the limits of robustness and they spur
learning and future research, particularly from specification choices that
suggest a lack of robustness of the baseline model estimate.

Chapter 4 on the concept of robustness lies at the very heart of the book's
first part. Here we define robustness as the degree to which an estimate using
a plausible alternative model specification supports the baseline model's
estimated effect of interest. We propose a quantifiable measure of robustness
that varies from 0 to 1 and defend our continuous concept of robustness
against a dichotomous arbitrary distinction into robust versus non-robust.
We argue why our definition of robustness as stability in effect size is superior
to conceptions of robustness as stability in the direction of an effect and its
statistical significance. We introduce partial robustness, which becomes relevant in all non-linear models and even in linear models if analyses depart from
linear, unconditional or homogeneous effects. In these cases, a baseline model
estimate can be partially robust, that is, can be robust or more robust for some
observations but less robust or non-robust for other observations.

Five types of robustness tests are distinguished in chapter 5: model variation, randomized permutation, structured permutation, robustness limit, and placebo tests. We discuss their relative strengths and weaknesses as well as the conditions in which they are appropriately used and refer to examples from leading political science journals in which they have been employed. Importantly, the different types of robustness are best seen as complementary, not substitutes for each other. In fact, the three main aims and goals of robustness testing – exploring the robustness of estimates, identifying the limits of robustness and learning from findings – positively require the use of multiple types of robustness tests.

Chapter 6 argues that there are no alternatives to robustness testing. Model specification tests and model selection algorithms cannot find the one "true" model specification. Model averaging across a huge number of specifications will include many models that are implausibly specified. Other research designs represent alternatives to regression analysis of observational data but, since their results are also based on a large number of specification choices that could have been undertaken differently, they too warrant robustness testing. While this book focuses on tests for regression analysis of observational data, we are confident that many proponents of case selection research designs, "identification techniques," and social science experiments will find the logic of robustness testing appealing and will want to adapt some of the tests we suggest for their own purposes.

The second part of the book analyzes what we regard as the most important dimensions of model specification, identifies the causes of uncertainty for each dimension, and suggests robustness tests for tackling these model uncertainties. Examples illustrate many of these tests with real world data analyses. We start with the population and sample in chapter 7, which, because of the relentless focus on unbiased estimation (internal validity), has received little attention. Scholars are uncertain about the population for which a theory claims validity and uncertain which population the results from the analysis of any particular sample can be generalized to. We include the issue of missing observations as an aspect of sample uncertainty, which threatens both internal and external validity.

Hypothesis testing requires data and data need to be collected. Social scientists refer to the act of collecting data as measurement. Measuring the social world constitutes a more difficult task than measuring the natural world. In the social world, many or perhaps most concepts of interest cannot be directly observed. These unobservable factors need to be captured with proxy variables. Chapter 8 addresses uncertainty about the validity and measurement of social science concepts.

In contrast to both population and sample uncertainty and measurement uncertainty, if one dimension of model specification has attracted much attention in the extant literature, it is the set of explanatory variables. Chapter 9 argues that including all variables of relevance to the data-generating process and excluding all irrelevant ones is impossible. In the vast majority of analyses, omitted variable bias is inevitable. Standard econometric fixes can do more harm than good. We thus suggest alternative and more flexible ways of dealing with uncertainty about potentially confounding unobservable and unobserved variables.

Linearity is the default functional form assumption and, if combined with robustness tests, not a bad choice given the need to simplify (chapter 10). Similarly, while the social world is marked by causal heterogeneity and context conditionality, the assumption of homogeneous and unconditional effects can be justified as a necessary simplification (chapter 11). Nevertheless, researchers are uncertain about when they need to deviate from these simplifying assumptions and robustness tests can explore if the baseline model's estimates and the inferences derived from them depend on these assumptions. Both dimensions of model uncertainty are closely linked since misspecified functional forms can erroneously suggest causal heterogeneity or context conditionality, and vice versa.

Chapter 12 discusses temporal heterogeneity, defined as variation in the effect strength of a variable over time. Temporal heterogeneity can be caused by structural change in the form of trends, shocks or structural breaks. Parameter homogeneity across time, the standard operating assumption of the vast majority of cross-sectional time-series analysis, seems a strong assumption to make in datasets covering several decades. Such samples cover a long enough period of time for disruptive events to have taken place or simply for actors to change how they respond to stimuli. Robustness tests set one or more of the estimated parameters free for all or a subset of cases, allowing the parameters to vary over time.

We turn to a problem related to temporal heterogeneity in chapter 13: dynamics. Researchers typically reduce dynamics to employing techniques that eliminate the serial correlation of errors and, almost haphazardly, impose simple and rigid dynamics on the effects of variables. However, the true data-generating process most likely contains more complex effect dynamics. If researchers strive to capture these dynamics, they need to model the onset and duration of effects and the functional form of effects over time and consider the possibility of dynamic heterogeneity across cases. Robustness tests either relax the constraints that the baseline model specification imposes on the dynamics of effects or model the dynamics differently from the baseline model.

Chapter 14 deals with a dimension of model specification that should in principle stand at the core of social science research: actors do not act independently of each other. After all, social interaction and interdependence are constitutive elements of life. Actors not only learn from and exert pressure on each other, their actions (and non-actions) also generate externalities on others. As a consequence, we find it difficult to imagine a data-generating process that does not incorporate spatial dependence in one form or another. Even so, the vast majority of social science research treats spatial dependence as a nuisance to be ignored. Robustness tests for these baseline models give up the assumption of independence and model dependence in either the independent variables or the error term, typically assuming that geographically more proximate units exert a stronger spatial stimulus. Analyses that explicitly test theories of spatial dependence have recently surged, however. Robustness tests have to deal with the fact that true spatial dependence is difficult to identify since many causes are spatially correlated or units experience spatially correlated trends and shocks. Equally importantly, they have to explore the robustness of estimates toward modelling the spatial-effect variable differently.

Chapter 15 concludes with our thoughts on what needs to change for robustness testing to fulfil its great promise. We believe that robustness tests are too important to be left exclusively to authors. Instead, we advocate that reviewers and editors also take responsibility and identify relevant robustness tests and ask the authors to undertake them when they review and decide on manuscripts. Taken seriously, robustness testing requires significant additional investments in time and effort on the part of authors, reviewers, and editors but we know of no better way for improving the validity of causal inferences based on regression analysis of observational data.

PART 1

Robustness – A Conceptual Framework

2 Causal Complexity and the Limits to Inferential Validity

Doing statistics is like doing crosswords except that one cannot know for sure whether one has found the solution.
John W. Tukey according to David Brillinger (2002: 1547)

Once the model is known, the inferential puzzles that remain are trivial in comparison with the puzzles that arise in the specification of a model.
Edward Leamer (1978: v)

2.1 INTRODUCTION

Causal inference is much more than the mere identification of a cause–effect relationship which dominates the current debate in the social sciences. Social scientists do not only wish to establish the existence of a causal effect, they also intend to estimate the size of the effect, they wish to find out whether the estimated effect represents all cases included in the sample, they aim at understanding the mechanisms by which causes take effect and they attempt to identify the population to which the estimated causal effect can be generalized.

Causal complexity of the social world renders the traditional science-derived concept of causality unsuitable for social science research. The traditional concept of causality assumes deterministic relations and homogeneity – assumptions that are problematic for the social sciences. Given causal complexity, all models – theoretical *and* empirical models – of social outcomes necessarily simplify and no empirical model can ever capture the true data-generating process.

The way forward, we suggest, begins with moving away from the concept of model misspecification toward model uncertainty. Rather than trying to specify models correctly (an impossible task given causal complexity), researchers should test whether the results obtained by their baseline model, which is their best attempt of optimizing the specification of their empirical model, hold when they systematically replace the baseline model specification with plausible alternatives. This is the practice of robustness testing. By providing additional evidence from plausible alternative models, robustness tests potentially increase the validity of inferences compared to inferences based only on the baseline model.

In this chapter, we put forward our understanding of causal inference in social science research. We show that causal complexity of the social world renders the traditional science-derived concept of causality ill-suited and the quest to find the correct model specification futile. No model can be known to be correctly specified and we introduce robustness testing as the logical answer to the ensuing model uncertainty. Lastly, we make the case that robustness testing can improve the validity of causal inferences despite the fact that each single estimation model is likely to be misspecified.

2.2 SOCIAL SCIENCE RESEARCH AND CAUSAL INFERENCE

For Heckman (2005: 1), "causality is a very intuitive notion that is difficult to make precise without lapsing into tautology." He argues that two concepts are central for a scientific definition of causality: a set of possible outcomes and manipulation of one (or more) of the determinants. However, causality may exist where manipulation of causes is impossible and it may exist without change. For example, a perfectly stable equilibrium that resists change will have causes. A black hole does not emit light and will never do, but this state is *caused* by its gravitational force. In other words, causality exists beyond the realm of causes that can be manipulated.

In the currently dominant paradigm, social scientists refer to the idea of counterfactuals to express causality (Rubin 1974; Holland 1986; Pearl 2000; Morgan and Winship 2015). In this perspective, causality could be observed if at the same time a research design allowed to treat and not treat a single case and observe the consequences thereof. In our view, causal inference reaches well beyond the identification of the existence of causality, however. Causal inference consists of five distinct elements:

1. the identification of a causal relation between two variables (cause and effect);
2. the estimation or computation of the strength of the effect;
3. the identification and understanding of the causal mechanism;
4. the generalization of the estimated effect to all cases included in the sample;
5. the generalization from the observed cases to the set of cases defined as the population.

Importantly, causal inference not merely encompasses the identification of a causal effect and an estimate of its strength, but also the generalization of causal findings to all cases included in the sample (internal validity)[1] and the larger set of cases defined as the population (external validity). It also includes the identification and understanding of a causal mechanism since the causality of an "identified" association is not understood unless the mechanism is understood.

For some methodologists, the provision of sufficient plausibility that an observed co-variation between two variables is actually causal is more important than the provision of evidence that the identified causal effect exists in an identifiable class of cases beyond the ones studied (Rosenbaum 2010: 56). This implied preference for internal over external validity is potentially dangerous for the social sciences (for a similar view, see Cronbach 1982): if theories developed by social scientists ought to be useful for guiding political, social, cultural, or economic decision-making, then stakeholders of social science research do not merely need to know that a causal effect has been established for a particular sample of cases; they also need to know under what circumstances the treatment effect – the effect of a cause – can be utilized for other cases.[2]

The identification of a causal effect and an unbiased estimate of its strength differs from understanding the causal mechanism – the chain of events that ultimately brings about the effect. Consider the causal effect of Aspirin on headache. The headache does not disappear because a patient swallows an Aspirin pill. It disappears because the pill has an ingredient, salicylic acid, stopping the transmission of the pain signal to the brain. Consequently, Aspirin does not necessarily eliminate the origin of the pain

1 Our definition of "internal validity" differs from the currently dominating perspective, which focuses on the local average treatment effect. Assume a randomized controlled trial and assume there is causal heterogeneity across two groups of individuals. For treated individuals from the first group the treatment reduces mortality by 50 percent, whereas for the second group the treatment reduces mortality by 10 percent. If the treatment groups include an equal number of participants from each group, the local average treatment effect is 30 percent. According to the common definition of internal validity, this result is internally valid. For our definition of internal validity, the local average treatment effect is not internally valid, since it does not represent the true treatment effect in either group.

2 For others (Altmann 1974), internal validity serves as a logical prerequisite for external validity: "[T]o the extent that we have not eliminated alternative explanations for the results within our sample, we cannot rule them out of any generalization or interpretation derived from the sample" (Altmann 1974: 230). In our view, this conflates internal with external validity. External validity requires that the sample represents the population in all relevant characteristics, which is different from and independent of Altmann's concern whether what is generalized is internally valid.

but prevents the brain from noticing the pain. The molecules of salicylic acid attach themselves to COX-2 enzymes, which blocks these enzymes from creating those chemical reactions that will eventually be perceived as "pain." Clearly, identifying causation – the pain disappears after taking a pill – is distinct from understanding causal mechanisms.

Undoubtedly, causal mechanisms are an almost infinite regress (King et al. 1994: 86) slowly approaching the quest for the "first cause": knowing that Aspirin reduces the reception of pain is one thing, understanding why the treatment works is another. Accordingly, finding a causal mechanism gives rise to questioning the mechanism behind the mechanism. In our example, we may now ask how and why COX-2 enzymes produce the notion of pain and we may perhaps find another way of reducing the notion of pain.

The infinite regress of causal mechanisms ends with "acts of god" or the "big bang." Approaching these metaphysical questions runs into limits of knowledge or leads to metaphysical answers. This infinite regress may be one reason why many quantitatively oriented social scientists focus on the identification of a causal effect rather than on causal mechanisms. However, we need to identify and understand causal mechanisms for the purpose of policy and decision-making (Deaton 2010). The simple proof that medicines made from willow reduce pain did not suffice to develop Aspirin.

With the central focus on causal mechanisms, theory has a dominant role to play in making causal inferences. Theory provides the formulation and justification of a mechanism that links effects to causes. Claims of causal mechanisms remain shallow if no sound and logical theoretical basis for them is offered. Theory should guide every step of the research design for making causal inferences. And yet, with theory alone comes no knowledge, and empirical research is therefore needed to undertake causal inferences.

2.3 CAUSAL COMPLEXITY

The causal complexity that characterizes the social world hampers causal inference. In table 2.1, we compare traditional science-derived concepts of causality to the logic of causality in the social world. We stress that the traditional concept of causality used in the social sciences comes from traditional physics. It does not necessarily apply to other sciences and is increasingly questioned even by physicists as the rise of quantum physics testifies. We employ it as a backdrop to illustrate how ill it fits to the social world despite many modern social science methodologists putting their faith in inferential techniques that would be well suited only to the traditional science-derived concept of causality.

The first dimension of causal complexity is that practically all cause–effect relationships in the social world are probabilistic instead of

Table 2.1: Concepts of Causality and the Social World		
	Traditional concept of causality	**Data-generating process in social sciences**
Causal effect	deterministic	probabilistic
Strength of causal effect	homogeneous and unconditional	heterogeneous and conditional
Dynamics of causality	determined by causal mechanism	influenced by agents' autonomous decisions
Sequence of causality	cause precedes effect	distorted by rational expectations
Effect on non-treated units	none (homogeneous)	possible, due to effect on expectations (placebo, nocebo) and to spill-overs

deterministic and that causes only contribute to effects instead of being sufficient. The probability of an effect is a continuum from 0 (a cause does not have an effect) to 1 (the cause is deterministic).[3]

The second dimension of causal complexity is the existence of conditional causal effects and heterogeneous causal effects. Some causes only have effects if certain conditions are satisfied (Franzese 2003). Unless these conditions are given, the causal factor has no effect. More common are conditional causal effects, in which other factors condition the strength of the effect of x on y. Causal heterogeneity exists when agents respond differently to the same treatment. Causal heterogeneity must be distinguished from stochastic error. That the mean sample effect size differs from the predicted effect for each case in the sample can be because of stochastic error in the estimation model and does not, as such, generate a problem for causal inference.

The third dimension of causal complexity is the timing of cause and effect. Scholars all too often implicitly assume that an effect occurs immediately after a cause and, given temporal aggregation, contemporaneously with the cause. Yet, effects can occur with a delayed onset, the duration of the effect can be long or short, and the temporal functional form of the causal effect can be complex if effect strengths evolve over time, all of which renders causal inference more difficult. Response delays can also be systematic and caused by actors' strategy (Fernandez and Rodrik 1991; Rodrik 1996; Alesina and Drazen 1991; Alesina et al. 2006) or by institutions (Tsebelis 1995, 1999). Causal mechanisms have heterogeneous, or even

---

3 The likelihood of an effect given a cause needs to be distinguished from the likelihood of a cause and from the strength of an effect: a supernova explosion is an unlikely event, but if it occurs it will destroy all planets within a given range with certainty. In other words, supernova explosions, though unlikely, have a deterministic and strong effect.

unknown dynamics. For example, the mechanisms that link investment to growth are likely to have different dynamics depending on the sector in which the investment takes place, the organization of the firm that makes the investment, and so on.

The fourth dimension of causal complexity is that in the living world effects can precede causes. Human beings have rational expectations about potential future treatments and may already act on their expectations rather than on the treatment itself. Consequently, if actors expect an exchange rate intervention, they may adjust their behavior before the intervention is announced or takes place and an exchange rate effect may occur without any actual intervention. Investors do not have to wait until inflation rises to shift investments from bonds into stocks, they can shift their portfolio composition based on their expectations of a rise in the inflation rate. Political leaders do not have to wait until another country attacks their country – they can launch preemptive strikes. Expectations blur the "causes precede effects" law that scientists believe in. The *cause-precedes-effect* assumption could be rescued only if social scientists traced back all behavioral changes to alterations of agents' expectations – an avenue of causation few are willing to take.

The fifth and final dimension of causal complexity is that treatments can affect non-treated cases. Because human actors act on expectations and even their internal biological processes react to expectations, positive or negative treatment effects are possible even if individuals have not actually been treated (placebo and nocebo effects). In the social world spill-over effects from the treated to the untreated are likely. Known as spatial dependence among cases, spillover effects can render it challenging to identify a causal effect of treatment. More generally, failure to adequately account for spatial dependence can result in biased estimates of causal effects. Conversely, confounding factors hamper the identification of spatial dependence effects if these confounders generate spatial patterns in the data – an inference problem known as Galton's (1889) problem.

2.4 FROM MODEL MISSPECIFICATION TO MODEL UNCERTAINTY AND ROBUSTNESS TESTING

To capture the true data-generating processes of a complex world, analysts would need to precisely know the set of regressors, include all relevant variables and exclude all irrelevant variables, operationalize and measure these variables correctly, precisely and without systematic measurement error, model the functional form of each variable correctly, get all conditionalities right, correctly account for temporal heterogeneity, dynamics, and spatial dependence among units, and so on. There is no way of knowing.

Theories cannot provide this knowledge, for two reasons. On the one hand, all empirical evidence is theoretically under-determined (Duhem 1954; Quine 1951), that is, empirical evidence is consistent with more than a single theoretical explanation. And on the other hand, theories have to simplify in order to identify causal mechanisms that explain some observable variation. Social science theories do not aim at explaining the true data-generating process (Freedman 1991). Rather, with few exceptions they focus on identifying and clarifying a single or at most a few causal mechanisms. Accordingly, theories in general and social science theories in particular tend to be underspecified.

It is a short logical step from underspecification to misspecification. Social scientists know at least intuitively that estimation models do not even try to model the data-generating process of reality and instead have to simplify – just like theories do. And just as with theories, so with empirical models: simplification is desirable. The only alternative to simplify reality is to copy it – in which case social scientists would not get any closer to an understanding of reality, but merely copy the lack of understanding of the original world over to the new world. Simplification is not a necessary evil, but an inevitable and important component of the process of understanding. Simplification requires knowledge and the skill to understand and to detect the important patterns of causal mechanisms in the complexity of reality.

At the same time, analyses based on misspecified models – models that simplify causal complexities – cause biased estimates[4] and may result in invalid inferences. The trick is to know how much an empirical model can simplify without losing the ability to recover the effect of interest in a sufficiently valid way. Researchers must find the optimal trade-off between simplicity and generality. To illustrate what we mean look at maps as a model of the real world.[5] All maps are wrong; they simplify and transfer three-dimensional spaces and contours onto a two-dimensional plane. Maps can also provide wrong information, though. For example, early maps like the Fra Mauro map of the fifteenth century represent the world as round, with oceans at the edge of the world. Mauro even failed to represent well the world known at his time. The British Isles exclude Scotland, Scandinavia is much larger than in reality, the Americas are – for obvious reasons – entirely missing, and so are the Bay of Bengal, Australia, New Zealand, and Japan. Accordingly, there exists an important

---

4 Under strong assumptions, it is possible to generate a data-generating process in which model simplification does not cause bias. For the analysis of observational data this possibility may also exist with a small probability, but one cannot be certain.

5 For a similar use of maps as analogy for theory, see Clarke and Primo (2012).

difference between simplification and misrepresentation – both of which open a gap between reality and model. Simplification is inevitable and desirable in the social sciences – misrepresentation is not. Scientific progress reduces misrepresentations, but not simplification.

An alternative to the impossible task of specifying a model that exactly matches the data-generating process is to accept model uncertainty. While the concept of model misspecification calls for all specification problems to be solved, the concept of model uncertainty and robustness testing takes the lack of knowledge about the correct model specification seriously. Model uncertainty is the uncertainty over which of all the necessarily misspecified models provides the best trade-off between simplicity on the one hand and generality on the other hand. Robustness testing explores the impact of taking alternative plausible model specification choices which, given model uncertainty, could have provided the best trade-off between simplicity and generality.

2.5 ROBUSTNESS TESTING AND CAUSAL INFERENCE

The probability that social scientists manage to specify an empirical model exactly right is fairly close to zero. The probability that social scientists derive valid inferences based on regression analysis of observational data despite estimating misspecified models is much larger. Yet, model misspecification and causal inference appears to be a contradiction in terms. At least, many social scientists seem to believe that unless an estimate is unbiased with certainty, causal inferences are invalid.

How can social scientists make valid causal inferences from misspecified estimation models and estimated effects that are likely to be biased? One of the first methodologists who argued that causal inference with observational data requires strong assumptions was Hubert Blalock (1964: 176):

We shall assume that error terms are uncorrelated with each other and any of the independent variables in a given equation. (...) In nonexperimental studies (...) this kind of assumption is likely to be unrealistic. This means that disturbing influences must be explicitly brought into the model. But at some point one must stop and make the simplifying assumption that variables left out do not produce confounding influences.

Blalock correctly states that full validity of causal inferences depends on the absence of excluded confounders and he seems willing to assume that no such confounder exists. This is an assumption that fewer and fewer contemporary social scientists share.

Yet, causal inferences can be valid despite model misspecification. To start with, a trivial strategy to improve the validity of causal inferences relies on formulating the hypothesis tested in a way that renders inferences trivially valid. The more "weakly" or "softly" causal inferences are formulated the more likely it is that they will be valid. Take the inference that higher education on average exerts a positive effect on income and social status (Griliches and Mason 1972). This effect can already be inferred from the fact that individuals voluntarily attend higher education – a behavior that would not occur as a mass phenomenon and as an evolutionary stable strategy if higher education had no positive effect for the average student.

More importantly, even non-trivial inferences can be rendered more valid despite model misspecification. The production of scientific knowledge is a social process. Social scientists do not make causal inferences based on any single study alone. Authors may do so but the community of scholars does not. Social scientists can learn about causality and make causal inferences from "misspecified models" because they

- do not use empirical analysis alone for making inferences but also rely on theory,
- do not rely on a single prediction (or hypothesis) when testing a theory, but instead derive and test multiple predictions of that theory,
- do not derive causal inferences from a single estimate, but rather validate findings by other estimates from other studies and interpret inferences by multiple analyses of various aspects of a theory using different methods, research designs, and samples.

Causal inference as a social or collaborative scientific process does not rely on empirics alone or on a single analysis. It relies on sophisticated theories that make multiple predictions and on a multitude of relevant analyses generating similar or consistent findings. In other words: causal inference is an outcome of academic debate and scientific progress that evolves over time.

Here robustness testing comes in. It provides multiple analyses already in a single study, namely estimates based on multiple plausible model specifications. By exploring the robustness of the baseline model's estimated effects it provides additional evidence. The uncertainty about the baseline model's estimated effect size shrinks if the robustness test model finds the same or similar point estimate with smaller standard errors, though with multiple robustness tests the uncertainty likely increases. Either way, robustness tests can increase the validity of inferences. This follows from the fact that robustness tests provide information on the influence of alternative model specifications on results. This information is likely to reduce the certainty of the baseline model's specific point estimate, but not necessarily the validity of other inferences based on the estimates. For example, robustness tests may easily increase the range of an estimated effect size – thereby reducing the validity about the specific point estimate. At the same time, the robustness tests may show a remarkable insensitivity to changes in the model specification within this range of estimated effect size – thereby increasing the validity of the inference that the effect estimated by the baseline model exists, has the estimated direction, and lies within the range suggested by the baseline and robustness test model estimates.

Not all types of robustness tests estimate effects based on plausible changes in model specification. Robustness limit tests ask which change in a specific model specification choice would render an estimate non-robust. Here, robustness tests improve the validity of inferences by testing whether a particular potential model misspecification can plausibly be so large as to invalidate the inference. Consider the effect of smoking on lung cancer. In responding to the evidence provided by analyses of observational data which demonstrated a significant effect of smoking on lung cancer (Hammond 1964), the tobacco industry argued that the models used to establish this cause–effect relationship were misspecified because an unknown gene could cause both a higher propensity for smoking and a higher propensity for lung cancer (Fisher 1958). In modern language: the effect of smoking on lung cancer is not identified. Rosenbaum (2010: 111ff.) nevertheless manages to demonstrate that smoking very likely causes cancer. He shows that the effect of smoking on lung cancer is robust to assuming the existence of a "smoking gene." Correcting for the plausible effect size of such a gene does not eliminate the effect of smoking.

This research shows that model misspecifications do not need to be eliminated to make valid inferences and that potentially misspecified models employed in the analysis of observational data can be used to derive causal inferences that are not valid with certainty but certain enough to be almost consensually believed to be valid. In other words: causal inference based on regression analysis of observational data is possible despite the potential for model misspecification if researchers analyze the relevance of model misspecification for estimated effects and causal inferences.

2.6 CONCLUSION

This chapter has made two important arguments, which both run counter to contemporary wisdom in the social sciences: first, we have argued that, due to causal complexity in the social world, not only is it impossible to specify an estimation model that perfectly captures the data-generating process;[6] it

---

6 Causal complexity is not the only reason though. There is the additional problem that variables are typically based on theoretical constructs that are not directly observable in reality. This results in measurement uncertainty and measurement

is not even desirable to try to do so since all estimation models must and should simplify. As a consequence, all estimation models obtain biased estimates. Second, valid causal inferences can and in fact have been made based on biased estimates from misspecified estimation models.

Our second argument draws on the notion of science as a social or collective process: while social scientists do not learn much from a single biased estimate, they may under certain circumstances learn a lot from different analyses of the same causal effect. Robustness tests mimic the social process that leads to better and potentially more valid causal inferences. Robustness tests are an important strategy to learn from potentially biased estimates. They should form an integral part of research designs in the social sciences.

Estimated effects and inferences from a single model should never be perceived as either valid or not valid. Rather, their validity should be perceived as uncertain and the individual and collective research strategy should focus on trying to increase their validity. It is possible for social science as a social enterprise to collect enough evidence over time to call inferences about a causal effect valid with near "certainty." Candidate examples include the inferences of a positive effect of schooling on income, a positive effect of proportional electoral systems on the number of parties in parliament, and the effect of living in cities on the experience of stress. If these effects – all understood as average effects, not as holding for all cases let alone holding for all cases equally – are not known with certainty, they are known with close to certainty.

A rather different question is whether social scientists know or even can know the strengths of these effects with certainty. The idea that social scientists can identify the one "true" effect size of schooling on income, for example, reveals a severe lack of understanding of social systems. The one true parameter does not exist and the search for its identification is necessarily futile. These effects are conditioned by many factors, including the wealth of the country, its political system, the technologies companies use, individuals' characteristics including intelligence and network externalities, and so on. Causal effects vary across space and time, potentially due to conditioning factors, but potentially also for endogenous reasons. Thus, there is not *one* effect size of schooling on income, nor even *one* average effect size, but many.

The baseline model ought to represent the researchers' best attempt at trading off simplicity versus generality to account for causal

---

error. As chapter 8 explains in detail, measuring the natural world is very different from measuring the social world.

complexity. The resulting model is almost necessarily misspecified and estimates based on the chosen model cannot fully generate either internal or external validity. Robustness testing does not necessarily prompt the development of better estimation models – models that result in higher internal or external validity. But robustness testing can increase internal and external validity by generating further evidence, namely that other plausible model specifications suggest varying degrees of robustness. The next chapter develops further this logic of robustness testing.

3 The Logic of Robustness Testing

The analysis of specification error relates to a rhetorical strategy in which we suggest a model as the "true" one for the sake of argument, determine how our working model differs from it and what the consequences of the differences are, and thereby get some sense of how important the mistakes we will inevitably make may be. Sometimes it is possible to secure genuine comfort by this route.
Duncan (1975: 101–102)

3.1 INTRODUCTION

We are not the first to argue that empirical models are misspecified. As George Box states, "all models are wrong, but some are useful" (Box 1976; Box and Draper 1987). Similar claims have been made over and over again. Martin Feldstein (1982: 829), former president of the National Bureau of Economic Research and former Chairman of the Council of Economic Advisers, warned that "in practice all econometric specifications are necessarily false models." Political scientist Luke Keele (2008: 1) states: "Statistical models are always simplifications, and even the most complicated model will be a pale imitation of reality." According to Peter Kennedy (2008: 71), author of one of the best-known introductory econometrics textbooks, "it is now generally acknowledged that econometric models are false and there is no hope, or pretense, that through them truth will be found." These authors do not argue that empirical models can be misspecified. Instead, they articulate a widespread consensus that all models are *necessarily* misspecified; they cannot and do not match the true data-generating process.

If all models are necessarily misspecified, authors and readers alike cannot trust any single estimation model to provide a valid estimate of the effect of a variable x on outcome y. This casts doubt on inferences derived from the estimate. Nearly all scholars are aware of the limits of model specification: if they did believe that their model specification was correct (and that peers and reviewers shared this belief), they would present the results of a single estimation model. But usually they don't.

This chapter discusses the logic of robustness testing. We start by acknowledging intellectual heritage: Leamer's sensitivity analyses, Rosenbaum's bounds, Manski's non-parametric bounds, Frank's robustness limit tests, and others. Yet, despite this heritage rooted in econometric theory, robustness testing is a grassroots movement with no identifiable inventor. Consequently, no common standards and practices toward robustness testing have been developed, which results in deficient current practices and robustness testing failing to achieve its full potential. We propose a more systematic approach to robustness testing that proceeds in four steps: baseline model specification, identification of potentially arbitrary modelling assumptions, robustness test model specification based on alternative plausible assumptions, and comparison of estimated effects and the computation of the degree of robustness. We also discuss the multidimensionality of robustness and argue that robustness is best explored for each test separately, rather than averaged over all robustness test models. Lastly, we describe what we regard as the main aims and goals of robustness testing.

3.2 ROBUSTNESS TESTING IN THE SOCIAL SCIENCES

Edward Leamer was the first to systematically justify robustness testing as a means to tackle model uncertainty without the unrealistic aim of eliminating it. In Leamer (1978: v), he justifies his departure from what was then contemporary methodology: "Traditional statistical theory assumes that the statistical model is given. By definition, nonexperimental inference cannot make this assumption, and the usefulness of traditional theory is rendered doubtful." To deal with uncertainty about model specification, Leamer developed what he called *sensitivity tests*. Leamer understood sensitivity testing broadly: "One thing that is clear is that the dimension of the parameter space should be very large by traditional standards. Large numbers of variables should be included, as should different functional forms, different distributions, different serial correlation assumptions, different measurement error processes, etcetera, etcetera" (Leamer 1985: 311). Despite his ambitions, those who have taken their inspiration from Leamer have almost exclusively focused on analyzing permutations to the set of regressors.[1]

---

1 Much of this early literature (Levine and Renelt 1992; Feld and Savioz 1997; Temple 1998; Sala-i-Martin 1997) was motivated by uncertainty with respect to the correct set of explanatory variables in economic growth models. Sensitivity tests soon reached other social sciences, but in political science (Neumayer 2002;

Some intellectual heritage of robustness testing derives from scholars like Paul R. Rosenbaum and co-authors (see Rosenbaum 2002, though there are many earlier contributions with many co-authors), Charles F. Manski (1990, 1995), Ken Frank and co-authors (Frank 2000; Pan and Frank 2003; Frank and Min 2007) and others who have developed what in chapter 5 we will call robustness limit tests, which represent one of five types of robustness tests. These tests explore how much a specific model specification needs to be changed for a baseline model's estimate to become non-robust.

Despite its intellectual heritage, contemporary robustness testing has arisen as an independent grassroots movement. Robustness tests have always been around. The first publication that presented two regression estimates with the same dependent variable implicitly conducted a robustness test of some kind. The oldest robustness test must be to add an additional regressor to the existing list of explanatory variables. This constitutes a robustness test even though it took decades until somebody used the label for such a simple change in model specification. Unfortunately, we have not been able to identify the first-ever use of the term "robustness test" with the specific meaning social scientists attach to it now. Over time, robustness testing became a *best practice of empirical research*, with authors integrating robustness tests into their manuscripts as a strategy to deal with anticipated model specification issues raised by reviewers.

The number of articles reporting robustness tests increases exponentially in the social sciences, though the growth rate appears to be higher in some disciplines, most notably in economics and political science, than in others, e.g., sociology and business studies. Despite this uneven take-up, robustness tests today form an important element of the scientist's toolbox. Between 2008 and 2013 alone, the number of articles indexed in the Social Sciences Citation Index that explicitly reported robustness tests doubled.[2] Today, robustness tests are used across all the social sciences.

While the increase in the number of articles reporting robustness tests over the last decade is impressive, roughly half of the articles published in leading political science journals over a ten-year period that we surveyed do not present the estimation results of the robustness tests in the body of the

---

Scheve and Slaughter 2004; Gerber and Huber 2010) and sociology (Frank 2000) the meaning of these tests broadened, varying many aspects of the model specification to test the robustness of results.

2 Many more articles presumably report robustness tests without being explicit about it. If we cross-check this trend using Google Scholar, we find that the number of articles mentioning robustness tests increased from 1,280 in 2008 to 2,600 in 2013.

article, the appendix, or the online appendix.[3] Robustness is more often than not a mere claim, and it hardly ever becomes an explicit part of the research strategy.

To make matters worse, the vast majority of these articles do not justify their choice of robustness tests. Authors could, therefore, potentially have reported tests selected not because they really test the robustness of the estimates in the presence of model uncertainty, but simply because their baseline model proves to be robust to the carefully selected tests. Unless scholars provide a good justification for their chosen set of robustness tests or robustness tests are chosen not by the authors but instead by journal editors or reviewers, the value of robustness tests remains questionable.

According to our review of political science journals, the most widely reported robustness tests are the inclusion of additional control variables, alternative measures of the dependent or central explanatory variables, changes in the sample, and alternative measurement scales or functional forms. These tests are conducted in 20–30 percent of articles that report robustness tests published in leading political science journals we surveyed. Alternative estimators, alternative functional forms, and alternative dynamics are used in about 10 percent of those articles. All other robustness tests are even less frequent. They occur occasionally, but scholars do not use these tests systematically. Nevertheless, some researchers conduct tests that account for structural breaks, alternative lag structures, conditionality, spatial dependence, missing observations, crucial cases (jackknife), or endogeneity (instruments). Yet, a glaring gap remains to be bridged between the number of model uncertainties potentially relevant to a baseline model and the frequency with which they are explored in robustness tests.

While the arbitrary selection of robustness tests might be the most evident and important problem in the current practice of robustness testing, it is not the only one. In addition, few scholars justify the robustness tests they conduct. Not justifying robustness tests is as bad as not justifying the baseline model. A lack of robustness between a plausibly specified empirical model and an implausibly specified model is irrelevant. More importantly, a robustness test model that only makes a minuscule change to the baseline model specification or that has been carefully selected because it supports the baseline model estimate rather than because it represents a real test does not add much to the validity of inferences, if at all.

---

3 We identified more than 500 articles published in selected political science journals in which authors reported at least a single robustness test. Overall we found that explicit robustness tests are employed in approximately one out of four empirical papers published in these journals.

Exceptions of good practice exist. Consider Scheve and Slaughter's (2004) analysis of the influence of foreign direct investment on what they call "economic insecurity" defined as volatility in the demand for labor that causes volatility in wages and employment. They analyze an individual's perception of job security. In their baseline model, Scheve and Slaughter regress this perception of economic volatility on a dummy variable capturing the presence of foreign companies, an individual's education, age, income, union membership, manufacturing employment, and sector unemployment rate plus year dummies. Scheve and Slaughter report five well-justified robustness tests: first, they replace the FDI dummy with "alternative measures of FDI exposure" (2004: 670), namely FDI total share and FDI inward share. Second, they admit that their baseline model "does not allow (...) to differentiate between the idea that persistence in observations of insecurity is accounted for by the influence of past experiences of insecurity on present perceptions and the alternative idea that certain individuals just have unobserved characteristics that lead them to have certain types of perceptions" (2004: 670). Accordingly, they use Arellano-Bond's first-differenced estimator to account for dynamics. As a third robustness test, Scheve and Slaughter admit that perceptions may influence an individual's choice of industry (which would render their model partly endogenous). They deal with endogeneity by lagging their FDI variable, which does not, however, solve the endogeneity issue if FDI is announced one year before it actually occurs or if FDI is serially correlated. In a fourth robustness test, Scheve and Slaughter add six additional covariates to explore the extent to which estimates depend on the choice of regressors. In their fifth and final reported test, they repeat their analyses based on a broader sample. What makes their article a candidate for good practice in robustness testing is not so much the specific choice of robustness tests, but the discussion they devote to derive robustness tests from specific dimensions of model uncertainty.

For a second noteworthy example consider Gerber and Huber (2010), who study the association between partisanship and economic assessments. They find that large partisan differences between Republican and Democratic voters in the United States exist and conclude that the observed pattern of partisan response suggests partisan differences in perceptions of the economic competence of the parties. Naturally, the self-description of voters in a survey can be subject to measurement error. Not only does the existence of neutrals pose a specification issue, the degree to which a survey respondent supports Democrats or Republicans also varies largely in a way not appropriately reflected by the survey. Gerber and Huber's robustness tests seek to address these issues. In different model specifications, they exclude independents, they change the coding scale of party identification toward fewer and more categories, they allow for a flexible effect of partisan affiliation by converting the categorical measure into separate exhaustive dummy variables, they employ matching to test whether the effect of partisanship is influenced by the linear functional form specification of the control variables, they control for spatial sorting of individuals by including a measure of partisanship at the aggregate state level, and they control for unobserved state heterogeneity by including state fixed effects. They conclude from conducting these tests (Gerber and Huber 2010: 167):

> [T]hese robustness checks suggest that the pattern of partisan response (...) is not driven by particular functional form assumptions or the behavior of independents. Rather, across a variety of measurement and model specifications, Democrats reacted to the 2006 election by becoming more optimistic in their economic forecasts for the national economy, while Republicans became more pessimistic.

3.3 ROBUSTNESS TESTING IN FOUR SYSTEMATIC STEPS

Since robustness testing developed as a grassroots enterprise, few if any common standards and practices have been developed. To provide a more systematic approach, we suggest that analyses of robustness require four steps:

1. Define a model that is, in the researcher's subjective expectation, the optimal specification for the data-generating process at hand, i.e. the model that optimally balances simplicity against generality, employing theory, econometric tests, and prior research in finding it. Call this model the baseline model.
2. Identify assumptions made in the specification of the baseline model which are potentially arbitrary and that could be replaced with alternative plausible assumptions.
3. Develop models that change one of the baseline model's assumptions at a time. These alternatives are called robustness test models.
4. Compare the estimated effects of each robustness test model to the baseline model and compute the estimated degree of robustness.[4]

The first step – the singling out of a model – appears to be the most controversial decision researchers have to take. Why do we think that the formulation of a baseline model and the resulting hierarchy between baseline model and robustness test models are good ideas? Conceptually similar approaches such as Leamer's sensitivity analysis and model averaging across

---

4 The next chapter deals with the fourth step. The entire second part of the book identifies potentially arbitrary modelling assumptions for different aspects of model specification and develops robustness tests for tackling them.

a large number of models refrain from suggesting the choice of a baseline model with all models in the model space having an ex-ante equal probability of being the best model.

The formulation of a baseline model and the testing of robustness against the baseline model require the provision of theoretical or other justifications for each model specification choice because the specification of the model has to be plausible. In fact, baseline models should be the researchers' *best bet* for an optimal specification of the data-generating process balancing simplicity versus generality. In addition, robustness test models need to represent plausible alternatives to specific baseline model specification choices.

Known or demonstrable misspecifications disqualify models from serving as a robustness test model. We distinguish here between three categories of empirical models. First, models known to be correctly specified – a category that is empty, at least in the study of observational data. Second, and on the other end of the spectrum, models that are known or at least strongly suspected to be misspecified. Structure in the residuals provides hints for model misspecification, but does not offer final proof. Likewise, if models are used for testing theories, they have to be consistent with the theory's assumptions and test its predictions. Models that do not are known to be misspecified. Third, models which are not obviously misspecified, but equally are not known to be correctly specified either. Even if the odds are diminishingly small, they could in principle or potentially at least be correctly specified. We call the specification of such models plausible. Both baseline and robustness test models should fall into this category.

Thus, the difference between Leamer's approach and robustness testing is the latter's focus on plausible model specifications. Leamer's definition of model space, by contrast, does not avoid the inclusion of models known to be misspecified. Rather than estimating and averaging across millions of models, many of which must be misspecified, robustness testing relies upon estimating a small number of plausibly specified models or a small number of sets of plausibly specified models (since randomized permutation tests can themselves employ hundreds or thousands of models varying one specific dimension of model specification).

3.4 THE MULTIDIMENSIONALITY OF ROBUSTNESS

Robustness is a multidimensional concept. The robustness of empirical estimates to changes in, say, the sample and assumed conditionality structure differ. Just like steel constructions are subjected to different robustness tests, so baseline models should be subjected to different robustness tests addressing different potential sources for potential lack of robustness.

Hence, the question is not whether the baseline model's estimates are robust in general, but whether they are robust to a specified change in a particular aspect of model specification. In other words: robustness is not an overall or general property of an estimate, but a property that differs from robustness test to robustness test.

While it seems possible to distinguish between important and irrelevant robustness tests, it is not possible to conduct "all relevant robustness tests." Every empirical model consists of multiple specification decisions. Scholars are usually uncertain about numerous aspects. In addition, few specification decisions are dichotomous, so that in each dimension a large number of alternatives may appear to be plausible. As a consequence, the possibility space for plausible model specifications is typically too large to try all permutations of all plausible assumptions of all aspects of model specification. There will always be possible alternative models which remain unknown or at least unchosen. In other words: the robustness tests that a researcher conducts are a selected subset of the entire model space of plausible models.

Given the multidimensionality of robustness, and the diversity of robustness tests that can be conducted within each dimension, averaging results over a large number of robustness tests is not useful either. While it is technically not difficult to average over different point estimates by taking weighted or unweighted means of point estimates or by adding the sampling distributions of these estimates, the result will inevitably depend on assumptions concerning the plausible model space and the model selection algorithm.[5] It would be convenient to compute a single parameter and single measure of uncertainty for the "overall averaged model" (baseline plus robustness test models) or for the "average robustness test model." Yet, the multidimensionality of model specifications should not beguile researchers to summarize over these dimensions in order to identify "the robustness" of an estimated effect. Strong robustness in one or more dimensions should not cover up the lack of robustness in other dimensions. At the very least, the multidimensionality of robustness testing requires that – regardless of the definition of model space and the averaging algorithm used – a single measure of overall robustness necessitates dimensionality reduction. This

---

5 Both Bayesian and frequentist methodologists have developed model averaging approaches (Hoeting et al. 1999; Claeskens and Hjort 2008). In model averaging, quantities of interest (point estimates, standard errors) are expressed as a weighted average of the same quantities from the models to be averaged. The weights used in these procedures differ. Where measures of model fit are used as weights results tend to be substantively similar since measures of model fit tend to be highly correlated.

will result in a loss of information unless all robustness tests were perfectly correlated, which they are not.

Knowing that a baseline model's estimate is robust on average is less useful than knowing that it is robust in, say, six dimensions of model specification and lacks robustness in a seventh dimension. Lack of robustness in a particular dimension is important information that gets lost by computing average robustness. It is therefore best to explore robustness in multiple dimensions of model specification separately without averaging across all robustness test models.

3.5 AIMS AND GOALS OF ROBUSTNESS TESTING

The purpose of robustness testing is *not* the demonstration that estimates, results, or findings are robust and all inferences are valid. Though practically all reported robustness tests conclude with a statement like the above, robustness tests do not demonstrate, let alone prove, the validity of inferences – especially not when the tests are selected by the authors. Instead, we suggest three main aims and goals of robustness testing:

- exploring the robustness of estimates,
- identifying limits of robustness and
- spurring further research via learning from variation in estimates across model specifications.

Exploring whether estimates are robust to specific plausible changes in the model specification is the principal aim of robustness testing. It is not the same as setting out to demonstrate that estimates are robust. The former task is driven by a sincere and serious attempt at exploring the robustness of estimates whereas the latter task seems driven by a desire to move the manuscript past reviewers and editors. Exploring robustness is part of a well-designed research strategy, whereas setting out to demonstrate robustness is merely part of a publication strategy.

The second goal of robustness testing is the identification of limits of robustness. Many of the most misleading inferential errors in the social sciences result from the concentration on and over-generalization from average estimated effects. Social scientists tend to infer internal and external validity from statistically significant point estimates. By doing so, they over-generalize findings and ignore that inferences tend to be limited in space and time. Robustness tests may bring the relevance of cases and historic time back into focus. Robustness tests can explore whether the estimated point estimate of the baseline model represents the effects in all units of analysis. Likewise, robustness tests can investigate whether the mean effect represents the entire period under investigation, or whether effect strengths vary over time. Robustness limit tests explicitly ask where the boundaries are. For example, scholars may ask how large measurement error needs to become to render the baseline model estimate non-robust. However, even other types of tests beyond robustness limit tests can nevertheless shed light on the limits of robustness.

Finally, though robustness tests are not primarily an instrument for model improvement, they can, by recognizing model specifications that lack robustness, identify areas where further research seems most promising or even necessary. In an ideal scientific world researchers abandon their preference for "robust" findings and employ robustness tests to identify important future avenues for research. An identified lack of robustness in a dimension of model specification poses questions that complementary research might be able to answer. Consider the simple example that two or more competing proxies for a latent variable exist, as is the case with ethnic diversity or democracy. Now assume that replacing one by the other proxy reveals a lack of robustness. In addition to stating that estimates are not robust to a change in the operationalization of the explanatory variable, researchers could thus investigate which cases drive the differences in results and discuss which operationalization appears to be more appropriate and how an optimal proxy variable for ethnic diversity or for democracy would be defined and measured.

Single robustness tests typically do not achieve all of the aims and goals of robustness testing. For the first and primary goal, the best robustness test provides the best insight into the dependence of estimated effects on model specifications. From a learning perspective, the best robustness test potentially offers the deepest insights into the causes for the observed variation in estimates of effect sizes. While robustness tests are often specialized for single purposes and only achieve one or perhaps two of these aims and goals, a shrewd combination of robustness tests can achieve all aims simultaneously.

3.6 CONCLUSION

By providing insights into the stability of estimates and into the factors that may inhibit this stability, by identifying the limits of robustness and by illuminating relevant areas of further research, robustness tests can contribute to the production of scientific knowledge. If properly undertaken, robustness tests can dramatically improve the perceived validity of causal inferences based on regression analysis of observational data.

Yet, despite the success and rise of robustness tests in social science practice, we argue that we are far away from this ideal and that a change in the practice of robustness testing is required. In this chapter, we have provided the foundation for a systematic approach to robustness testing. We have argued against general, average or overall robustness. The multiple dimensions of model uncertainty need to be explored separately and strong robustness in one dimension cannot compensate for lack of robustness in other dimensions.

Robustness tests are necessarily selected from a "possibility space." It is not possible to conduct all possible or all relevant robustness tests – just as it is not possible to conduct all permutations of plausible models. Nevertheless, there can be robustness tests that are so crucial that the baseline model's failure to pass them will cast serious doubt on the baseline model's estimated effect. While it is not possible to predefine robustness tests that are crucial for all research projects, it is often possible to predefine (and possibly even pre-register) crucial robustness tests for specific research projects.

4 The Concept of Robustness

Humans desire certainty, and science infrequently provides it. As much as we might wish it to be otherwise, a single study almost never provides definitive resolution for or against an effect and its explanation (...) Scientific progress is a cumulative process of uncertainty reduction that can only succeed if science itself remains the greatest sceptic of its explanatory claims.
Nosek and 268 co-authors (2015: aac4716)

4.1 INTRODUCTION

Robustness relates to the behavior of an object under stress and strain. In technical language, robustness refers to the ability to tolerate perturbations that potentially affect the object's functions. In order to fall in line with this concept of robustness, we need to answer three questions:

1. What is the object?
2. What is the stress and strain to which we subject the object?
3. How can we compute robustness?

The object of robustness depends on the research question and the inferences researchers wish to make. In most cases, an analysis aims at testing the predictions from a theoretical model about the effect of one or more variables on an outcome. In this case, the object of robustness tests is the baseline model's estimated effect of x on y. Note that we write "effect" here rather than "coefficient" because similar effects are consistent with dissimilar coefficients in non-linear models, models that allow for non-linear functional forms, conditionalities, and so on. Conversely, similar coefficients may also imply very different effects. In a simple linear model without non-linear or conditional effects the robustness of an estimated effect is identical to the robustness of its estimated coefficients. In all other cases, this does not hold and analysts need to compute effects and state at what values of the explanatory variables they assess robustness or, preferably, analyze partial robustness, which we define further below. Yet, researchers may instead be interested in forecasting, in which case the predicted effect of the entire model becomes the object of robustness tests. If, for example, an analysis forecasts population growth, the object of robustness tests is the forecast that the baseline model makes. In the remainder of this book, we will talk about the effect of a variable x on y as the object of robustness, but readers should keep in mind that the object may be different.

Researchers impose stress and strain on the above object by changing the specification of the baseline model in systematic and plausible ways. It follows that implausible model specifications are not valid robustness tests. Models known or strongly suspected to be misspecified do not qualify as robustness test models.

In this chapter, we define robustness and propose as a measure of robustness the extent to which a robustness test model estimate supports the baseline model estimate. We suggest that this measure, which varies from 0 to 1, offers several useful properties, including that it measures robustness continuously rather than declaring an estimate as robust or non-robust at an arbitrarily chosen threshold. Our definition of robustness is independent of the level of statistical significance of either the baseline or robustness test model and we contend that robustness is most usefully understood as stability in the estimated effect, which is inconsistent with a definition that relates to statistical significance, even if this departs from how many interpret robustness in current practice. We also introduce the concept of partial robustness, which is relevant in all non-linear models and even linear models that estimate a non-linear, conditional or heterogeneous effect. The concept of partial robustness allows the degree of robustness to differ across observations in all such models.

4.2 DEFINITIONS AND CONCEPTS OF ROBUSTNESS IN CURRENT PRACTICE

Robustness tests are common practice. An increasing number of researchers report the results of robustness tests and an even larger number claims that their baseline model proved robust to specific changes in the model specification without showing the results. However, though robustness tests are fashionable, neither a common practice of core tests nor a common understanding of the meaning of robustness has evolved. Indeed, social scientists disagree about what they mean by robustness, what ought to be robust, and where they see the threshold between robust and not robust.

No commonly accepted definition of robustness exists. Researchers conducting robustness tests rarely ever define robustness when they claim their results are robust. Instead, robustness is typically regarded as given by a situation in which estimates from robustness tests do not "deviate much" from the estimates of the baseline model. Specifically, scholars see robustness as given when estimates "are quite similar" (Bailey and Maltzman 2008: 379) or "close" (Gehlbach, Sonin, and Zhuravskaya 2010: 732), "results uphold," coefficients remain "substantively similar" (Lipsmeyer and Zhu 2011: 652) or "do not change" (Braumoeller 2008: 86; Hafner-Burton, Helfer, and Fariss 2011: 701; Mukherjee and Singer 2010: 50) and thus "remain essentially the same." Yet, how similar estimates have to be to qualify as "fairly similar," "essentially the same," or "close" is almost never operationally defined. The vagueness in the conceptual definition implies that virtually all authors can interpret their results as "robust." To make matters worse, social scientists do not agree on what ought to be robust: is it effects, their level of statistical significance or inferences? In the next section, we offer an operational definition of robustness.

4.3 DEFINING ROBUSTNESS

Robustness tests explore the stability of the baseline model's estimated effect to systematic alternative plausible model specification changes. We define robustness as the degree to which the baseline model's estimated effect of interest is supported by another robustness test model that makes a plausible change in model specification. Higher levels of robustness imply a higher degree of support for the baseline model's estimated effect, lower levels of robustness suggest a lower degree of support.

The baseline model provides a point estimate for the effect of interest. Naturally, sampling variability means that the point estimate is unlikely to exactly capture the population parameter. If analysts draw another finite random sample from the population, they will get another point estimate because the distribution of random errors will be different. The estimated standard error of the point estimate allows the construction of 90- or, more typically, 95-percent confidence intervals. A confidence interval provides an estimate for a plausible range for the estimated parameter, given sampling variability (Cumming 2012: 79).

As we have argued before, the baseline model, like the robustness test models, falls into the category of plausible models – that is, models which are neither known to be misspecified nor known to be correctly specified either. Hence, researchers cannot claim that the baseline model captures the "truth" with any level of confidence. Likewise, robustness tests do not seek and cannot find the truth, but they analyze the extent to which estimates from different model specifications support the estimate from a baseline model specification. In this sense, the baseline model marks a researcher's best effort at constructing an estimation model. It is therefore not just any model, it is the model against which other robustness test models that make other plausible specification assumptions should be compared to.

Given our above definition of robustness, and taking sampling variability into account, robustness becomes the extent to which social scientists can be confident that the plausible range for the estimated effect of the robustness test model supports the plausible range for the estimated effect from the baseline model. To be precise, we define robustness as the degree to which the probability density function of the robustness test model's estimate falls within the confidence interval of the baseline model.

Assume for simplicity a linear and unconditional model such that coefficients represent effects. Formally, let

$$f(a_b, \hat{\beta}_b, \hat{\sigma}_b) = \frac{1}{\hat{\sigma}_b \sqrt{2\pi}} e^{-(a_b - \hat{\beta}_b)^2 / 2\hat{\sigma}_b^2} \qquad (4.1)$$

be the probability density function of parameter estimate β_b, which is the point estimate of the effect of variable x and σ_b its standard error. This density function is normally distributed by construction: since econometric theory assumes that errors are normally distributed, the probability density function of the parameter estimate is also normally distributed. If methodologists make alternative assumptions about the error process, a different probability density function for ρ or some transformation of the original equation is required. Fox (1991) argues that the assumption of normally distributed errors appears arbitrary. We disagree for two reasons. First, the assumption is not arbitrary but roots in theories of random processes and in experiments with stochastic processes. And second, the central-limit theorem proves that, in the limit, the sum of random distributions approaches a normal distribution. We therefore know no other general assumption about error processes which is as plausible as the normal one.

As equation 4.2 suggests, we define the degree of robustness ρ (rho) as the share or percentage of the probability density function of the robustness test model that falls within the 95-percent confidence interval of the probability density function of the baseline model,[1] which is

$$\rho(\hat{\beta}_r) \equiv \frac{1}{\hat{\sigma}_r \sqrt{2\pi}} \int_{\hat{\beta}_b - C\hat{\sigma}_b}^{\hat{\beta}_b + C\hat{\sigma}_b} e^{-(a_r - \hat{\beta}_r)^2 / C\hat{\sigma}_r^2} \, da. \qquad (4.2)$$

Again, the probability density function of the robustness test model is assumed to be normally distributed by econometric convention.

---

1 Note that C decreases from approximately 2.04 to approximately 1.96 as the sample size grows toward infinity.

This definition has some useful properties. Assume, for simplicity, that the coefficients of the baseline and the robustness test models are identical. Under this assumption, the estimated degree of robustness ρ depends entirely on the standard error of the robustness test model compared to the one from the baseline model. If the standard error were exactly the same in both models, then $\rho = 0.95$. This makes sense: with the robustness test producing the exact same result as the baseline model we are 95 percent confident that the robustness test estimate falls within the 95-percent confidence interval of the baseline model. If the standard error of the robustness test is smaller than the baseline model, ρ becomes larger than 0.95 and converges to 1.00 as the robustness test standard error becomes smaller and smaller. This, again, represents a useful property: the smaller standard error of the robustness test model suggests researchers can be more confident that the robustness test estimate falls within the 95-percent confidence interval of the baseline model. Conversely, if the robustness test standard error is larger than the one from the baseline model, ρ is necessarily smaller than 0.95 and declines as the robustness test error becomes larger, if we keep point estimates constant.[2] Figure 4.1 illustrates the logic for a baseline model with a coefficient of 1.0 for the variable of interest and a standard error of 0.3 and a robustness test model with a coefficient of 1.0 and a standard error of 0.5 (light grey shading).

The calculated value of ρ for figure 4.1 equals 0.760. Thus, 76 percent of the probability density function of the robustness test model falls within the 95-percent confidence band of the baseline model. The robustness measure ρ provides information on the stability of the baseline model's estimated effect: since the robustness test model has the same coefficient but a larger standard error, the confidence in the baseline model's estimate declines.

We now relax the unrealistic assumption that the point estimates of the robustness test and the baseline models are identical. In this case, ρ is determined by both the difference in point estimates and the standard errors. Figure 4.2 displays the same baseline model but the robustness test model has a different point estimate. As a comparison of the two figures shows, ρ declines as the difference between the point estimates of the baseline model and the robustness test model increases. In example 2 (figure 4.2), with the robustness test model giving a point estimate of 1.5 and standard

---

2 The 0.95 threshold at which one becomes either more or less certain is precise for all robustness tests that hold the sample constant. If, however, a robustness test varies the sample, the sampling variation between the baseline and the robustness test model will push the value of ρ downward, all other things equal. In principle, one would therefore want a lower threshold of ρ for robustness tests that do not hold the sample constant.

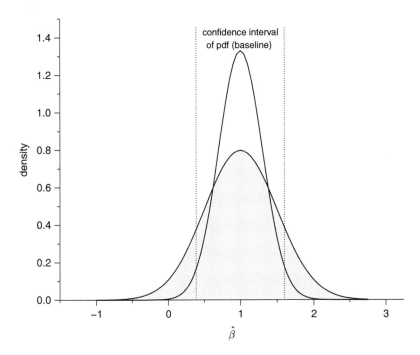

Figure 4.1: Example 1 of Degree of Robustness ρ

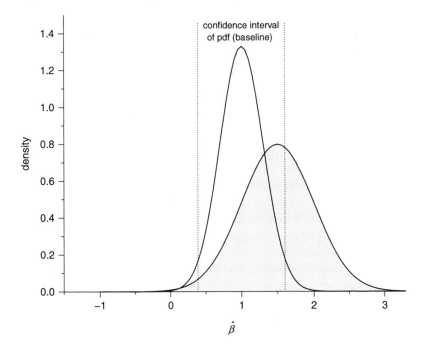

Figure 4.2: Example 2 of Degree of Robustness ρ

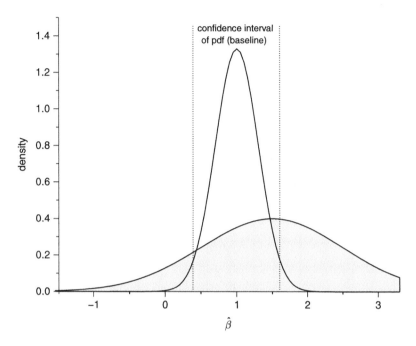

Figure 4.3: Example 3 of Degree of Robustness ρ

error 0.3, ρ is 0.615. Our third example (figure 4.3) doubles the standard error in the robustness test estimate to 1.0. By increasing the standard error, ρ declines to 0.397 in this example.

Table 4.1 shows the joint influence of the difference between the point estimates and the standard error of the robustness test model on ρ for a baseline model point estimate of 1 with standard error of 0.3.

Table 4.1 demonstrates several properties of ρ. First, robustness is left–right symmetric: identical positive and negative deviations of the robustness test compared to the baseline model give the same degree of robustness. It does not matter for ρ whether the estimate of the robustness test model is larger or smaller than the one of the baseline model. Only the difference matters. Second, if the standard error of the robustness test is smaller than the one from the baseline model, ρ converges to 1 as long as the difference in point estimates is small. If the robustness test coefficient is estimated with high precision, its probability density function can lie almost entirely within the baseline model's confidence interval even if the point estimates differ, as long as they do not differ too much. Third, for any given standard error of the robustness test, ρ is always and unambiguously smaller the larger the difference in point estimates. Not surprisingly, for any given level of uncertainty around a robustness test estimate, the larger the

Table 4.1: Degree of Robustness for Various Robustness Test Estimates					
	s.e.=0.1	s.e.=0.3	s.e.=0.5	s.e.=0.7	s.e.=1.0	s.e.=2.0
β=−0.50	0.000	0.001	0.034	0.095	0.162	0.176
β=−0.25	0.000	0.014	0.093	0.168	0.221	0.191
β=0.00	0.000	0.085	0.204	0.266	0.284	0.204
β=0.25	0.053	0.295	0.369	0.381	0.345	0.216
β=0.50	0.811	0.615	0.555	0.490	0.397	0.224
β=0.75	1.000	0.867	0.704	0.570	0.431	0.229
β=1.00	1.000	0.950	0.760	0.599	0.443	0.231
β=1.25	1.000	0.867	0.704	0.570	0.431	0.229
β=1.50	0.811	0.615	0.555	0.490	0.397	0.224
β=1.75	0.053	0.295	0.369	0.381	0.345	0.216
β=2.00	0.000	0.085	0.204	0.266	0.284	0.204
β=2.25	0.000	0.014	0.093	0.168	0.221	0.191
β=2.50	0.000	0.001	0.034	0.095	0.162	0.176

Note: Baseline model β = 1.0; s.e. = 0.3, 95-percent confidence interval

difference in the point estimates the lower the support for the baseline model's estimate. Fourth, differences in point estimates have a strong influence on ρ if the standard error of the robustness test is small but a small influence if the standard errors are large. Robustness test models estimated with large sampling variability remain uninformative – they are not powerful enough to increase the certainty of the baseline model estimate but at the same time not powerful enough for signaling complete lack of robustness.

Perhaps surprising at first sight is the complex influence of the sampling distribution of the robustness test model estimates on ρ. The impact of increasing standard errors on ρ is ambiguous as it depends on the difference in point estimates between the robustness test and baseline model relative to the baseline model's confidence interval. If the difference in point estimates is such that the robustness test point estimate lies *within* the baseline model's confidence interval, i.e. if $|\beta_b - \beta_r| < C\sigma_b^2$, then increasing standard errors of the robustness test model's estimate unambiguously decrease ρ. The highest probability of the robustness test estimate lies within the baseline model confidence interval but increasing uncertainty around the robustness test estimate increases the uncertainty as to whether the robustness test supports the baseline model estimate. Conversely, if the difference in point estimates is such that the robustness test point estimate lies *outside* the baseline model's confidence interval, i.e. if $|\beta_b - \beta_r| > C\sigma_b^2$, increasing standard errors of the robustness test model first increase ρ and then decrease it as the standard error becomes larger and larger. This may seem counterintuitive but is easily explained: the highest probability of the robustness test estimate lies outside the baseline model's confidence interval. With small standard errors researchers can be fairly confident that the robustness test model does not support the baseline model estimate. In the extreme, almost the entire probability density function of the robustness test lies outside the baseline confidence interval and ρ converges to zero. As the standard error increases, one of the tails of the robustness test probability density function moves closer to or, if already inside, moves further into the baseline model's confidence interval. Researchers thus become less confident that the robustness test does *not* support the baseline model. Eventually, with larger and larger standard errors, the tail of the robustness test probability density function moves outside the other end of the baseline confidence interval and reduces the confidence that the robustness test supports the baseline model. Figure 4.4 displays the joint effect of changes in the difference between point estimates and changes in the standard errors of the robustness test model on ρ (based on the assumption of a baseline model point estimate of 1 with standard error of 0.3).

Figure 4.5 displays the same information in a different way, namely as a heat plot. It shows the nonlinear bivariate relation between the difference

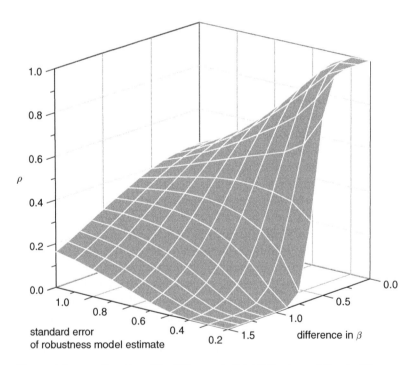

Figure 4.4: ρ as a Function of the Difference in Point Estimates and Standard Errors
Note: Baseline model β=1; s.e.=0.3.

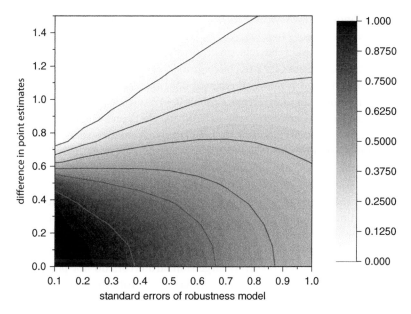

Figure 4.5: ρ as a Function of the Difference in Point Estimates and Standard Errors (Heat Plot)

Note: Baseline model β=1; s.e.=0.3.

in the point estimates of the baseline and the robustness test model and the standard error of the robustness test model (based on the assumption of baseline model point estimate of 1 with standard error of 0.3 as before). This distribution resembles a bivariate Weibull distribution. It asymptotically goes to 0 in three of the four corners and to 1 in the remaining fourth corner. Accordingly, if the difference in point estimates goes to infinity, ρ goes to 0 (top left corner). Similarly, if the standard error of the robustness test goes to infinity, ρ goes to 0 (bottom right corner). The same holds if both the difference in point estimates and the robustness test standard error go to infinity (top right corner). Conversely, ρ goes to 1 if either the difference in point estimates goes to 0 and the robustness test standard error is smaller than the one from the baseline model or if the robustness test standard error goes to 0 and the difference in point estimates remains sufficiently small.

Figure 4.5 also displays selected isolines, which represent equal degrees of robustness. The ones starting just above and just below 0.60 on the difference in point estimates scale illustrate that if the difference in point estimates is below the crucial threshold of approximately 1.96 times the baseline model estimate's standard error (here around 0.59), ρ monotonously decreases with larger standard errors of the robustness test model. If it stays above that threshold, ρ first increases and then decreases, i.e. it is non-monotonous. Asymptotically, both converge to 0 as the robustness test standard error goes to infinity.

Note that for relatively small differences in point estimates, it takes large standard errors for ρ to converge to 0. For example, for a difference of 0.20 or 0.40 and a standard error of 0.90 (i.e. three times the size of the baseline model standard error), ρ equals 0.447 and 0.476, respectively. Even with a standard error as large as 5.00 for the same differences in point estimates ρ is 0.094 and 0.093, respectively. It takes a standard error of around 9.50 for ρ to drop below 0.05. When the robustness test estimate lies within the baseline model's confidence interval, the degree of robustness will not be low unless the standard error becomes sufficiently large. In other words, robustness test models with even fairly large uncertainty around their estimates do not render the baseline model estimate non-robust, unless the sampling uncertainty becomes extremely large. Conversely, if the difference in point estimates is relatively large, small standard errors signal lack of robustness, but even relatively large standard errors do not produce high degrees of robustness. If the point estimate of the robustness test lies outside the confidence interval, ρ can never be higher than 0.50 no matter what the standard error.

Critics might wonder whether our definition of robustness creates strategic incentives for authors to specify their baseline model sub-optimally in order to maximize the chances that their results will appear robust. After all, all other things equal, a baseline model estimate that has wider confidence intervals is more likely to be found robust than one with narrower confidence bands. This is only logical: the larger the uncertainty of the baseline model, the smaller the extent to which robustness tests can add further to the uncertainty. But all other things are not equal. If researchers intentionally specify their baseline model less well than they can, the degree of robustness of the baseline model's estimate will likely increase for some tests but decrease for others. Particularly if the choice of robustness tests is not left to researchers alone but partly determined by reviewers and editors, a strategic misuse of robustness may backfire, thus diminishing the incentive.

4.4 CONTINUOUS VERSUS DICHOTOMOUS ROBUSTNESS

According to our definition, the degree of robustness ρ is a continuous measure, ranging from 0 to 1. We think this has important advantages. A continuous concept of robustness reflects the fact that robustness comes in degrees and not as a dichotomy. Higher values of ρ represent a higher degree of robustness and lower values represent a lower degree of robustness. Robustness tests can increase the confidence in the baseline model's estimated effect size if ρ exceeds 0.95. Yet, the majority of robustness tests will result in a ρ smaller than 0.95, which suggests a higher level of uncertainty than the baseline model implies. Robustness tests provide a more realistic picture of the uncertainty of the baseline model's point estimate. The true uncertainty stems not only from sampling variability expressed by the baseline model estimate's standard error but also from model uncertainty and its consequences.

Nonetheless, researchers are familiar with critical values of, for example, statistical tests and might crave a criterion for when to regard a robustness test estimate as suggesting non-robustness. Generally speaking, we do not believe that the arbitrary creation of critical values for robustness is useful, just as we do not believe that the arbitrary distinction between statistically significant and statistically insignificant – with its consequence of arbitrary rejection decisions (of null hypotheses and of manuscripts in the review process) – has served the social sciences well (Gill 1999). Arbitrary thresholds provide a major obstacle to the accumulation of scientific knowledge. With this caveat in mind, if scholars wanted to look for a critical value for ρ, it is likely to be 0.05 since in this case 95 percent of the probability density function of the robustness test estimate lies outside the baseline model's confidence interval. Accordingly, the robustness test model estimate does not support the baseline model estimate.

We nevertheless urge scholars to abstain from clinging to arbitrary bounds for "robust" versus "non-robust." The important element of robustness testing is not to define arbitrary thresholds in order to dismiss certain findings as irrelevant. Both high and low degrees of robustness provide important information. High degrees of robustness indicate that model specification does not exert much influence over the estimated effect. An apparent lack of robustness indicates large uncertainty about the estimated effect. We believe that all non-trivial estimation models will lack robustness to some degree in some dimension. A lack of robustness signals an important research question, it does not falsify a theory, a prediction, or a hypothesis.

4.5 ROBUSTNESS AND STATISTICAL SIGNIFICANCE

Despite all known shortcomings and flaws of Fisher significance (Gill 1999; Rainey 2014; Gross 2015), social scientists are used to basing their inferences on whether an estimated effect is statistically significant. The widespread recognition of model uncertainty and the rise of robustness testing put an end to the idea that a single model, a single parameter estimate and its sampling error can be used to make valid statistical inferences. It did not, however, put an end to statistical significance as the predominant criterion for making inferences, which maintained its status through the back door by becoming the dominant way in which robustness is assessed.

Starting from Leamer's idea of sensitivity testing (Leamer 1978), most applied scholars even today define robustness through an extreme bounds analysis: a baseline model estimate is robust to plausible alternative model specifications if and only if all estimates have the same direction and are all statistically significant.[3] Let us call this "Leamer robustness" for short.

In stark contrast, our definition of the concept of robustness, and our measure of the degree of robustness ρ based on this concept, are independent of the level of statistical significance of the effects in either baseline or robustness test models. All that matters for computing ρ are the point estimates and the standard errors of the baseline and the robustness test model.[4] We contend that the logic of robustness testing is incompatible with Leamer robustness and that useful definitions of robustness must refer to stability in estimated effect sizes or effect strengths as in our definition.[5]

On a fundamental level, Leamer robustness ignores that the difference between a statistically significant baseline model result and an insignificant robustness test result need not be statistically significant. For the same reason a statistically insignificant result in a replication exercise does not necessarily demonstrate that a statistically significant prior result has proven non-replicable (Goodman 1992). Gelman and Stern (2006: 329) correctly point out that if one were to make statistical significance the criterion for inference from multiple estimations, then "one should look at the statistical

---

3 For example, in robustness tests for their analysis of the presence of multiple veto players on the credibility of monetary commitments, Keefer and Stasavage (2002: 772) find that the "test statistics are significant in most cases at the one percent level and in all but one case at the ten percent level of confidence." In a paper analyzing how the stock values of seven European defense companies respond to EU summit decisions on defense policy, Bechtel and Schneider (2010: 219) conclude their robustness test as follows: "The coefficient of the summit outcome variable (...) remains positive and statistically significant". Nordås and Davenport (2013: 934f.) find that "the results for youth bulges remain highly significant (at the 1% level)" in robustness tests for their analysis of the effect of large youth cohorts on state repression. We could cite many more examples, including from our own publications.

4 Thus, with a baseline model that has a point estimate of 1.0 with standard error of 0.3, ρ is 0.72 regardless of whether the robustness test point estimate is 0.5 with standard error 0.4 or is 1.5 with standard error 0.4: the difference in point estimates between the baseline and the two robustness test models, the standard errors of the robustness test models, and the 95-percent confidence interval of the baseline model are all identical.

5 We acknowledge that ours is only one way of defining robustness in terms of effect stability.

significance of the difference" in two results "rather than the difference between their significance levels."

Leamer robustness is at odds with an understanding of robustness as the extent to which the robustness test estimate is compatible with and supports the baseline model's estimate. This cannot be assessed without direct reference to the baseline model's estimated effect size and confidence interval. The robustness of the baseline model estimate is not tested by merely checking whether the robustness point estimate has the same sign and remains statistically significant when the actual point estimate and its associated confidence interval can be very different from the baseline model estimate. Would social scientists really call a baseline model estimate of 10 with small standard errors robust to a robustness test estimate of 2 with sufficiently small standard errors below 1 so that it too is statistically significant?

Equally importantly, due to the fact that multiple models can never all be assumed to represent the optimal trade-off between generality and simplicity, employing Leamer robustness to reject null hypotheses is based on a flawed inferential logic. At best, Leamer robustness provides a one-sided test: if all estimates have the same sign and remain significant, analysts can reject the null hypothesis with greater confidence. However, the opposite inference that the null hypothesis is correct – usually that there is no effect – cannot be derived from the fact that not all models generate estimates with the same sign and the minimum level of statistical significance since one of the models could be severely misspecified or inefficiently estimated. In other words, Leamer robustness has an extremely low probability for making false positives errors but an unreliably high probability for committing false negatives errors (Plümper and Traunmüller 2016). Rejecting hypotheses based on a lack of Leamer robustness, thus, potentially allows the worst specified model or the model estimated with lowest efficiency to determine the overall inference. Since both errors are equally problematic and can lead to costly faulty policy recommendations (Lemons et al. 1997), there is no "conservative research design strategy" excuse for adopting Leamer robustness.

This problem of one-sidedness is exacerbated by the fact that in a number of robustness test models standard errors increase *by design*. The estimated effect may well become statistically insignificant, but this does not necessarily cast doubt on the robustness of the baseline model estimate. For example, many authors employ robustness tests in which they restrict the sample in some way and thus discard some observations. Naturally, the reduced sample size lowers the efficiency of the estimates and renders finding a statistically non-significant estimate more likely.[6] This

---

6 In the study by Bechtel and Schneider (2010), for example, one robustness test restricts the sample to estimating immediate effects (abnormal returns on the day

similarly applies to other robustness tests that discard information – for example, unit fixed-effects robustness test models that drop all the between-variation in the data.

In contrast, in our definition of robustness, estimation models with large power exert a potentially large influence, namely when the estimated effects differ. In our definition of robustness, the consequences of efficiency for the degree of robustness depend on the location of the robustness test model's point estimate. If it is far from the baseline model's point estimate, small standard errors of the robustness test signal non-robustness, not robustness. Larger standard errors signal greater robustness but never high degrees of robustness. If the robustness test point estimate is close to the baseline model's point estimate, robustness test models that lack efficiency (that come with fairly large standard errors) are not informative: these estimates do not signal non-robustness unless the size of standard errors substantially exceeds the size of the baseline model estimate's standard error.

Finally, the hunt for statistical significance has always incentivized the selection of model specifications according to p-values. Adopting Leamer robustness as the inferential criterion with a small number of highly selected robustness tests – most social scientists report only few robustness tests – will fuel the undesirable tendency to find everything significant and hence robust in empirical analyses. Ever since Fisher's (1925) original proposal of null hypothesis significance testing, social scientists have learned how to "tweak" significance and to conceal the lack thereof. Coupled with the fact that "undisclosed flexibility in data collection and analysis allows presenting anything as significant" (Simmons et al. 2011: 1359), published empirical social science research seems to be robust to an astonishing degree.[7]

In sum, the logic of robustness testing conflicts with defining robustness as effects remaining statistically significant with the same sign. Defining robustness instead as stability in effect size embraces the logic of robustness testing. It perfectly fits with the call by a growing number of authors for

---

after the summit). The estimated effect becomes statistically insignificant at the 5-percent level. The increase in standard errors is obviously triggered by the sharp decline in the number of observations (from 1,554 to 222). Why would a result become not robust only because researchers artificially reduce the available information used to estimate the effects?

7 Negative findings are important and in need of robustness testing as well. We wholeheartedly agree with the editors of eight health economics journals who issued an editorial statement on negative findings that clearly states that results from well-designed studies "have potential scientific and publication merit regardless of whether such studies' empirical findings do or do not reject null hypotheses that may be specified" (Editors 2015: 505).

social scientists to focus on the substantive importance of their estimated effects (Ziliak and McCloskey 2008; Esarey and Danneman 2015). As Gill (1999: 657f.) has put it: "Finding population-effect sizes is actually the central purpose of political science research since any difference can be found to be statistically significant given enough data."

4.6 PARTIAL ROBUSTNESS IN NON-LINEAR AND LINEAR MODELS

Up to this point, we have defined robustness as stability of the estimated effect of a variable, implicitly assuming a single estimated effect. In all non-linear estimation models, however, coefficients do not represent effects and estimated effects are a function of the values of all explanatory variables in the model. Non-linear models, thus, do not have a single effect of variable x on outcome y. In practice, authors often report the marginal effect at mean values or at median values or at other specified variable values that for some reason are of particular interest, or at variable values as observed in the sample and averaged across all observations (called the average marginal effect).

Hanmer and Kalkan (2013) make the case for basing inferences to the population on the average marginal effect. Cameron and Trivedi (2010: 340) suggest that for policy analysis one might want to look at either the average marginal effect or at targeted specified values. We agree with the latter suggestion: if researchers know to what part of the population they intend to generalize findings, they should compute the effects for cases that are similar to the part of population to which they wish to generalize. In most cases, problems occur if no case represents the entire population and if researchers do not intend to make targeted generalizations. This is a problematic practice if effect strengths vary with covariates: in non-linear models or in linear models with non-linear effects, conditional effects, or causal or temporal heterogeneity. In all of these cases, predicted effects which are representative for the entire sample do not exist.

Whenever effect strengths differ across cases, the degree of robustness differs too. It may well be that robustness is high for some parts of the sample and low for other parts of the sample. For these situations, we have developed the concept of partial robustness that applies our definition of robustness to the predicted effect and its standard error for each observation. The predicted effect varies across observations in non-linear models and in all linear models that allow for non-linearity, conditionality or causal or temporal heterogeneity. Partial robustness means that the baseline model's estimated effect can be robust or more robust for some observations but non-robust or less robust for other observations.

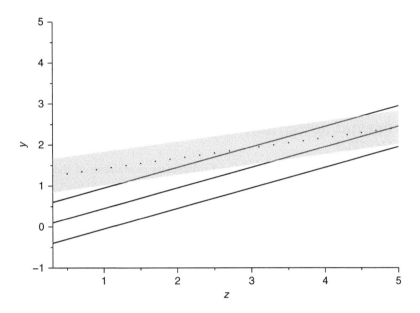

Figure 4.6: An Example of Partial Robustness
Note: Grey-shaded area represents confidence interval of baseline model.

To illustrate, assume a linear baseline and robustness test model that both estimate effects of x on y that are conditioned by z. The two models are specified differently; as a result, the estimated conditionality of x in the baseline model is weaker than in the robustness test model. Figure 4.6 shows point estimates with associated confidence intervals for the effect of x as a function of varying values of z for the baseline and robustness test model.

For values of z smaller than 1.6, the estimated degrees of robustness are below 0.05. At $z=1.6$, the degree of robustness is 0.05 and continues to increase to 0.98 as z increases to 4.9, the point where the point predictions are identical. Figure 4.6 thus demonstrates partial robustness: 0 or low degrees of robustness at low levels of z and high degrees of robustness at high values of z.

4.7 CONCLUSION

This chapter filled the concept of robustness with meaning. While the object of robustness depends on the research question and the intended inferences, the baseline model's estimate should be subjected to robustness testing in the form of systematic plausible changes to model specification. Robustness comes in degrees, we have argued, rather than as robust versus non-robust.

We have defined the estimated degree of robustness ρ as the degree to which the probability density function of the robustness test model's estimate falls within the 95-percent confidence interval of the baseline model. Put simply, ρ measures the extent to which the robustness test model supports the baseline model's estimated effect. Like all definitions, ours is neither right nor wrong. But it is useful, we have argued, since it has desirable properties. It both pays heed to how close the point estimates are and considers the sampling variability of both estimates.

There is another sense in which robustness comes in degrees. Whenever the estimation model is non-linear, the estimated degree of robustness will differ across observations, unless analysts restrict their analysis to effect sizes at specified variable values such as mean, median or targeted values or to the average of marginal effects across observations. Whenever they estimate non-linear, conditional or heterogeneous effects, the estimated degree of robustness will inevitably differ across observations even in a linear estimation model. We call this concept partial robustness: the effect can be more robust for some observations and non-robust or at least less robust for other observations.

Our definition of robustness conflicts with the implicit or explicit ad hoc definition of many who seem to equate robustness with an effect continuing to be statistically significant with the same sign in the robustness test model. According to our definition, an effect can be robust to a high degree or can be non-robust (be robust to a low degree) independently of whether the baseline or robustness test model's estimates are statistically significant. Robustness differs conceptually from statistical significance.

5 A Typology of Robustness Tests

We may at once admit that any inference from the particular to the general must be attended with some degree of uncertainty, but this is not the same as to admit that such inference cannot be absolutely rigorous.
Ronald Fisher (1966)

5.1 INTRODUCTION

The number and variety of possible robustness tests is large and, if tiny details and small differences matter, potentially infinite. The research project and its design as well as the degree of uncertainty about specific modelling assumptions determine the choice of robustness tests. Not every possible robustness test is relevant for each research project. To the contrary: each project requires a distinct set of tests, as the relevance of each test depends on the specificities of model uncertainty, the intended inferences, and the data structure.

The great variety and large number of tests appears bewildering. To cut through this diversity, we suggest in this chapter a typology of robustness tests. Specifically, we distinguish between five types: model variation tests, randomized permutation tests, structured permutation tests, robustness limit tests, and placebo tests. Model variation tests vary one specific aspect of model specification in a discrete way. Randomized permutation tests randomly select robustness test models from a large space of plausible alternative models. Structured permutation tests exhaustively select all plausible alternative models from a small space or select a few models in a structured way with the aim of representing the entire distribution of models in the larger space of plausible alternative models. Robustness limit tests ask which model specification, which could represent a model misspecification, renders the baseline model estimate non-robust. Placebo tests either replace the dependent variable with a placebo variable to test that the variable of interest has no effect under conditions in which no effect is to be expected, or replace the treatment variable with a placebo variable to test that this placebo variable has no effect. Alternatively, researchers assume that the baseline model is correctly specified in a certain dimension and placebo tests intentionally introduce a model misspecification given this assumption to test whether the baseline model estimate of the variable of interest remains robust despite the introduction of a model misspecification. Placebo tests of this kind represent the exception to the general rule that robustness test models should not be implausibly specified.

5.2 MODEL VARIATION TESTS

Model variation tests are as old as regression analysis. In model variation tests, researchers change their baseline model in discrete ways. The first scholar who added a control variable to his or her baseline model was probably the first person ever to conduct a robustness test.

Most researchers conduct this type of robustness test – usually without referring to it as robustness test at all. Yet, model variation tests go well beyond the addition or removal of control variables. They are flexible and can be applied to all dimensions of model uncertainty. In addition to adding and removing explanatory variables, it is possible to change the operationalization of the variable of interest and the controls, the sample, the functional form, to add or remove conditionalities, to change the specification of structural change, dynamics, spatial dependence, and so on.

Model variation robustness tests can be specified so that the baseline is nested in the robustness test model, so that the robustness test model is nested in the baseline model or so that the two models are non-nested. Nestedness requires that the baseline (robustness) test model is a special or constrained case of the robustness (baseline) model. For example, the baseline model might opt for greater simplicity by estimating a linear effect of variable x, whereas a robustness test model might add the square of the variable to allow for a non-linear (quadratic) effect and greater complexity. In this case, the baseline model is nested in the robustness test model, which contains the baseline model as a special case. Conversely, the baseline model might opt for greater complexity by estimating a conditional effect of variable x, whereas a robustness test model might estimate an unconditional effect, thus exploring the robustness of baseline model estimate to a simpler robustness test model that is nested within the baseline model. Lastly, the two models are non-nested if neither represents a special or constrained case of the other. For example, scholars might operationalize democracy in the baseline model with one measure and explore the robustness of the estimate with another measure of democracy in a robustness test model.

Examples of model variation tests in the literature abound. For example, in one of the most extensive early robustness tests, Tucker, Pacek, and

Berinsky (2002) use alternative survey questions, re-code the answer categories, and estimate models that exclude "don't know" answers to analyze attitudes towards EU membership in transition countries. Carey and Hix (2011: 389) are concerned about their arbitrary decision of a functional form: "We do not know whether some other functional form might describe the shape of the diminishing returns even better." They therefore replace their baseline specification by robustness test models adding first the squared, then the squared and cubic terms. Gibler and Tir (2010: 959) replace their baseline model autocracy–democracy threshold by both higher and lower thresholds.

A popular model variation robustness test seems to be to split the sample at a defined line. Muckherjee and Singer (2010) use this test in their analysis of the influence of the IMF on capital account liberalization. Likewise, Nielsen et al. (2011) split their sample into small and large conflicts. In an interesting study, Boix (2011: 819) analyzes the influence of democracy on per capita income using a structural equation model with instruments. As a robustness test, he varies the instruments, ranging from trade share to initial income ratio times the time trend. Though instrumental variables models estimate local effects and cannot be expected to give identical results, Boix's estimates at least all point in the same direction.

As these examples demonstrate, model variation tests are best suited for model uncertainty with a small set of discrete plausible alternatives. If, for example, a variable can be plausibly operationalized in two ways, the design of the model variation robustness test is fairly straightforward: use both operationalizations. In practice, these situations occur, but they are rare. For the majority of specification choices, a larger number of plausible alternatives exist and sometimes this number is very large or even infinite, in which case other types of robustness tests become attractive. Still, even in this case it is possible to test the robustness of the baseline model in comparison with the most common, the most plausible or the most drastic of alternative specifications. The argument for the most plausible test is simple, albeit a bit tautological: different potential robustness test model specifications differ in their degree of plausibility, and researchers should opt for the test that appears to be the most plausible. An alternative strategy employs the most common alternative specification. The advantage here is that the majority of peers will find the robustness test relevant. The most drastic specification is one that, in expectation, puts most strain on the baseline model, i.e. the test that offers the highest ex-ante likelihood to result in non-robust findings. Care must be taken not to choose a model that is not plausible since models known to be misspecified are not valid robustness tests. Despite these options for employing model variation tests even in situations where the number of plausible specifications in the uncertain dimension is large, other robustness test types become more attractive. The next three types can all deal with a large number of alternatives.

5.3 RANDOMIZED PERMUTATION TESTS

Model uncertainties for which a large number of alternatives exist can be dealt with by either randomized or structured permutation tests. We refer to the former as randomized permutation tests because the uncertainty of a model specification is dealt with by randomly selecting a limited number of specifications from a larger set of potential specifications (the relevant model space) for the same specific dimension of model uncertainty. The number of random draws and of model iterations must be large enough to represent the relevant model space.

The challenge for randomized permutation tests lies in the definition of relevant model space. Care must be taken that only plausibly specified models are included by ex ante restricting the space to an exclusive model space or by minimizing the impact of implausibly specified models on the robustness analysis via ex-post evaluation of model specification (see Plümper and Traunmüller 2016). If the model space cannot easily be restricted either ex ante or ex post, the results from randomized permutation robustness tests become difficult to interpret. Findings that cast doubt on the robustness of estimates may be due to lack of robustness or due to the inclusion of implausibly specified models into the model space. The definition of the model space forms the Achilles heel of randomized permutation tests.

The problem of defining the model space becomes apparent in the best known randomized permutation test: Leamer's (1978) sensitivity analysis. Practically all of Leamer's followers have applied sensitivity analysis to the choice of explanatory variables, in which regressors are selected from a large set of possible variables via randomized permutation, though some variables are always included in order to limit the overall model space. In Leamer's original formulation, robustness requires that all estimates have the same sign and all estimates are statistically significantly different from zero. Since early sensitivity tests of economic growth theories (Levine and Renelt 1992) demonstrated that few variables pass this extreme bounds test, Xavier Sala-i-Martin (1997: 179) argues that extreme bounds analysis "is too strong for any variable to pass it: if the distribution of the estimators of βz has some positive and some negative support, then one is bound to find one regression for which the estimated coefficient changes sign if enough regressions are run. Thus, giving the label of non-robust to all variables is all but guaranteed." Instead, he suggests measuring robustness by the density function of the weighted model averaged estimates. If 95 percent of this density function lies to either side of zero, the effect of a variable can be considered robust.[1] He suggests two variants of model weighting depending on whether the distribution of estimates is assumed to be normal or not normal, both based on the integrated likelihood of estimated models.[2] As Sala-i-Martin (1997: 180) himself admits, such goodness-of-fit weights need not be a good measure of the quality of model specification. In fact, clearly misspecified models can exhibit high goodness-of-fit, for example due to variables being endogenous. Consequently, we regard this kind of sensitivity analysis as failing the requirements for a valid robustness test.

Randomized permutation tests are not limited to sensitivity testing of the set of explanatory variables. For example, researchers may explore the robustness of a baseline model in the presence of measurement uncertainty. Researchers can randomize the extent of artificial measurement error injected into variable values across the plausible potential range of error. Instead of eliminating measurement error from the data, this test explores whether measurement error of a defined maximum magnitude affects the robustness of estimates and potentially invalidates inferences based upon them. The bounds of artificial measurement error should not be larger than the largest measurement error that likely occurs in reality. While this may sound cryptic, social scientists usually have information that allows them to justify the bounds of measurement error. For example, the January 2010 Haiti earthquake placed a plausible limit on measurement uncertainty in respect of mortality from large quakes in locations where reliable measurement appears difficult.

The split sample test provides another example of a randomized permutation test. The test aims at exploring the internal validity of causal homogeneity typically assumed in baseline models. The sample is randomly split in two halves and each observation in each half-sample is duplicated. If causal homogeneity holds, the baseline model estimate based on the causal homogeneity assumption will be robust to the estimates from these two split samples. While a single split sample estimate does not mean much, 1,000 split sample estimates can cover the relevant model space. This raises the question of how to assess robustness across the 1,000 estimates. Contrary to Leamer's sensitivity test, none of the models randomly selected by the split sample and the artificial measurement error tests is implausibly specified.

1 In a re-analysis of Levine and Renelt (1992), Sala-i-Martin (1997) found only one variable robustly related to growth based on extreme bounds. Using a model averaging approach, he identified 22 of the 59 tested variables as robust.

2 In Sala-i-Martin, Doppelhofer, and Miller (2004), the authors move to what they call a Bayesian averaging of classical estimates approach for model weighting.

We therefore suggest averaging the unweighted estimates of the permutations to assess robustness.

5.4 STRUCTURED PERMUTATION TESTS

In contrast to randomized permutation tests, structured permutation tests deal with uncertainty of a specific dimension of model specification by selecting either all alternative specifications or a limited number of specifications from a larger set of potential specifications according to some guiding principle. In other words, structured permutation tests are non-randomized and cover the model space either exhaustively or selectively but in a structured fashion.

The requirements for structured permutation tests are similar to the requirements of their randomized cousins: the model space and the robustness criterion have to be defined, but a rule to select models replaces the randomization algorithm. The same challenge to appropriately restrict the model space applies. In terms of assessing robustness, since with structured permutation tests the number of test models will typically be small to moderate, ρ can be computed and reported for each one.

Exploring the entire relevant model space in a systematic fashion can be done in either one of two ways. If the number of plausible alternative models is small, all models of the model space should be selected. For example, a variable x can be conditioned by more than one potential factor or analysts can relax the functional form assumption by estimating polynomial models of increasingly higher order up to a certain degree. If the model space becomes large because minuscule variations are possible, researchers have to make a discrete choice of plausible models – a choice that represents the entire distribution of plausible models or, put differently, the relevant model space.

With a large model space, the question becomes whether the space can really be represented by structured selection. If this is questionable, randomized permutation might be preferable. Covering the entire model space can quickly become computationally infeasible. Consider the example of an exhaustive structured variant of Leamer's sensitivity analysis. Rather than randomizing models, one would either estimate all possible combinations of explanatory variables (inclusive model space) or estimate all combinations which are not considered to be misspecified (exclusive model space). The number of possible permutations equals 2^k-1, where k is the number of considered explanatory variables. Thus, if 20 variables are known to potentially influence an outcome, the number of possible models reaches a shade above 1 million. If the number of potential explanatory factors doubles to 40, the number of possible models increases to 1,099,511,627,775. Assuming that a single estimate takes

0.1 second on average, the sensitivity test would need almost 3,500 years to finish on a single computer and still 3.5 years on 1,000 efficiently clustered computers. While randomized permutation tests have their advantages when the model space becomes very large, structured permutation tests have their strengths with relatively small model spaces or if the selected structured permutations represent the entire distribution of models.

A frequently used structured permutation robustness test is based on the jackknife method, which drops one unit or one group of units of analysis at a time, thereby exploring the extent to which estimates depend on the inclusion of single units or groups. They thus indicate a lack of internal validity or – potentially – causal heterogeneity. Jackknife tests are popular. Egorov, Guriev, and Sonin (2009), Lipsmeyer and Zhu (2011: 654) and Martin and Swank (2004, 2008) exclude one country at a time in their analyses. As another example of a structured permutation robustness test, in an excellent robustness test section Scheve and Slaughter (2004: 672) gradually expand the sample size and move away from what they consider to be the sample "for which the theoretical framework most directly applies."

A common structured permutation test relates to the aggregation of a continuous or categorical variable into two or more sub-categories. In these cases, the "true" cut-off points are unknown. Accordingly, robustness tests can vary the chosen cut-off point to explore whether results are independent of the threshold. Take the *polity2* measure of democracy as an example. Besley and Reynal-Querol (2011) use a dichotomous distinction between autocracies and democracies setting the cut-off point at 0, i.e. democracies are defined as scoring 1 or higher on the scale that runs from –10 to 10. Cut-off points are arbitrary and thus controversial, and this example is no exception. Other authors prefer a higher threshold. Fearon and Laitin (2003), for example, use a cut-off point of 5, others use the even higher score of 6 (Bigsten 2013: 31) as threshold. A structured permutation test uses *all* plausible cut-off points.

As a final example of structured permutation tests, Michael Bailey (2005) employs a simple but appealing "varying control group approach" to analyze the migration response of poor single mothers who receive the treatment of a specific welfare benefit. Recognizing that his research design "requires that I include in the sample a 'control group' that is not eligible for welfare but otherwise resembles the 'treatment group' of poor single mothers" (Bailey 2005: 127), he follows two previous studies in using three different control groups of people who were not eligible for the particular welfare benefit. In his baseline model he uses poor women, but changes the control group to, separately, poor men without children and to married women with children. He chooses these groups to explore the robustness of findings (Bailey 2005: 127): "No group perfectly matches the welfare population, but all match in some way the skill profiles and economic circumstances of poor single mothers. Using multiple specifications should increase confidence in the robustness of the results."

ROBUSTNESS LIMIT TESTS

The vast majority of robustness tests ask whether the baseline model estimates remain robust to plausible changes in model specification. However, not all robustness tests seek to check the degree of robustness given plausible alternative specifications. Robustness limit tests, which are inspired by "Rosenbaum bounds" (Rosenbaum 2002), though others like Frank (2000), Pan and Frank (2003), and Frank and Min (2007) have independently developed similar ideas, instead ask by how much the specification of a model needs to change to render the baseline model estimate non-robust.

Consider, as an example, the choice of functional form. Rather than analyzing whether the estimated effect is robust to a change in functional form of the variable of interest, researchers can ask to what degree the functional form needs to change to render the baseline model estimate not robust. Robustness limit tests work particularly well with model specifications that can be altered in a continuous fashion. For example, a set of estimates can explore what the correlation between a random placebo variable and the variable of interest needs to be to render the estimated effect non-robust.

Rosenbaum (1991, 2002) develops his idea of the bounds of hidden bias based on the example of the effect of smoking on lung cancer. His analysis draws on two previous works: Cornfield, Haenszel, Hammond, Lilienfeld, Shimkin, and Wynder (1959) were the first to use the logic of a bounds test. In an argument worth citing despite its convoluted English, they claim (p. 194):

If an agent, A, with no causal effect upon the risk of a disease, nevertheless, because of a positive correlation with some other causal agent, B, shows an apparent risk, r, for those exposed to A, relative to those not so exposed, the prevalence of B, among those exposed to A, relative to the prevalence among those not so exposed, must be greater than r. Thus, if cigarette smokers have 9 times the risk of nonsmokers for developing lung cancer, but this is not because cigarette smoke is a causal agent, but only because cigarette smokers produce hormone X, then the proportion of hormone X-producers among cigarette smokers must be at least 9 times greater than that of nonsmokers. If the relative prevalence of hormone X-producers is considerably less than ninefold, the hormone X cannot account for the magnitude of the apparent effect.

Based on this logic, the authors came to conclude that the evidence for smoking causing cancer is "beyond reasonable doubt," just as a Study

Group appointed by the National Cancer Institute, the National Heart Institute, the American Cancer Society, and the American Heart Association had proclaimed two years prior.[3]

The second study on which Rosenbaum relies is an analysis of matched pairs (Hammond 1964). This analysis identified 36,975 heavy smokers and nonsmokers who were (almost) identical in respect of age, race, time of birth, residence, occupational exposure to dust and fumes, religion, education, marital status, alcohol consumption, sleep duration, exercise, nervous tension, use of tranquilizers, current health, history of cancer and heart disease, stroke, and high blood pressure. Of these pairs 12 nonsmokers and 110 heavy smokers died of lung cancer. The lung cancer mortality rate among heavy smokers was thus below 0.3 percent ($p=0.002975$), but still more than 9 times higher than the lung cancer mortality among nonsmokers, which stood at 0.000325. The probability that the gap is random if we had a perfect random draw from a population was 0.0001.

Rosenbaum uses this information for what he calls a sensitivity test. He asks by how much an unobserved lung cancer propensity factor of heavy smokers has to exceed that of non-smoking individuals to render the causal effect of smoking statistically insignificant. Rosenbaum (2002: 114) concludes: "To attribute the higher rate of death from lung cancer to an unobserved covariate u rather than to an effect of smoking, that unobserved covariate would need to produce a sixfold increase in the odds of smoking, and it would need to be a near perfect predictor of lung cancer."

As Rosenbaum demonstrates, robustness bounds can be computed analytically. However, it is possible and in many cases easier to conduct robustness limit tests. These tests gradually increase the degree of "pressure" on the baseline model. It works best where researchers have a clear idea about a potential model misspecification that is difficult or impossible to correct, for example because of potential confounders that are unobservable or unobserved due to measurement problems. To stay in the example of the effect of smoking on lung cancer, the correlated artificial variable test proposed in chapter 9 on the choice of explanatory variables plays with two "moving elements" of an artificial variable that "by design" leads to cancer: the probability that a latent variable causes cancer and the correlation between this variable and smoking. As both

---

3 This logic depends on numerous untested assumptions. Most importantly, the authors assume that treatments are either present or absent and if absent either equally strong or, if strength matters, the strength is irrelevant for the causal effect. For example, the true causal effect may well be that smoking is correlated to an intensified production of hormone X, which has to exceed a certain threshold to stimulate the occurrence of lung cancer. Hence, it may well be that smokers only have 30 percent higher production of hormone X, but they may be nine times as likely to pass the threshold required for cancer.

factors go up, the predicted effect of smoking declines (while the uncertainty of an effect of smoking increases). In addition to the robustness limit scholars might be interested in the uncertainty of the estimate.

Robustness limit tests have drawbacks. Most importantly, the interpretation of results is not straightforward. Interpretation is easy if and only if researchers have sufficient information to conclude that the model that reaches the robustness limit is misspecified. Rosenbaum argues exactly this: the effect of a lung cancer phenotype correlated with smoking necessary to overturn the effect of smoking would have to be too large to plausibly exist. In other cases, it remains contested what to make of the robustness limit test: does the test suggest that the baseline model estimate fails the robustness test or does it instead suggest that the baseline model estimate is robust because the model that reaches the robustness limit is misspecified?

As a corollary, if the limit is known beyond which a model becomes clearly misspecified, analysts have two options: firstly, they can use a randomized or structured permutation test and assess the robustness of the baseline model estimate within the boundary. Alternatively, they can go beyond this boundary to study where the robustness limit lies, knowing that models which reach the robustness limit are misspecified. Take the example of measurement uncertainty. If the bounds of plausible measurement error can be established, a randomized or structured permutation test can explore robustness within the boundary. Alternatively, a robustness limit test can find the extent of measurement error that needs to be injected to render the estimate non-robust and can then assess whether this extent of measurement error falls within the boundary of plausible measurement error.

Robustness limit tests are rare in the social sciences. Imai, Keele, Tingley, and Yamamoto (2011) propose such tests as part of their methodological contribution on how to learn about causal mechanisms in observational and experimental studies:

Given that the identification of causal mechanisms relies upon an untestable assumption, it is important to evaluate the robustness of results to potential violation of this assumption. Sensitivity analysis provides one way to do this. The goal of a sensitivity analysis is to quantify the exact degree to which the key identification assumption must be violated for a researcher's original conclusion to be reversed.

(Imai et al. 2011: 774)

We agree with the authors that robustness limit tests always explore robustness in one specific dimension of model misspecification, not in other or all dimensions. Imai et al. (2011: 774) correctly warn readers about the limitations of their robustness limit test:

Although sensitivity analysis can shed light on whether the estimates obtained under sequential ignorability are robust to possible hidden pretreatment confounders, it is important to note the limitations of the proposed sensitivity analysis. First, the proposed method is designed to probe for sensitivity to the presence of an unobserved *pretreatment confounder*. In particular, it does not address the possible existence of confounders that are affected by the treatment and then confound the relationship between the mediator and the outcome.

Robustness limit tests are powerful in directing future research. Assume a researcher wishes to explore whether controlling for time-invariant "unobserved heterogeneity" renders the baseline model estimate non-robust. One option is a model variation test that includes unit fixed effects. As chapter 9 shows, this strategy may have severe drawbacks, including testing a hypothesis that differs from the theoretically derived hypothesis as well as potentially inappropriately throwing away variation that belongs to the estimated effect – thereby throwing out the baby with the bath water. As an alternative, we propose a between-variation test that can find the percentage of between-variation that needs to be dropped to render the baseline model estimate non-robust.[4]

5.6 PLACEBO TESTS

Up to this point, we have argued that, other than for robustness limit tests, models used in robustness tests must be plausibly specified. Placebo tests are different. To understand why, we first make a detour into medical trials.

Placebo analyses are most commonly used in experimental research with human participants. Placebo-controlled studies are a way of testing a medical therapy in which, in addition to a group of subjects that receives the treatment to be evaluated, a control group receives a placebo treatment specifically designed to have no real effect. Placebos have to be employed in blinded trials where subjects do not know whether they are receiving real or placebo treatment. Often, the experiment includes a third group that does not receive any treatment at all.

The placebo treatment aims at accounting for the placebo effect. This effect is caused by the treatment act – the psychological effect of receiving attention from health care professionals – rather than by the proper treatment, that is, a substance or procedure that supposedly has an effect. Typically, social scientists define the treatment effect as the net effect of the observed change in the treated group minus the observed change in the placebo group. If it were ethically possible and if an appropriate placebo

---

4 Additional research can analyze which factors usually assumed to be time-invariant such as history, institutions, culture, and geography can account for this between-variation and whether the estimated effect is robust with these additional time-invariant control variables included.

existed, researchers could study the effect of smoking on lung cancer by giving the treatment group cigarettes and the control group placebos which are identical to cigarettes in all dimensions except one: they do not contain carcinogenic substances.

Placebo robustness tests in regression analysis of observational data are similar, but not identical to placebo analysis in experiments. They come in two variants. In the first variant, researchers intentionally "misspecify" the model by either switching the dependent variable to one for which the variable of interest is expected to not have an effect (i.e., becomes a placebo variable) or by keeping the same dependent variable but switching the treatment variable to a placebo variable which is expected to not have an effect on the original dependent variable. Instead of testing the robustness of the baseline model's estimate, a placebo test asks whether the placebo variable that replaces the treatment variable does or does not have an effect on the original dependent variable or whether the variable of interest loses its explanatory power if we replace the original dependent variable with a placebo variable.

In the second variant of placebo robustness tests, researchers make a specification change that, under the assumption that the baseline model is correctly specified in a certain dimension, represents a misspecification. For example, scholars can add a placebo variable to the estimation model that in expectation does not affect the robustness of the baseline model estimate for the variable of interest. In this variant, analysts continue to estimate the degree of robustness similar to other types of robustness tests. Placebo robustness tests of the second variant have to be permutation tests. For example, it does not make sense to add a single randomly distributed placebo variable to the model since by pure chance it could affect robustness. Rather, a large number of permutations are needed – we recommend at least 1,000 permutations if computationally feasible – to render such chance impact unlikely.

For placebo tests of the first variant a single model run will not be conclusive either since pure chance can suggest relevant effects where none exist and suggest no effects where they do exist. However, it may not be feasible to undertake permutations since there may exist only one alternative dependent variable for which the treatment variable should have no effect or only one option to switch the treatment variable into a placebo variable. For the same reason, placebo robustness tests of this variant are somewhat limited since they require either the existence of an alternative dependent variable which is independent of the variable of interest or the possibility to transform the variable of interest, the treatment variable, into a placebo variable.

Folke, Hirano, and Snyder (2011) provide a clever example of the first variant of a placebo robustness test. While the baseline model demonstrates that parties in power were able to use patronage to improve their chances of winning at later elections, their placebo test demonstrates that no such relation exists for prior elections. Similarly, Gerber and Huber (2009: 415) show that partisanship has no placebo effect "under conditions where our model predicts partisanship and consumption should be unrelated."

Occasionally, placebo tests can be a part of a structured permutation test in which a treatment variable becomes more and more a placebo variable. Consider the effect of democracy on an outcome where analysts use a dichotomous cut-off point to distinguish autocracies from democracies, which raises the question where to set the cut-off point. Of course, no "true" cut-off point exists. Democracy is a latent variable, proxy variables will be measured with error, and no consensus exists on where the true cut-off point is, not least because even in theory regime type falls along a spectrum instead of into a clean dichotomy. At the same time, certain cut-off points are not plausible and can thus function as placebo tests. For the example of the *polity2* measure of democracy which runs from –10 to 10, reducing the cut-off point to lower values represents a structured permutation test. At some point, further decreasing the cut-off point should result in the test finding the baseline model estimate to be less and less robust, just as it is designed to be.

A prime example of a placebo test of the second variant adds a random variable. It is of no interest whether the estimate for the placebo variable turns out to be statistically significant or not. By construction, random variables become statistically significant at the 95-percent level in roughly 5 percent of cases because the placebo variable is correlated to the random deviation of the errors from the assumed normal distribution of residuals. If the random placebo variable turns out to be significant in a substantially higher share of cases, the placebo variable is likely to be correlated to systematic structure in the residuals. This finding suggests some form of model misspecification though identifying the type of misspecification based solely on the structure in the residuals is not normally possible.

Placebo robustness tests become more informative when researchers do not add a purely random variable, but give the placebo variable a certain structural property to account for a potential specification error that is non-existent in the baseline model. Assume that researchers believe that they have specified their baseline model correctly in a certain dimension. For example, they believe that they have included relevant control variables that sufficiently account for time-invariant unobserved heterogeneity or that they have adequately modelled dynamics and temporal heterogeneity. Introducing time-invariant placebo variables or strongly trended placebo variables should not affect the stability of the baseline model's estimate for the variable of interest. However, in cases like these, placebo variables may become statistically significant in more than the expected 5 percent of permutations. In both cases, the impact of the inclusion of the placebo variable on the effect of the variable of interest matters.

In chapter 14 on spatial correlation and dependence we propose a structured spatial placebo test. Assume that the baseline model tests a theory of spatial dependence. As we have argued elsewhere (Neumayer and Plümper 2016a), the weighting matrix models the causal mechanism of a theoretical argument for spatial dependence. The connectivity variable employed in the weighting matrix and its specification must capture this mechanism. The placebo robustness test replaces the theoretically informed connectivity variable in the weighting matrix by a random variable. Since the weighting matrix is multiplied with the spatially lagged dependent variable, the spatial lag becomes statistically significant in more than 5 percent of permutations – not least because it will be correlated with the spatial-lag variable that employs the theoretically informed connectivity variable. Nevertheless, if the baseline model is not obviously misspecified, the effect of the spatial-lag variable based on the theoretically informed connectivity variable will remain robust to adding this spatial placebo variable.

5.7 CONCLUSION

The degree to which robustness tests contribute to the validity of inferences derived from regression analysis of observational data depends on the extent of uncertainty about model misspecification, on the theoretical justification and design of robustness tests as well as on the type of robustness tests chosen for dealing with this uncertainty. The vast majority of social scientists rely on simple model variation tests, which seem to have the advantage to scholars that they can be done easily and carefully selected to not render the baseline model estimates non-robust. These tests merely aim at providing additional arguments for journal editors and reviewers to accept a manuscript.

This standard practice stands in remarkable contrast to the best work in empirical social science. Indeed, an increasing number of authors conduct intelligently designed, increasingly complex robustness tests of multiple types, going well beyond simple model variation tests. To us, robustness tests are an essential element of causal inference based on regression analysis of observational data, where researchers cannot guarantee the correct specification of the baseline model. Yes, replacing one variable operationalization by another constitutes a robustness test as do other model variation tests, but randomized permutation tests, structured permutation tests, robustness limit tests, and placebo tests, if well specified, offer deeper insights into the validity of causal inferences. If used optimally, robustness tests allow scholars to improve the validity of causal inferences and to identify their limits, for example, the limits of generalizability. However, to seize this great opportunity, social scientists need to take robustness testing seriously and stop misusing them as a means to increase their publication chances. In best practice, robustness tests are no longer part of a publication strategy, they become an essential part of the research strategy.

6 Alternatives to Robustness Testing?

No amount of experimentation can ever prove me right.
Attributed to Albert Einstein

6.1 INTRODUCTION

Robustness tests provide social scientists with the means to improve the validity of statistical inferences based on the analysis of observational data. Regressions analyses of observational data will remain at the heart of the methodological toolkit for quantitative social science research though they are fraught with model uncertainty.

Robustness tests are not the only methodological option on offer for solving the problem of model uncertainty. Methodologists have developed alternative methods for analyzing observational data. They have also suggested that specific research designs strongly improve the probability of valid inferences from observational data. In addition, there are many who believe that the analysis of observational data cannot be free from ambiguities and that social scientists should simply follow the experimental turn in the sciences.

In this chapter we argue that these alternative methodologies offer no alternative to robustness testing. In short, an alternative methodology that allows researchers to formulate inferences that are valid with certainty does not exist – at least not if researchers intend to go beyond mere description. This provides the most fundamental reason why all methodologies require robustness testing: if no single research design, estimation procedure or analytical technique allows the derivation of perfectly valid inferences then every design, procedure or technique warrants subjecting its results to plausible alternative specifications to explore whether these generate sufficiently similar (robust) estimates.

Our argument may surprise those who have fallen under the spell of identification techniques and, particularly, social science experiments, erroneously believing that these alternative designs are not only unambiguously superior to regression analyses of observational data but also identify the true causal effect of a factor with certainty and therefore obliterate the need for robustness testing.

We concentrate here on what we regard as the most important alternatives to regression analyses. For each alternative methodology that we discuss, we identify the – in our view at least – most important specification uncertainties it suffers from. We make no pretense of being comprehensive in the choice of specification uncertainties we identify. Our objective is merely to persuade those readers who remain skeptical that indeed no methodology is free of specification uncertainty and consequently requires robustness testing for improving the validity of inferences based on these methodologies.

We start by staying within the realm of regression analyses and discuss why comprehensive model specification tests or model selection algorithms cannot result in identifying or at least sufficiently approximating the one "true" model. Acknowledging that it is not possible to find this model and that estimates based on any model are sensitive, some seek solace in averaging across a very large number of models. We then move to more recent methodological advances in the form of research designs based on the selection of cases (regression discontinuity, matching, and synthetic control), effect isolation via instrumental variable estimation and social science experiments.

6.2 MODEL SPECIFICATION TESTS

Econometricians have long since developed econometric tests aimed at detecting model misspecification. The hope is that a battery of tests will allow researchers to find the true model, or at least get sufficiently close to it. Econometric tests fall into three categories:

First, relative tests which say nothing about the absolute quality of a model, but compare two or more models. Yet, the best-fitting misspecified model remains misspecified. Often, as in the Hausman test, a comparison draws on whether the estimates from an estimator assumed to be consistent and an estimator assumed to be inconsistent are significantly different. Implicitly, these tests depend on the absence of other model misspecifications that render the "consistent" estimator inconsistent, e.g. time-varying omitted variables or misspecified dynamics in the classical Hausman test that compares a fixed-effects to a random-effects specification.

Second, model fit tests that assess the overall quality of a model with adjusted R-squared statistics, F-tests, and chi-squared tests as well as more complex "goodness-of-fit" measures. Often, the indicators become inflated by econometric patches which do not belong into the true model but are included in the hope that they account for omitted variables the researcher cannot or does not want to control for, e.g. unit fixed effects. This invalidates the goodness-of-fit test. Moreover, strong and implausible assumptions are required for making the claim that better-fitting models are better specified. For example, proponents of this claim would have to argue that over-fitting is impossible and to claim that better-fitting models are always better specified. Unfortunately, goodness-of-fit can be improved much more easily than model specification.

Third, model fit tests that analyze the residuals for structure. From our perspective, these tests are better suited than other tests to evaluate the quality of a model specification. We advocate the careful use of such tests for finding a baseline model. However, these tests will not find the "true" model and whether they always improve a model specification is debatable.

The main problem with econometric tests, even those that analyze the residuals for structure, is that they may signal the existence of a problem, but they fail to identify the problem's cause. For example, Ramsey's specification test is usually employed for detecting functional form misspecification, but a rejection of the null hypothesis can indicate a large number of other specification errors. A correlation between the regressors and the residuals can be caused by too many regressors, too few regressors, wrong regressors, wrong functional form, wrong interaction effect, and wrong functional form of interaction effect. The same holds for other specification tests (McAleer 1994: 330f.).

But what about a test contest of plausible models? Researchers could develop a set of plausible model specifications and then subject each of these model specifications to those tests that appear to have sufficient power to identify misspecified models. In principle, there is nothing wrong with this idea. However, the problem is that econometric tests remain inconclusive: whatever the specification test, more than one model will pass the test. Even if we could interpret a set of tests as a single model specification test that empirical models need to pass, there would still be more than one model specification that passes all econometric tests simultaneously. As Peach and Webb (1983: 697) already demonstrated in the 1980s, "econometric testing as sole criteria for discriminating among competing (...) models is inconclusive."

Accordingly, we currently see no possibility of conclusively discriminating between plausible models, that is, models that are not obviously misspecified. As a consequence, in order to improve the validity of their inferences researchers have to use robustness tests to analyze whether the estimated effects of these plausibly specified models are sufficiently similar.

6.3 MODEL SELECTION ALGORITHMS

The idea that model specification tests can find the "true" specification and that the process of finding "the truth" can be handed over to a computer program has been championed by David Hendry and his disciples. His "testing-down approach" (Krolzig and Hendry 2001; Hendry and Krolzig 2005) starts with a general statistical model that is "congruent" with the dataset: It "matches the data evidence on all the measured attributes" (Campos, Ericsson, and Hendry 2005: 7). The objective is to reduce the complexity of this model as much as possible by eliminating statistically insignificant variables. Here, "as much as possible" means that the more specific model must pass specification tests and must be congruent with the dataset. Specification tests are, in other words, used to establish the congruence of the general model and are repeatedly used to discard invalid reductions of the general model.

The general-to-specific approach has been criticized, because it "would require an enormously complex exercise, with a complete model of the joint distribution of all variables, allowing for non-linearities, heteroscedasticity, coefficient drift and non-Gaussian errors" (Hansen 1996: 1411). Magnus (1999: 61–62) similarly argues that the testing-down approach "does not work. If you try to estimate such a large model, which has everything in it that you can think of, you get nonsensical results."

Hendry and his followers are aware of this critique (Campos, Ericsson, and Hendry 2005: 6), but believe their approach can recover the so-called local data-generating process (Hendry 2002: 599). Yet, it remains unclear whether a "local data-generating process" exists at all and, if it does, whether the convenient error structure that researchers assume to exist is exactly matched in the real data-generating process.

In the specification search from the general to the specific model two principal errors can and indeed are likely to occur: variables are eliminated that should be retained in the model, while other variables are retained even though they should be eliminated. Its supporters contend that their highly sophisticated multiple-path search and testing algorithms minimize the risk of both errors and provide Monte Carlo evidence to this effect (Hoover and Perez 1999, 2004). Yet, there is no guarantee that relevant variables are retained and irrelevant ones eliminated, particularly not if variables are correlated with each other as they typically are and if models are misspecified.

In consequence, the results of testing-down approaches depend crucially on arbitrary decisions about model misspecification. For example, it is not possible to simultaneously include all possible functional forms, conditionalities, and dynamic specifications into the "general" model. Likewise, it is not possible to simultaneously include different samples into a testing-down experiment so that more than one plausible model and more than one effect estimate emerge as a result. In fact, testing-down approaches are hardly suited to deal with more than the selection of right-hand-side variables and perhaps functional form assumptions. In conclusion, model selection algorithms cannot address all dimensions of model uncertainty and cannot solve those dimensions they do address.

6.4 MODEL AVERAGING

Leamer (1978) pioneered the idea of basing inferences not on the results from a single model but on a potentially very large number of models. Methodologies which draw conclusions from multiple estimates require an aggregation rule. In Leamer's original analysis a single model exercised a veto right over inferences, as a particular result had to pass the test – of statistical significance in Leamer's definition of robustness – in every single model.

Followers of Leamer have adopted statistical significance as the criterion of robustness, which runs counter to our definition of robustness as stability in effect strength. More importantly, however, for the purpose of this chapter is that Leamer's disciples moved away from granting a single model veto right and instead adopted what is known as model averaging. Model averaging serves as a label for very different techniques; it can be combined with numerous inferential rules and with virtually infinite definitions of the model space included across which results are averaged. For example, our randomized and structured permutation tests also employ model averaging techniques within robustness testing. In this sense already, model averaging is an integral part of robustness testing and not an alternative. Many proponents of model averaging agree, including Bayesians. Montgomery and Nyhan (2010: 266), for example, suggest that Bayesian Model Averaging "is best used as a subsequent robustness check to show that our inferences are not overly sensitive to plausible variations in model specification."

This does not mean that model averaging is not regarded by some as an alternative technique to robustness testing as proposed in this book. Model averaging techniques require the following specification decisions:[1]

1 This discussion follows Plümper and Traunmüller (2016).

1. A definition of the parameter of interest and its computation;
2. A definition of the model space: the set of all models potentially included;
3. A selection rule that draws models from the model space;
4. A stop function that determines the number of estimated models;
5. An aggregation and weighting rule;
6. An inferential rule, which decides how to interpret the weighted mean of parameter estimates.

Consider model averaging for estimating the effect of educational attainment on economic growth as the parameter of interest. Even if researchers exclusively focus on one aspect of model uncertainty, namely the set of explanatory variables, the model space can become extremely large. The model space is usually constructed from the set of all combinations of explanatory variables that in the past have been used in growth regression studies, giving us at least 50 different variables. Including 50 variables into the set of explanatory variables from which to generate all potential permutations results in a model space of more than 1,000 trillion models. Yet, researchers who employ model averaging usually estimate only a few million models, that is, a very small fraction out of every possible model variant. A popular model selection rule has been suggested by Levine and Renelt (1992), who limit the model space by the 1+3+3 rule; the first variable is the variable of interest, then three variables are specified which are always included, and the final three variables are a random draw from the remaining 46 variables – thereby shrinking the model space to a little more than 15,000 models. Researchers have also used different weights, ranging from unweighted to the Bayesian or Akaike information criterion. Since model fit parameters tend to be correlated, the choice of a weight exerts considerably less influence than the decision to use weights rather than an unweighted mean of all estimates. Finally, at least in principle, scholars could use numerous different inferential rules. In practice, however, most researchers have followed Leamer and adopted statistical significance by looking at the share of the distribution around the (weighted) mean of all point estimates that crosses the threshold, usually of zero.

Model averaging lacks a clear intuitively plausible foundation. A model space of thousands, millions, let alone billions of models will include many utterly implausibly specified models. More importantly for our argumentation here, model averaging techniques rely on numerous model specification assumptions for which plausible alternatives exist – for example, on the functional form of an effect, the conditionality between variables, the definition of the population from which a sample is drawn, the definition of the model space, model selection rules, and the choice of weights. As a consequence, model averaging techniques require subjecting their results to robustness tests for improving the validity of inferences based on this technique.

6.5 CASE SELECTION RESEARCH DESIGNS

The recent rise of identification approaches in the social sciences brought case selection techniques back into the social scientists' toolbox. When done well, a careful selection of cases has two consequences: on the one hand, the selection of cases increases the homogeneity of cases analyzed. The more homogeneous the cases, the fewer confounding factors need to be controlled for to make valid inferences. Ideally, cases become not just more homogeneous but identical in all but the relevant dimension (the treatment), in which case it becomes possible to directly compute the causal effect, distorted only by the difference in the average random errors between treatment and control group. On the other hand, however, selection reduces the number of cases and the types of cases included in the sample. Since real world cases are likely to be characterized by causal heterogeneity and context conditionality, as selection gets stricter and stricter the sample properties become increasingly different from the population properties.

Research designs that employ selection rules aimed at improving the internal validity of estimates include regression discontinuity, matching, and synthetic control. Regression discontinuity designs exclusively compare cases that only just met the criteria to receive treatment in the treatment group with cases that only just failed to receive treatment in the control group – by assumption both sets of cases ought to be very similar to each other provided subjects did not exercise control over whether they received treatment or not. Matching selects cases from a larger sample, matching treated cases to similar, and ideally otherwise identical, untreated cases on the values of observable variables, with all other unmatched cases being discarded. Synthetic control designs employ some weighting rule to artificially create a control case (or a set of control cases) that closely resembles a treated case (or a set of treated cases). Thus, rather than finding an identical or sufficiently close twin of a specific case, researchers synthetically produce an almost identical twin by taking shares of other cases.

Selection-based research designs can deal fairly well with two specification problems: observable confounders and their functional form. Yet, all other model uncertainties remain. For example, since it is not possible to match or create a synthetic case control based on unobserved confounders, these techniques provide no solution to unknown confounding factors, but only against potential misspecification of the functional form of known confounders (Sekhon 2007, 2009). Specifically, matching gives unbiased results if and only if cases are matched based on the true model. If the matching algorithm excludes one or more variables which are included in the true model, matching estimates are biased.

Research designs that are based on case selection can only be generalized to a population that has properties identical to the selected sample. Unless the population of cases is characterized by strict causal homogeneity, the selected cases do not represent a random sample of the true population and the population to which results can be inductively generalized from the selected cases is therefore not the true population for which researchers seek to make causal inferences. Matching almost inevitably produces deviations of the sample from the population particularly in those parts of the population where the number of observations remains small so that perfect "matches" become unlikely. As a consequence, the matched samples will no longer represent the population. While it may be possible to "match" a sample in which, in principle, all permutations of treatments and conditionalities are represented, we are not aware of any attempt to produce such a matched sample in any study. Similarly, in regression discontinuity designs, the deviation of cases at the discontinuity threshold from other treated and untreated cases is likely to be non-negligible. The return on investment in higher education for somebody who almost failed to be accepted by a university ought to be smaller than the returns to the average student or the superstar among students.

It is questionable, in our view, whether it pays to trade off a potential increase in internal validity against a certain loss in external validity. In any case, robustness tests with different selected cases, possibly with entirely different analyses, are required to establish the extent to which the estimated effect can be generalized.

Beyond uncertainty about causal heterogeneity, selection-based research designs are also subject to other model uncertainties regarding the population, concept validity and measurement, dynamics, and spatial dependence. Consider spatial dependence: to analyze learning effects and externalities, a full sample is required. Missings and selection usually bias the results from spatial analyses. Accordingly, spatial dependence and selection-based research designs do not go well together. Selection-based research designs have to match cases based on their spatial dependence, regression discontinuities have to demonstrate that networks are identical on both sides of the discontinuity, and the synthetic case has to have identical ties and links to real cases. We are not arguing here that it is not possible to achieve this, but there must be a reason that no selection-based research design we have seen incorporates spatial dependence into the selection. In sum then, selection does not comprehensively solve the problem of model uncertainty. Selection-based designs quite successfully solve some dimensions of model uncertainty but maintain and even exacerbate others. As a consequence, selection-based research designs warrant robustness tests as much as regression analyses.

6.6 EFFECT ISOLATION VIA INSTRUMENTAL VARIABLE ESTIMATION

According to econometric wisdom, instruments can be used to isolate the causal effect of a variable from the effect of unobserved confounders. As Morgan and Winship (2015: 291) claim:

If a perfect stratification of the data cannot be enacted with the available data, and thus neither matching nor regression nor any other type of basic conditioning technique can be used to effectively estimate a causal effect of D on Y, one solution is to find an exogenous source of variation that affects Y only by way of the causal variable D. The causal effect is then estimated by measuring how Y varies with the portion of the total variation in D that is attributable to the exogenous variation.

Instrumental variable (IV) estimation gives an unbiased estimate of the effect of D on Y if

1. the instrument is perfectly correlated with the exogenous part of the covariation of D and Y,
2. the instrument is perfectly orthogonal to the endogenous part of D,
3. the instrument is perfectly orthogonal to any other model misspecification.

If these conditions are not satisfied, then the estimated instrumented effect of D on Y is biased: it differs from the true effect of D on Y.

Since conditions 2 and 3 need to be assumed and cannot be tested for or taken for granted, IV estimation does not solve uncertainty about model specification. Robustness tests are required to establish the stability of IV estimates for different plausible model specifications. For example, IV estimation does not help against dynamic or spatial misspecification: the instrument may suffer from measurement error which can be correlated to the endogenous part of the covariation between D and Y or with other misspecifications, such as those resulting from population uncertainty or sampling uncertainty. If an endogenous variable is conditioned by other factors, there will be great uncertainty whether an instrument for the endogenous variable closely mirrors the conditionality structure. All of these uncertainties warrant robustness tests.

Condition 1 is never fulfilled. Instrumental variable designs therefore do not "identify" the average population treatment effect, but only the treatment effect for those cases which have experienced variation in treatment as a result of variation in the instrument. Since different valid instruments are correlated with a different part of the exogenous variance, different but equally valid instruments often produce significantly different point estimates, sometimes even in different directions. This would not be possible if IV estimation identified the true average population treatment effect; it therefore gives researchers the possibility of fine-tuning the desired result. As a consequence, IV estimates are not conclusive but require robustness testing. This seems to be perfectly clear to Angrist (2004: C80), who admits that "the external validity of IV estimates is ultimately established (...) by replication in new data sets and, of course, by new instruments," in other words: by robustness tests.

6.7 SOCIAL SCIENCE EXPERIMENTS

The most severe problems in empirical social science result from the analysis of observational data. Observational data are messy and their data-generating process unknown. Researchers have no control over who receives treatment and cannot eliminate the influence of potential confounders. It therefore seems only logical to replace the analysis of observational data with the analysis of experimentally generated data.[2] At the very least, this research strategy has the advantage of bringing the social sciences closer to what is regarded by many as the gold standard for causal inference in the sciences (Banerjee 2007; Rubin 2008; Falk and Heckman 2009; Angrist and Pischke 2009; Imbens 2010).

Social science experiments come in three variants: *lab experiments* usually observe responses of selected participating individuals to experimentally provided and randomized stimuli (treatments) in an artificial (laboratory) setting. *Field experiments* randomize a real treatment in the real world. Participants usually have to consent to participating due to ethical concerns about experimenting with humans without their consent. *Natural* and *quasi-experiments* are real-world situations in which a treatment appears to be randomized by some naturally-occurring phenomenon or some policy intervention.

---

2 However, experiments cannot answer the vast majority of relevant research questions in the social sciences because experiments are simply not feasible, are too costly or would be unethical since experiments must not cause substantial harm to participants. As Winship and Morgan (1999: 659f.) correctly point out "... in most social science research done outside of psychology, experimental designs are infeasible. (...) For these reasons, sociologists, economists, and political scientists must rely on what is now known as observational data – data that have been generated by something other than a randomized experiment – typically surveys, censuses, or administrative records."

The case for experiments is simple: observational data does not allow eliminating the effect of confounders, which therefore have to be controlled for; experiments however can eliminate the effect of confounders by controlling the environment in which treatment is given, by blocking on all known confounders and by randomizing treatment status across a very large number of cases. As the number of participants approaches infinity, any differences between the treatment and control group vanish, leaving only random correlation between the confounders and the randomized treatment. If the experiment manages to hold all confounders constant, the causal effect of the treatment can be inferred from experiments simply by the difference in outcomes in the treated compared to the control group.

Real-world experiments are typically undertaken with small sample sizes, for which it becomes questionable whether uncertainty about potentially confounding variables has been solved. Whether the properties of confounding variables in the treatment and control group become sufficiently similar depends on how rare relevant properties are. The rarer these properties, the larger the number of participants has to become for any given level of bias. Robustness tests which either use different samples or which condition on potential confounders can answer these uncertainties.

Experiments therefore require robustness tests even for the dimension of model uncertainty for which they are most powerful. Other uncertainties also remain as does therefore the need to employ robustness tests. Critics often doubt the concept validity of treatments given in lab experiments, pointing to a potential gap between real-world treatment and experimental treatment. Knowledge about participating in an experiment can result in behavioral adjustment of participants to the experimental situation (Hawthorne bias).[3]

---

3 Experimenters might interact more with the treatment group than with the control group and participants might learn to "play" experimental situations (Bracht and Glass 1968). Natural and quasi-experiments are the only form of experiment in which the participants do not know that they are exposed to an experimental design. They are also the only "experiments" based on observational rather than generated data. They do not rely on a randomization of treatment, but on the assignment of treatment by a rule, which happens to be more or less orthogonal to structure in the covariates of behavior and in outcomes (e.g., assignment by alphabetical order or by lottery number). The hope is that the treatment assignment is haphazard and as if randomly distributed across cases. Natural and quasi-experiments are both rare and contested. Keane (2010: 12) and Shadish, Cook, and Campbell (2002) warn that many of the actual allegedly natural or quasi-experiments found in the social science literature are of low quality as often it remains questionable whether treatment was quasi-randomly assigned across groups and whether the two groups were sufficiently similar.

The conductors of lab experiments cannot necessarily know what real-world behavior their experimental findings represent, since the experimental treatment and setting differ from the real-world treatment and setting (Cobb-Clark and Crossley 2003), again casting uncertainty on the concept validity of the treatment. For example, many social science experiments transfer real-world stimuli and incentives into monetary lab incentives. The concept validity of the experimental treatment needs to be checked against other values of the monetary incentives and against other incentives.

In principle, field experiments perform better with regards to uncertainty about concept validity. However, even in field experiments participants typically know that they participate in a randomized experiment for a certain period of time and may adjust their behavior accordingly, whereas in the ideal experiment no participant knows in which group she is, nor do those handing out treatment know whether they are administering a genuine treatment or a placebo (Cartwright 2010: 63). Robustness tests therefore need to explore the impact of uncertainty about concept validity on estimated effects even in field experiments.

Other specification uncertainties also require more attention than they typically receive. Uncertainty about the functional form of treatment requires tests that go beyond dichotomized treatment status or simple, often linear, functional form assumptions. Uncertainty about dynamics requires tests that overcome the typical comparison of only two points in time: before the experiment and after the experiment. Uncertainty about spatial dependence is essentially assumed away in field experiments by ignoring spill-over and general equilibrium effects (Ravallion 2012: 105). In reality, however, many treatment effects depend on the degree of social interaction. Lab experiments may mirror this setting by placing participants in a situation of competitiveness or co-operation among participants. Yet, the choice of strategies played by real actors varies with the level of competitiveness or co-operation, and so robustness tests that vary these factors are required.

The largest uncertainty that experiments face is with regards to causal heterogeneity and context conditionality, however. Real-world lab experiments often draw participants from pre-selected convenience samples of, for example, students. Yet, randomizing treatment within a pre-selected group will not solve pre-selection bias, not even asymptotically, and will not produce an unbiased effect of the average population treatment effect if there is causal heterogeneity (Ho et al. 2007: 205; Heckman et al. 1997). Analyses of randomized treatments in convenience samples trade internal validity for external validity and any increase in the former often comes at the expense of a sharp decline in the latter. The limited external validity could in principle be overcome if researchers managed to randomize treatment in a sample that is randomly drawn from the deductively derived population (Shadish, Cook, and Campbell 2002: 91f.). More realistically, robustness tests are needed to tackle uncertainty about causal heterogeneity in lab experiments based on convenience samples. The external validity needs to be checked by conducting experiments with participants drawn from alternative social groups and strata. Without such tests, the only inference from lab experiments based on convenience samples one can draw is that the treatment can make a difference in some samples.

Field experiments also take place in particular settings and conditions (Shadish, Cook, and Campbell 2002: 18; Cartwright 2010; Cartwright and Hardie 2012). It cannot be guaranteed that an estimate derived from a randomized controlled experiment among individuals from a certain village in a certain region in north India in 2010 can be generalized to different settings and to the population of interest. Uncertainty about causal heterogeneity and context conditionality implies that, in the absence of robustness tests, the experimental result cannot be known to be valid beyond the specific setting or beyond the values of the conditioning factors as found in the experiment. The results should not be transferred and generalized to alternative settings or alternative values of the conditioning factors without robustness tests demonstrating the stability of the estimated effect.

In sum, then, for every experimental design there exist numerous plausible alternative experimental designs. Rather than being assumption-free, experimental design requires making a very large number of modelling assumptions, just as regression analysis of observational data does. The experimenter cannot simply assume that results are robust to plausible alternative specification assumptions of her experiment. Accordingly, social science experiments represent no alternative to robustness tests but instead themselves require robustness tests.

6.8 CONCLUSION

The methodological toolbox available to researchers has never been better equipped. Recent advances enable social scientists to study the phenomenon of interest with a plethora of methodologies. As this chapter has made clear, no research design, estimation procedure or analytical technique solves the problem of specification uncertainty. They all depend on specific modelling choices taken for which plausible alternatives exist. Therefore, no research design, estimation procedure or analytical technique represents an alternative to robustness tests as such. At best, they can provide a partial substitute for some robustness tests. For example, moving to experimental design can reduce the necessity to conduct robustness tests dealing with omitted explanatory variables. However, at the same time it makes robustness tests analyzing the impact of alternative concept definitions and operationalizations as well as uncertainty about causal heterogeneity and context conditionality much more important. Every tool in the methodological toolbox of social scientists requires robustness tests to improve the validity of inferences based upon it.

Modern experimental designs and identification techniques have their role to play in the development of the social sciences. However, we wish their proponents would develop a more realistic assessment of the strengths and weaknesses of these techniques and the validity of results generated. Social scientists should not equate *identification* with *valid inference* and the "methodological triumphalism" (Barrett and Carter 2010: 516) of experimentalists and proponents of identification techniques is an unjustified self-marketing exercise. Imai, King, and Stuart (2008: 493) similarly caution against any presumed inferential superiority of any technique: "Experimentalists may envy the large, randomly selected samples in observational studies, and observationalists may envy the ability of experimentalists to assign treatments randomly, but the good of each approach comes also with a different set of constraints that cause other difficulties."

Social scientists will learn with time that the findings from experiments, quasi-experiments, and identification techniques need to be subjected to robustness tests just like any other analytical technique. Robustness testing should play an important part in the social sciences regardless of the research design and recognition of this fact is starting to spread. To give a laudable example: Lassen and Serritzlew (2011), in their quasi-experimental analysis from a large-scale municipal reform in Denmark of the effect of jurisdiction size on political efficacy, have a "preferred specification" (we call it baseline model) but they undertake a large number of different estimates (we call them robustness test models) to explore the robustness of their results. They find that

the result that population size has a causal, significant effect on IPE [internal political efficacy] is robust across samples and estimators, and we demonstrate that local variations in the amalgamation process, as well as changes in local public finances and municipal political control following reform, do not affect this relationship.

(Lassen and Serritzlew 2011: 239)

When in one robustness test they employ matching additionally to their baseline differences-in-differences specification and find significantly stronger effects, they explore reasons for these differences. The differences could stem from the sample changing because matching drops observations or from the fact that matching makes no functional form assumption. To find the true reason, the authors re-estimate the baseline (parametric) model based on the sample of their matching (non-parametric) model and "observe results essentially similar to those identified by the matching analysis" (p. 252). Accordingly, the observed difference is caused by the change in sample, which suggests the existence of causal heterogeneity or unobserved conditionality. What is remarkable about Lassen and Serritzlew's analysis is that firstly they judge the lack of the robustness of their findings based on the estimated effect size and not merely on the direction of the effect. This finding motivates them to dig deeper into the nature of administrative reform and municipality size. And second, the robustness analysis, while based on research design and empirical model specification, also has important theoretical implications, which open the avenue for additional research.

Like modern techniques, old-fashioned regression analyses continue to be a valuable tool for social scientists. Regression analysis retains an unrivalled strength: its modelling flexibility and its almost unlimited versatility. Social science is full of questions, which cannot be answered with randomized experiments (Ravallion 2012), and it worries even its most fervent proponents that the emphasis on this inferential technique "may lead researchers to avoid questions where randomization is difficult, or even conceptually impossible, and natural experiments are not available" (Imbens 2010: 401).

Regression analysis does not require a random treatment; it can be used with all sorts of observational data. Real-world causal complexity in the form of conditionalities, temporal dynamics, spatial dependence, and so on can in principle be modelled and their effects interpreted. More often than with alternatives, it is possible to draw a random sample from the population. As Deaton (2010: 445) argues: "... a biased nonexperimental analysis might do better than a randomized controlled trial if enrolment into the trial is nonrepresentative." But, without doubt, regression analyses of observational data are fraught with model uncertainty, and the remainder of this book suggests tests for exploring the robustness of results for important dimensions of model uncertainty.

PART 2

Robustness Tests and the Dimensions of Model Uncertainty

7 Population and Sample

7.1 INTRODUCTION

Population, sample, case, and observation are important ontological elements of statistics. A population is a set of cases or subjects (such as individuals, groups, institutions, countries etc.). It exists if and only if its subjects can be distinguished from other subjects that do not belong to the population (Ryder 1964). Definitions of a population must therefore, implicitly at least, justify the set of cases included given the causal mechanism studied. A case is the unit of analysis that can but need not be observed more than once, e.g. over time. A sample ought to be a strict subset of the population. Samples can be selected or random. To be a perfect random sample, all cases included in the population need to have an identical a priori probability of being drawn into the sample, while all cases that do not belong to the population have an a priori probability of zero of being drawn into the sample.

Social scientists are not per se or at least not predominantly interested in description but in generalizing findings from the analyzed sample to the population. They want to learn from the past and they seek to transfer knowledge from the analysis of some cases to many other cases. This transfer is called inference. In an optimal world, social scientists would validly infer findings from the analysis of a subset or sample of cases to the entire universe of cases, the population. In other words, their inference would be perfectly externally valid.

Though reflections on how social scientists define and identify populations are rare, we are far from the first to recognize the importance of population and sampling for empirical model specification (e.g., Heckman 1979; Hug 2003; Strijbis 2013). Nevertheless, given the importance of generalizing from the sample to the population for empirical analysis, the scant attention this process receives in econometric theory baffles us.[1]

Ideally, social scientists use theory to define the boundaries of their population. In other words, a population is the set of cases for which a theory claims validity. In practice, few theorists define the boundaries or limits of the validity of their theory. As a consequence, social scientists define the boundaries of the population inductively instead, asking to which set of cases their results based upon the study sample can be generalized.

Yet, starting with the sample instead of the population does not help social scientists because they know of only two strategies that render generalizations valid: a random draw from the population and stratification of the sample to mimic population properties. A random draw becomes impossible when the sample comes first and the population is "induced" (or shall we say: assumed), and stratification from the sample to the population presupposes knowledge of the relevant properties of the population. In other words, social scientists often conduct an empirical analysis that represents an unknown population, if it represents a population at all.

This chapter discusses three population- and sampling-related questions of causal inference:

1. Do researchers know the population?
2. Can researchers be sufficiently certain that the properties of the sample are identical to the properties of the population?
3. To what extent do missing cases threaten external validity by reducing the correlation between population properties and sample properties?

The first question asks whether inferences suffer from *population uncertainty*. Population uncertainty exists when social scientists do not know to which cases outside the set of analyzed cases their findings extend. The second question addresses the issue of *sample uncertainty*. Sample uncertainty exists when social scientists do not know whether their findings can be generalized to the population they wish to generalize to. The third question addresses a special case of sample uncertainty that results from the effect that missing cases might have on inferences. If missings are non-random, they reduce the similarity between the sample and the population and potentially invalidate the external validity of findings.

Since population and sample uncertainty has received little attention in the extant literature, we discuss this dimension of model uncertainty more extensively than others. We start by showing how populations can either be deductively or inductively derived and how these options are related to the

---

1 For example, "population" is not listed in the indexes of standard econometric textbooks.

problem of selection. We then discuss separately sources of, respectively, population uncertainty and sample uncertainty together with robustness tests for dealing with these. Note, however, that in spite of the separate discussion population and sample uncertainty are connected: if uncertainty exists about what constitutes the population, it becomes impossible to ensure that one studies a sample randomly drawn from the population. Hence, population uncertainty causes sample uncertainty. Conversely, if researchers remain uncertain whether they have managed to draw a random sample or whether they can sufficiently correct for any non-random sampling (selection), it becomes difficult to know to which larger set of cases one can generalize findings. In other words: sample uncertainty generates population uncertainty.

7.2 DEDUCTIVELY AND INDUCTIVELY DERIVED POPULATIONS AND THE PROBLEM OF SELECTION

We can distinguish two approaches to generalization. The *deductive* approach starts with a theoretically justified notion of a population and in an optimal world either randomly draws a sample from the population or develops sampling techniques that result in a sample that is sufficiently similar on all relevant population properties. The *inductive* approach starts with a sample and in an optimal world generalizes findings from the given sample to a population which mirrors the relevant properties of the sample.

The deductive approach toward defining the population corresponds to the scientific ideal: it includes in the population those and only those cases for which a theory claims validity. In actual practice, social scientists often do not ask what theory has to say on the definition of population. Rather, they adopt a convenience definition of population. Jeffrey Wooldridge offers a canonical example: He defines population as "any well-defined group of subjects" (Wooldridge 2000: 699). This definition is a-theoretical and assumes away any selection bias – the existence and consequences of which have played a prominent role in econometrics (Heckman 1979, 1990; Vella 1998) – by simply defining the population as a well-defined group of subjects however non-representative they may be for the set of cases for which a theory claims validity. If researchers were free to define the population simply on the basis that the group of subjects can be distinguished from other subjects, then the group of Harvard alumni would be a possible "population" for the question whether an additional university year adds to income. Yet, asking whether an additional year at Harvard adds to lifetime income differs from asking whether an additional university year affects lifetime income.

A deductively derived population cannot be just any "well-defined group of subjects" but the one well-defined group of subjects or cases for which a theory makes a prediction and scientists like to learn something about. For deductively derived populations, it is therefore as important to carefully think about the boundaries for which a theory claims validity as it is to draw a random sample from the population. Only if all cases have the same probability to be drawn into the sample will the sample (if it is large enough) represent the population. In contrast, a random sample of a selected subset of the population – a convenience sample – is not a random sample of the population and will have divergent sample properties in expectation. For this reason, inferences from a randomly drawn sample of a pre-selected set of subjects suffer from selection bias and can be misleading.

An inductively derived population is the set of all observations to which an empirical result can be generalized. With induced populations, the question whether a sample suffers from selection bias depends on the limits of generalization. Typically, researchers know the sample and only then define the limits of inferences. Though induction does rest on a sample selected by some rule other than a randomized draw from a predefined population, an inductively derived population can nevertheless have the same properties as the sample. In principle, a finding from analyzing a non-randomly selected sample can be generalized to a population from which it is possible to draw a random sample that has the same properties as the non-randomly selected sample. In other words, the inductively derived population is the one for which the actually studied sample could have been a random sample.

No simple technique exists that allows generalizations in a valid way from a sample to the inductively derived population. Whether a broader set of cases exists to which research can inductively generalize depends on the analyzed model, the complexity of the causal problem, and the heterogeneity of cases. If the analyzed phenomenon is complex, the variation between cases increases and it may become difficult to identify additional cases to which a finding can be generalized. If the heterogeneity of the sample is so large that the estimated average effect is not representative for the entire sample, then no inductively derived population exists at all for this sample and at best only for a subset of cases of the sample. Estimates from a non-random sample can only be generalized to populations that have the same properties as the non-random sample if that sample is sufficiently homogeneous. In addition, if findings are only partially robust, that is, robust only for certain parts of the sample, we recommend generalizing findings only to an inductively derived population that has the same properties as the parts of the sample for which the finding is robust. In sum, only in the absence of causal heterogeneity can researchers validly generalize from a non-random sample to a broader population.

Inductively derived populations are defined by and dependent on the research design. Uncertainty about what constitutes the inductively derived population will always exist. A study of nationalization in Switzerland can possibly be generalized to a few other countries, but the result that committees are generally less inclined to discriminate against foreigners than the general public (Hainmueller and Hangartner 2013) cannot be assumed to hold globally. It is unclear whether these results can be generalized and, if so, to which other cases. And since the conditions under which these results hold are unknown, we cannot be certain that these findings can be generalized even to Switzerland's future either. If scholars analyze OECD countries, they might be able to generalize to other countries with similar properties to OECD countries, but probably not to developing countries; if they study a selection of British households they might be able to make inferences to other British households but probably not to households in other countries; and if they decide to conduct randomized controlled experiments with Oxford students they can make inferences to, well, Cambridge students perhaps – but even that may already be overly optimistic.

Researchers can easily avoid selection bias by not generalizing from the findings based on their selected sample, but that will turn the social sciences into a descriptive discipline and throw out the baby with the bathwater. With generalization as one of the main tasks of science, the population cannot be defined by "cases that are observed" or otherwise the task will not be fulfilled.

According to James Heckman, "[s]ample selection bias may arise in practice for two reasons. First, there may be self-selection by the individuals or data units being investigated. Second, sample selection decisions by analysts or data processors operate in much the same fashion as self-selection" (Heckman 1979: 153–154). The first problem occurs when cases were selected or selected themselves into treatment. Heckman discusses the case of migrants and stresses that non-migrants have chosen to not migrate, whereas migrants chose to migrate, which suggests that migrants and non-migrants are likely to be systematically different. If they are different, generalization from migrants to non-migrants is likely to be invalid. The second selection stems from the difficulties of defining the boundaries between cases that belong into the population and cases that do not. Consider the case of ethnic groups. According to Alesina et al. (2003: 157), the authors of one well known classification of ethnic diversity, "ethnic classifications are fraught with ambiguities." And Fearon (2003: 197), the author of an alternative classification of ethnic diversity, states: "[i]t rapidly becomes clear that one must make all manner of borderline-arbitrary decisions, and that in many cases there simply does not seem to be a single right answer to the question 'What are the ethnic groups in this country?'" As a consequence, given "[t]he theoretical difficulty (or even impossibility) of defining ethnic groups, the presence of selection bias [becomes] almost a certainty" (Hug 2003: 269).

The first selection problem as described by Heckman seemingly disappears with the inductive approach to populations. If researchers only sample migrants, they can only generalize inferences to other migrants and to an unknown group of all other individuals who are sufficiently similar to migrants, which is not the population of interest, however. Expressed in modern treatment terminology, the population is defined as the set of subjects that could have received a treatment. Thus, non-migrants belong to the population – their exclusion from the sample invalidates inferences to the population. It follows that all useful definitions of population must allow the possibility of selection. Letting the selection problem disappear does not help with generalizations. The trick merely shifts the problem from a solvable problem (selection) to an unsolvable problem (generalization to unknown "others").

The second selection problem, as described by both Heckman and Hug, also continues to exist with an inductive approach to population. If a classification is unlikely to be "correct," findings can only be generalized to a population in which the incorrect classification was correct – a population that probably does not exist in reality. Again, seemingly eliminating the selection problem makes matters worse.

By contrast, with a deduced population, selection generates a clearly defined problem that can, in principle at least, be addressed if perhaps not entirely solved. If scholars use a perfect random draw to sample from the population, differences between sample and population properties are expected to be unsystematic with the size of these unsystematic differences depending on the sample size relative to the population. As the sample size grows bigger, the differences become smaller. Yet, perfect random draws from the population are rare and selection remains widespread. Heckman (1979), Berk (1983), and, with greater clarity, Hug (2003) and Strijbis (2013) correctly draw a direct line from population uncertainty to selection bias. Whether selection models or ex-post stratification of the sample provide the optimal solution to population uncertainty remains an entirely different question. If the boundaries of populations remain fuzzy and uncertain, researchers cannot reliably specify the selection stage or undertake ex-post stratification. Robustness tests are therefore necessary for exploring the true impact of population uncertainty on estimates and, ultimately, on inferences.

7.3 POPULATION UNCERTAINTY AND ROBUSTNESS TESTS

Since theories tend to not specify the boundaries of their validity, scholars are uncertain what the deductively derived population should be (Frank and Min 2007). Rarely is it as easy to define the population as in our own research on earthquake mortality (Keefer et al. 2011). We define the population for our theory of the political determinants of earthquake mortality as all cases experiencing an observable event, an earthquake above a certain physical strength with potentially fatal consequences. Uncertainty can only occur as to the minimum strength of an earthquake that can kill human beings, which can be approximately known or at least derived from past experiences with earthquakes. The vast majority of research questions in the social sciences face considerably more population uncertainty.

Consider the effect of education on income. Do economic theories claim validity for the working population or the entire adult population? Do they claim validity for market economies or also for countries and regions in which little industry exists and in which the service sector is confined to the informal economy and to government agencies and other public service companies?

It is erroneous to believe that theory plays no role in inductively derived populations. The opposite is true: since one can only make inferences to a sufficiently similar population, theory needs to identify the dimensions in which cases have to be "sufficiently similar." In other words, theory has to help in determining the induced population for the sample studied. Under-specified theories hamper the process of making judgments on "how far" one can generalize the results.

This adds to uncertainty. While the inductive approach undoubtedly offers some leverage in defining the population, any generalization has to be justified. And since selected samples are not random draws, the justification has to be that for theoretical reasons, the *relevant* properties of the sample and the properties of the cases to which researchers generalize – the defined population without the cases in the sample – are sufficiently similar. Hence, with inductively derived populations, greater population uncertainty exists than with deductively derived populations. The gist of the problem encountered in inductively deriving the population is that scholars do not know "how far they can go" in generalizing.

Theories rarely specify the temporal domain to which they apply. Many seem to be formulated as if they claimed eternal validity, others with the present day and age in mind. The future poses problems for both deductively and inductively derived populations. For deduced populations derived from theories that claim validity for the future as well, an apparent problem is that no randomly drawn sample can be established, since future observations have not yet materialized.[2] Social scientists still need to be willing, to some extent at least, to generalize their findings into the future for their research to have any impact on policy-making. Otherwise a finding from a study of the past would provide no guidance on whether the future can be expected to be influenced in the way the finding suggests. For example, a finding that smaller class sizes improved the study performance of pupils in the past is only of historical value if this result cannot be generalized into the future. Here the deductive and inductive modes converge: even for a deductively derived population, the sample studied can only reflect the past up to, at best, the present and scholars need to justify that the results can be generalized into the future. As with induced populations, the further into the future one ventures in generalizing the findings the more problematic the validity of generalizations.

The past and present also cause problems. This becomes evident for all those cases in the present or the past for which a theory claims validity, but that cannot be included in the sample because data are missing. Missings apparently cause uncertainty about the extent to which the sample represents the population. For inductively derived populations, the question arises how far the findings can be generalized back into the past. This question becomes particularly acute if no past data has been collected and scholars cannot go back in time to collect data but still wish to generalize beyond the observed periods.

Another source of population uncertainty stems from unobservable boundaries, which leads to uncertainty about which cases form part of the population even if theory clearly defines the population. Under these conditions, researchers cannot know whether individual cases belong to the population or not.

As a final source of uncertainty, the population is not independent of the complexity of the estimation model. This seems to be evident for inductively derived populations: to which subjects a particular result based on

---

2 A special case is research that uses all available observations to test theories. For example, in our research on disaster mortality we use samples that include all cases for all time periods for which information is available. Even for exhaustive samples, the question of generalization to the same set of cases or other cases in the past or in the future is relevant. If, for example, in the future a structural break occurs – say, because geologists can forecast volcanic eruptions or earthquakes or because countries become politically, economically or socially different from the type of countries we know today – our findings would no longer be valid for making predictions.

a particular sample and estimation model can be generalized will be a function of the complexity of the estimation model. More complex models that account for more influential factors can be generalized to more cases than relatively simple models. Relatively simple models have to hold many factors constant; therefore they can be applied to the potentially few cases which are sufficiently similar in "all other dimensions." As a simple example, an estimation model that does not control for democracy can either include only democracies or only autocracies but not both if the democracy–autocracy distinction makes a difference for the dependent variable. Hence, results can only be generalized to either democracies or autocracies, depending on which type of country is included in the sample.

Population uncertainty can induce the formulation of a too-narrow or a too-wide definition of the population. In the first case, some cases from the true population are excluded; in the latter case some cases are included though they are not part of the true population. Population definitions can also be too narrow and too wide at the same time: the population definition includes cases which do not belong to the true population and at the same time exclude cases that do belong to the population. Once the definition of the population is wrong, the sample is unlikely to represent the true population. As a consequence, inferences cannot be externally valid (unless cases are strictly homogeneous) if the set of cases from which researchers produce a sample differs from the population about which they wish to make inferences. This problem becomes most apparent in the qualitative study of a few selected cases but also in modern inferential techniques such as experiments, quasi-experiments, regression discontinuity, and matching designs. Yet, it can similarly afflict regression analyses of observational data.

In the situation of a potentially too-broad definition of the population in the baseline model, the robustness test model can exclude cases that might not belong to the population. In principle, when population boundaries are uncertain, scholars should prefer to "over-sample" by employing a too-broad sampling strategy from the start that includes observations for which it is questionable whether they belong to the population and thus should be eligible for inclusion in the sample. The comprehensive sampling strategy is preferable because observations can more easily be eliminated from a sample than added.

Assume we believe that the set of cases A is the correct population for our theory, but there is some positive probability that the theory is valid for observations included in set B. By sampling once from set A for the baseline estimation model and sampling from the set union of A and B for the model that employs this *population boundary test*, it becomes possible to test the robustness of the estimated effect based on a sample drawn from set A alone toward the inclusion of observations also drawn from set B. Alternatively, the baseline model can be based on A and B and the *population boundary test* model based on set A only. Both are robustness tests of the model variation type. Alternatively, researchers can also undertake a structured permutation variant of the *population boundary test* in which they continuously shift the population boundary further and further in a specific direction – for example, by continuously varying the threshold of the Richter value of the earthquake for determining the inclusion of cases into the population in a study of earthquake mortality.

As an illustrative example for the model variation type test, we employ a dataset from our own research. In Keefer, Neumayer, and Plümper (2011) we show that countries with larger historical experience of earthquakes suffer lower mortality (holding the size of the actual quake constant) and that this effect – we call it quake propensity – is larger in less corrupt countries than in more corrupt ones. The argument is simple: countries with larger quake propensity face higher quake risk and stronger incentives to introduce quake-proof building regulations but less corrupt countries are likely to enforce these regulations better than more corrupt countries. We employ a negative binomial estimator for which estimated coefficients can be interpreted as semi-elasticities and the robustness analysis therefore simply refers to estimated coefficients. Baseline model m1, reported in table 7.1, is identical to model 5 in Keefer, Neumayer, and Plümper (2011). Higher quake propensity lowers mortality controlling for hazard strength and a number of control variables, but the effect is stronger in less corrupt countries[3] than in more corrupt countries.[4]

The population boundary test requires a sampling strategy that potentially over-samples and a population definition threshold that can be defined and thus shifted in a continuous, count or categorical way. The baseline model relies on a broad sampling strategy, in which we include all known earthquakes with a quake strength of 5 or above on the Richter scale. Quakes of strength at Richter magnitude below 6 can kill but most fatalities only occur in quakes of larger strengths. To test the robustness of the baseline model findings, we therefore exclude all quakes below Richter magnitude 6 in model 2. The coefficients of the variables of interest, quake propensity in more or less corrupt countries, both become smaller with the estimated negative mortality effect of higher quake propensity about 30 percent larger in less corrupt countries. Both coefficients are robust with $\rho = 0.66$ for the mortality effect in non-corrupt and $\rho = 0.55$ for the effect in corrupt countries.

---

3 Defined as scoring 4 or above on the control of corruption scale of the International Country Risk Guide running from 1 (most corrupt) to 6 (least corrupt).
4 In non-corrupt countries, an increase by one standard deviation in quake propensity lowers quake mortality by 61.5 percent.

Table 7.1: Population Boundary Test

	m1: baseline	m2: quakes ≥6 on Richter scale	p
Maximum quake magnitude	0.00577	0.00235	0.994
	(0.00489)	(0.00247)	
Magnitude population density	3.68e–05**	9.65e–05	0.263
	(1.72e–05)	(7.11e–05)	
Minimum focal depth	–0.00106	–0.0185	0.398
	(0.00727)	(0.0135)	
Democracy	–2.369***	–1.942**	0.839
	(0.770)	(0.987)	
Per capita income (ln)	–0.595***	–0.400*	0.869
	(0.218)	(0.206)	
Population (ln)	0.547**	1.015***	0.486
	(0.235)	(0.196)	
Lack of corruption	–0.173	0.469	0.422
	(0.290)	(0.373)	
Quake propensity in more corrupt countries	–0.00318	–0.000727	0.547
	(0.00195)	(0.00439)	
Quake propensity in less corrupt countries	–0.00770***	–0.00990***	0.663
	(0.00164)	(0.00229)	
p-value χ^2 test propensity corrupt vs non-corrupt	0.008	0.001	
Observations	698	335	

Note: Dependent variable is earthquake fatality. Negative binomial estimations. Constant not reported. Standard errors clustered on countries in parentheses. Statistically significant * at 0.1, ** at 0.05, *** at 0.01 level.

One consequence of a potentially too broad sampling strategy is that the sample may contain observations that do not belong into the population and therefore should not have been sampled. These cases may, but need not, show up as outliers and, conversely, any detected outlier may or may not belong to the population. A conventional technique for studying the robustness of estimates to the presence of outlying cases is offered by the jackknife technique and the bootstrap technique. The bootstrap technique was developed after the jackknife technique, and in most applications replaces the similar older technique. The *bootstrap test* has the advantage of holding the sample size constant, but has the disadvantage that it is at least difficult and often impossible to identify the causes of deviating standard errors. We therefore prefer the *jackknife test* for population uncertainty.

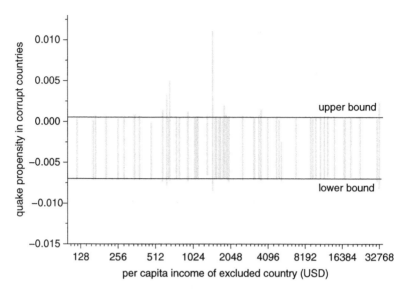

Figure 7.1: Jackknife Test: Corrupt Countries

The jackknife robustness test systematically excludes one or more observations from the estimation at a time until all observations have been excluded once. With a "groupwise jackknife" robustness test, researchers systematically drop a set of cases that group together by satisfying a certain criterion – for example, countries within a certain per capita income range or all countries on a certain continent.

Figures 7.1 and 7.2 display the results from a jackknife test dropping one case at a time for the effect of quake propensity on earthquake mortality in corrupt and non-corrupt countries. Cases are defined as countries and not as earthquake events, and the figures are ordered by the average per capita income of the excluded country over the sample period. These figures not only visualize the robustness of the baseline model to dropping single cases at a time, but also allow the identification of countries that exert large leverage on the baseline model estimates.

The country with the largest leverage on estimates is Iran, with an average per capita income of just below USD1,500. The exclusion of this country reduces the negative effect of quake propensity in non-corrupt countries and turns the effect in corrupt countries positive but with large standard error. Both effects from the baseline model remain robust, however, even if Iran is excluded, with $\rho = 0.63$ in non-corrupt and $\rho = 0.55$ in corrupt countries.

An alternative to the jackknife test that is more specific about the excluded cases employs either theory or conventional outlier tests to provide

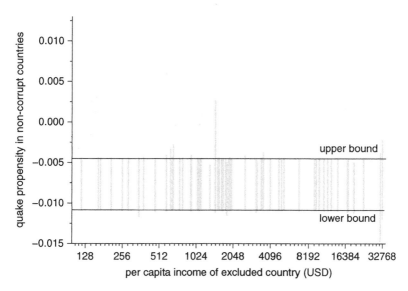

Figure 7.2: Jackknife Test: Non-corrupt Countries

insight into the robustness of estimates. Theory can be used to either formulate alternative justifications for the population or adjust the sample according to a narrower definition of population. Theory might allow researchers to distinguish a core group of cases that undoubtedly belong to the population from cases that may not belong to the population. The identified core group can be used to estimate a core group model, the results of which can be directly compared to the original sample. Alternatively, researchers can use the core group estimates to generate out-of-sample predictions for the cases which belong to the population only with some probability. The *core group test* works by testing whether the predicted values are statistically indistinguishable from the actual values of the excluded cases.

If theory does not help to identify a core group of cases that undoubtedly belong to the population, researchers can employ as a robustness test the potential elimination of outliers to redraw the boundaries of the sample (Belsley, Kuh, and Welsch 1980). The *outlier elimination test* assumes that in a well specified estimation model, selected or randomly drawn cases that do not "belong" to the population usually reveal their existence by comparatively large residuals. However, if the model is strongly misspecified, outlier tests are more likely to pick up the consequences of model misspecification than to detect true outliers (cases that are not part of the population), thereby making bias potentially worse. With this caveat in mind, we use a definition of outliers in negative binomial regression models from

Table 7.2: Outlier Elimination Test

	m1: baseline	m3: "outliers" excluded	p
Maximum quake magnitude	0.00577	0.00645***	1.000
	(0.00489)	(0.00171)	
Magnitude population density	3.68e−05**	4.01e−05***	1.000
	(1.72e−05)	(8.81e−06)	
Minimum focal depth	−0.00106	0.00244	0.879
	(0.00727)	(0.00851)	
Democracy	−2.369***	−2.366***	0.999
	(0.770)	(0.458)	
Per capita income (ln)	−0.595***	−0.543***	0.986
	(0.218)	(0.167)	
Population (ln)	0.547**	0.712***	0.999
	(0.235)	(0.0925)	
Lack of corruption	−0.173	−0.405*	0.945
	(0.290)	(0.211)	
Quake propensity in more corrupt countries	−0.00318	−0.00339***	1.000
	(0.00195)	(0.000953)	
Quake propensity in less corrupt countries	−0.00770***	−0.00791***	1.000
	(0.00164)	(0.000897)	
p-value χ^2 test propensity corrupt vs non-corrupt	0.008	0.000	
Observations	698	174	

Note: Dependent variable is earthquake fatality. Negative binomial estimations. Constant not reported. Standard errors clustered on countries in parentheses. Statistically significant * at 0.1, ** at 0.05, *** at 0.01 level.

Joseph M. Hilbe, who suggests that observations with so-called standardized deviance residuals greater than 2 can be regarded as potential outliers (Hilbe 2011: 278). Applying Hilbe's definition to our baseline model suggests that a large number of observations (524 out of 698) are potentially outliers (see table 7.2).

In our analysis, the estimated coefficients for the central variables remain close to the baseline model estimates with much smaller standard errors. Hence, outlier exclusion – not unexpectedly – increases the certainty of the point estimate and (in our case) does not influence the point estimates much. Of course, if the baseline model eliminates outliers and the robustness test brings them back in to test the robustness of the baseline model for the possibility of a too narrowly defined population, the opposite result will occur: the uncertainty of the point estimates increases.

7.4 SAMPLE UNCERTAINTY AND ROBUSTNESS TESTS

A perfect random sample requires that all cases have an identical ex-ante probability of being drawn into the sample. If the selection probability varies across cases, selection bias may occur and the sample does not exactly represent the population. Typically, sufficient information that allows researchers to draw a perfect random sample does not exist. Some cases are difficult or even impossible to actually observe. The specific situation of some cases amplifies the problem. For example, territories of failed states, in war areas or areas affected by natural disasters tend to be difficult to sample. On the micro-level, this holds for groups of the population that do not have a permanent address or a landline telephone number or that partly live abroad. All other things equal, a random sample can be more easily drawn in richer than in poorer countries and in democracies than in autocracies. Consider survey research that requires a random sample of the rural population in, say, Burundi or Malawi. The absence of reliable administrative records, the distances between villages, and poor infrastructure render it impossible to guarantee a sample that has properties identical in expectation to those of the population. Thus, random samples are difficult to draw, which creates sample uncertainty.

Survey analysts often enjoy the advantage over other social scientists that in principle their population is well defined by the set of individuals whose opinions, vote intentions or other characteristics they wish to survey. For example, their population may be the set of individuals eligible for voting in the US Presidential elections or the set of households in London. Yet, despite a well-defined population in principle, survey analysts face uncertainty about who forms part of a defined population and what their characteristics are, which renders it impossible to draw a truly random sample. Consider for example the problem posed by illegally residing residents. According to the UK's Home Office, the number of illegal immigrants in the UK lies between 310,000 and 570,000. A random sample of the population cannot be guaranteed if many subjects reside illegally. Clearly, an illegally residing immigrant does not have the same ex-ante probability of being drawn into the sample as, say, Mr. Eric Smith registered as living at 12 Roundhouse Avenue.

At least in private conversation, survey companies admit that they use second-best options and stratify the sample using census information where available. Unfortunately, census data, too, suffers from systematic and unsystematic nonresponse problems, from missing data, and from systematically under-represented hidden populations. In addition, census data tend to be relatively old as few countries organize more than one census per decade, if at all. Therefore, post-sampling stratification, while almost certainly moving the sample properties closer to the population properties, does not prevent selection bias.

Robustness tests for sample uncertainty focus on the plausibility of the assumption that the baseline model's estimated effects are representative of the population. If two entirely or partly different samples can both be considered representative of the population, estimation results will be robust toward using the same model specification for one sample and then for the other. This *cross-validation test* appears particularly warranted where researchers deliberately forego assembling a true random sample of the population in order to save on data collection costs as with case-control research designs for rare events data (King and Zeng 2001a, 2001b). In the sciences, cross-validations with different samples are frequent and belong to "normal science." In the social sciences, cross-validation tests remain rare, not least because scholars find it difficult to get these studies published. In addition, cross-validation tests are costly, time-consuming, and unfeasible when parts of the population are "hidden" and thus difficult to observe (Watters and Biernacki 1989; Salganik and Heckathorn 2004).

Additional robustness tests for sample uncertainty analyze whether selection or self-selection influence sampling or whether certain cases are systematically under-represented, both of which renders it questionable whether the sample represents the population. Robustness tests provide a new perspective on selection. Selection can occur at different levels of the research process. First, agents can be selected or self-select themselves into treatment. And second, the treatment may be sufficiently close to random, but not all cases can equally be observed and therefore selection occurs at the sampling level. In both cases, a selection model can (partly) correct selection bias. We discuss selection into treatment and under-representation in turn.

7.4.1 Selection and Self-Selection

Selection models need to capture the probability that a case is drawn into the sample – the inverse of the Mills ratio, in technical terms (Heckman 1979).[5] This can sometimes be easy, but at other times it appears almost impossible

---

5 Many more models going beyond Heckman's (1979) seminal model have been developed for the purpose of correcting for selection in specific research contexts – see, for example, Sartori (2003), Boehmke (2003), Hug (2003), and Boehmke et al. (2006).

to model the selection process appropriately. An example for a selection that is comparably easy to model comes from our own research on the negotiation of EU accession. EU accession negotiations constitute a selection problem because not all countries apply for EU membership. As a consequence, the EU and its member states negotiate only with self-selected member-states, but they may have in mind that the number of applicants increases if the EU grants easy entry. Modelling this self-selection process was relatively straightforward because theories exist which predict the conditions under which an outside country seeks EU membership (Plümper, Schneider, and Troeger 2006).

Other selection problems are less obvious and sometimes difficult or even impossible to model. Take the example of estimating the wage differential for legally and illegally residing migrants (Rivera-Batiz 1999). Assume researchers want to generalize findings to the population of all immigrants, both legally and illegally residing. Unfortunately, illegally residing immigrants cannot be sampled easily, thus raising serious doubts that they have the same ex-ante probability of being drawn into the sample as legally residing immigrants. A possible strategy to address the issue is to over-sample identifiable illegally residing immigrants. This requires knowledge or estimates of the share of illegal immigrants. Nonetheless, over-sampling does not guarantee that all types of illegally residing immigrants are equally represented in the sample.

Selection tests must compare the estimated effect from the baseline model that is based on the original sample without selection correction to the model with selection bias correction.[6] The estimated effect from the sample selection model must take into account the effect of variables onto both stages of the estimation – not just the second or outcome stage, but also the first or selection stage (Sigelman and Zeng 1999). For example, if scholars wish to test whether an estimate of the wage return of an additional year of schooling based on a sample of working adults is robust toward potential selection bias, they should compare this estimate to the wage effect of additional schooling that is the combined effect of an additional year of schooling increasing the likelihood of a person entering the workforce and increasing a person's wage once in employment.

Uncertainty is not limited to whether selection exists or not. The specification of the selection stage will also be uncertain. The econometric debate about selection models has focused on whether the inclusion of a variable that affects selection, but does not affect the outcome in the second stage (the so-called exclusion restriction), is strictly necessary for Heckman-

---

6 As an example of an article that tests the robustness of a selection model to a simple baseline model, see Beardsley and Asal (2009: 287).

style sample selection models (Leung and Yu 1996; Vella 1998; Puhani 2000). Without such a variable the selection model depends on the non-linearity of the inverse Mills ratio for identification, which some find highly dubious (Breen 1996; Wooldridge 2010). Variables that exclusively affect the selection stage but not the main stage are typically hard to find.

Whereas selection models try to model the selection process completely, instrumental variable techniques merely try to purge the second stage from the endogeneity that results from the self-selection of observations. Selection models depend on stronger distributional assumptions and a well-specified selection stage model (Caliendo and Hujer 2006). However, as we have argued in chapter 6, instrumental variables estimation often solves one selection problem by creating another selection problem, namely by basing the estimations on a sub-sample that may no longer be representative of the population. If the determinants of selection are time-invariant, differences-in-differences methods provide another option for dealing with selection since they erase time-invariant selection effects. Differences-in-differences designs not only select cases (throwing away those cases for which the assumption of parallel trends in the absence of treatment cannot be defended) but also variance: by eliminating between-variation, the differences-in-differences design estimates the immediate effect of a *change* in the treatment level on outcomes. This makes the problematic assumption that the effect of a treatment is independent of previous treatments. It also assumes a linear and unconditional treatment effect with homogeneous dynamics.

7.4.2 Under-representation

Robustness tests can help to reduce the problem of under-representation and at the same time explore whether findings are robust to potential corrections in the sample. For example, in survey research it is possible to correct the sample so that the properties of the sample and the properties of the census data population become more similar (Lohr 2009). However, if reliable census data do not exist, ex-post stratification becomes more difficult. Under these conditions, one can use over- and under-sampling techniques as well as the estimation of separate effects for different groups as robustness tests.

Assume, for example, a researcher suspects that ethnic minorities and illegally residing individuals are under-represented in the sample, but she cannot fully correct for under-representation since no reliable census data exist for individuals of these groups. In robustness tests, she can employ several different assumptions of presumed under-representation and over-sample subjects drawn from ethnic minorities and illegally residing individuals already contained in the sample. Researchers can also employ

Monte Carlo studies that mirror a bootstrap to repeatedly draw additional subjects from the under-represented group into the sample. Each of these estimates generates standard errors that are slightly too small, but researchers can correct them by estimating these resampling models repeatedly and by using the "resampling variation" as an additional source of uncertainty and adding it to the mean standard error of the estimates. Analysts can over- and under-sample cases interchangeably. Rather than drawing subjects from under-represented groups more than once into a sample, researchers can eliminate subjects from the over-represented group from the sample. *Stratification tests* either over-sample under-represented cases or under-sample over-represented cases. They can be employed to test robustness to each other. Of course, it is possible to over-sample under-represented and under-sample over-represented cases at the same time.

Returning to our example to illustrate robustness tests, natural disasters in developing countries tend to be under-reported relative to natural disasters in developed countries, which have superior monitoring and recording capacity. Even though this will be far less of a problem for earthquakes, which can be detected remotely, let us assume that developing country earthquakes are relatively under- and developed country earthquakes are relatively over-represented. In Monte Carlo simulations, we first over-sampled existing observations from developing countries, varying in defined percentage point steps from a chance between 10 and 90 percent to be sampled twice into the estimation sample. This randomized permutation robustness test gave us mean estimates across the simulations and mean standard errors of these estimates, to which we added the standard error of the mean standard error estimate to account for the additional source of uncertainty (see table 7.3). Based on the mean estimates and their standard errors, our finding of a larger effect in non-corrupt than in corrupt countries remained robust.[7] The estimated degrees of robustness averaged across all Monte Carlo simulation models without model weighting were $\rho = 0.92$ for the effect in non-corrupt countries (95 percent of simulations have $0.87 < \rho < 0.96$) and $\rho = 0.99$ for the effect in corrupt countries (95 percent of simulations have $0.96 < \rho < 1$).

In a second step, we under-sampled existing observations from developed countries, varying by one percentage point at a time their chance of being dropped from the sample by between 10 and 90 percent

---

7 If, much more radically, we do not look at mean estimates from the Monte Carlo simulations but at their full range, thus taking into account the extremes, one can no longer reject the hypothesis that the two effects are equal at the maximum estimate for corrupt countries and the minimum estimate for non-corrupt countries.

Table 7.3: Stratification Tests

Over-sampling of developing country observations

	mean	std. dev.	min.	max.
Quake propensity in corrupt countries	−0.0033	0.0004	−0.0041	−0.0024
Standard error	0.0013	0.0001	0.0010	0.0016
Quake propensity in non-corrupt countries	−0.0083	0.0004	−0.0090	−0.0072
Standard error	0.0017	0.0001	0.0014	0.0018

Under-sampling of developed country observations

	mean	std. dev.	min.	max.
Quake propensity in corrupt countries	−0.0033	0.0002	−0.0037	−0.0027
Standard error	0.0015	0.0001	0.0014	0.0017
Quake propensity in non-corrupt countries	−0.0088	0.0008	−0.0101	−0.0068
Standard error	0.0021	0.0001	0.0019	0.0024

(see again table 7.3). The estimated degrees of robustness averaged across all Monte Carlo simulation models without model weighting were $\rho = 0.80$ for the effect in non-corrupt countries (95 percent of simulations have $0.66<\rho<0.90$) and $\rho = 0.99$ for the effect in corrupt countries (95 percent of simulations have $0.97<\rho<0.99$).

Researchers may also use a robustness limit variant of the stratification tests and analyze how many additional observations of the under-represented group need to be added to the sample to render the estimated effects not robust. The limit test gradually increases the degree of over-sampling of the under-represented group. It is possible to turn this test into a structured permutation test by stepwise increasing the degree of over- and/or under-sampling.

7.5 SAMPLE UNCERTAINTY CAUSED BY MISSINGS

Missing values on one or more variables for cases that belong to the population represent a problem for sampling unless they were missing completely at random, in which case they solely reduce the efficiency of the estimate. In most cases, observations will not be "missing completely at random," but will merely be "missing at random" (see next paragraph), in which case the probability of a value being missing is a function of observable values. Worse still, they may even be missing not at random, in which case the probability of a value being missing is a function of both observable values and unobservable ones (Rubin 1976; King et al. 2001; Schafer and Graham 2002).

This standard terminology is somewhat confusing or "unintuitive (for historical reasons)" (King et al. 2001: 50): if values are called missing at random, many social scientists will expect that these are unsystematically missing values. Sticking to standard terminology, however, samples with observations that are not missing completely at random, i.e. that are either merely missing at random or are missing not at random, cannot constitute random draws from the population, and thus bias the estimations. For example, such missings will cause bias if they are systematically correlated with another regressor or if the missings prevent the detection of a non-linearity in the functional form. There are few instances in which missings are completely at random. Most missing data is missing for a reason.

We can further distinguish two types of missings. For the first type, no information can be established. This occurs when participants in a survey do not respond or with some "pariah" states in comparative macro-research. For example, Albania, South Africa, Taiwan, and North Korea did all at some time not report data to international organizations. Thus, little is known about these countries during these periods. In cases like these, it does not make sense to impute missings – research should simply abstain from extending inferences to these countries. For the second type, data is missing only for some variables but available for others. In this case, missing data can be imputed in various ways.

Researchers could in principle try to correct for the effect of missing observations by sampling techniques. For example, if observations for autocracies were more likely to be missing than observations for democracies then they could try to "over-sample" more observations from autocracies. This is problematic because missing observations from autocracies may differ from non-missing observations from autocracies in other aspects relevant to the estimation model. The dominant technique for dealing with missing observations is therefore to recover these observations via imputing missing values. Imputation comes in three main variants: interpolation/extrapolation, theory-based out-of-sample predictions, and multiple imputation techniques. All three can function as robustness tests to a baseline model that ignores missing values, which leads to listwise deletion of observations, or as robustness tests to each other.

The oldest and least sophisticated variant of imputation is interpolation and extrapolation. The *interpolation test* works best when earlier and later information is available, say when family income is known for 2004 and 2006 but is unknown for 2005. The odds are that the missing is similar to the adjacent known values and probably falls between the adjacent values of family income. The linear form of interpolation is most common. It assumes that the missing family income of 2005 is the mean of the 2004 and the 2006 income – an assumption that is not exactly correct (other than by coincidence), but probably close to the true figure. Linear interpolation is not the only possibility. Instead, analysts may wish to interpolate using the lower or the higher of the two adjacent values or some weighted average between the two. For example, in Plümper and Neumayer (2010a) we interpolate missing values of the *polity* variable from the Polity IV project (Marshall and Jaggers 2007) once linearly, once by the minimum, and once by the maximum of adjacent values. If extraneous information is available, one way of interpolating may be known or at least be suspected to be preferable to the other; otherwise multiple ones can be used in separate robustness tests. Of course, there is no guarantee that the true missing value will indeed lie between the adjacent known values. If the reason for missing values is that the case experienced a strong exogenous shock during the period of missing values then the true values may well lie outside the boundaries of adjacent known values.

Arguably, interpolation is more reliable than extrapolation. Extrapolation can only work reliably if there is no structural break in the data, but uncertainty grows with every additional data point extrapolated into the future or into the past. Linear extrapolation is again just one possibility. For series known to grow exponentially, for example, extrapolation based on the assumption of exponential growth may be preferable.

We prefer an *out-of-sample prediction test* over inter- and extrapolation. For example, in Plümper and Neumayer (2010a) we use a theoretical model of the determinants of democracy to make out-of-sample predictions for missing values of the *polity* variable from the Polity IV project that are due to interregnum and affected transition periods in countries. These predictions can then be used in lieu of the missing values. A similar solution has been suggested by Simon Jackman for survey non-response (Jackman 1999). Like ours, his method exploits "auxiliary information" from the same or similar surveys where it is possible to derive the relative amount of non-response bias and measurement error. He then averages over the auxiliary information to bound the quantity of interest, yielding an estimate corrected for both non-response bias and selection. These techniques require a good model from which predictions for missings can be derived.

A modern variant of the out-of-sample prediction technique relaxes the assumption that researchers necessarily know a useful theoretical model to generate these predictions, which leads to the *multiple imputation test*. The multiple imputation approach (King et al. 2001) uses all available information in the dataset to impute missing values and Markov Chain Monte Carlo (MCMC) techniques generate a probability density distribution of imputed values. Since standard imputation models often work poorly for time-series cross-section data because such data violate the assumptions of conditional independence and exchangeability of observations, the lags and leads of the variables that have missing values can be added to the imputation model in order to impose smoother trends on the variables to be imputed than what is typically generated by a standard imputation model. Priors in the form of existing expert knowledge can be included (Honaker and King 2010). Using the various imputed values for the missing observations in the estimation model gives a probability density distribution of estimated coefficients.

The multiple imputation approach thus implicitly already relies on the logic of robustness testing. It has the further advantage that it takes into account the added uncertainty that comes with the imputation of missing values, whereas interpolation/extrapolation and theory-based out-of-sample predictions replace missing values with single values as if they were known such that the standard errors in the estimation model are under-estimated since they fail to take into account the additional sampling uncertainty that results from imputation. Of course, in principle MCMC techniques can be applied to generate a probability density distribution of imputed values rather than unique imputed values for different inter- or extrapolation variants or different runs of theory-based out-of-sample predictions as well. The out-of-sample prediction provides information about the uncertainty of the point prediction. We can use this uncertainty to repeatedly replace missings by a random draw from the (normal) distribution around the point prediction. This gives us a distribution of estimates which – after averaging – provides the true uncertainty of the missing replacement. In any case, the results from multiple imputation techniques can and should be compared to other techniques for dealing with missing values including theoretically-based out-of-sample predictions and interpolation and extrapolation.

In the example that we used throughout this chapter, there are many missing values for one of our central explanatory variables, corruption. Interpolating values missing in between existing adjacent values does not make much difference since the sample only increases by 13 observations after interpolation.

Clearly, the vast majority of missing values stem from the entire lack of information on corruption in a good number of countries. We therefore employ in model m4, reported in table 7.4, the multiple imputation robustness test, employing a Bayesian iterative MCMC procedure for imputing the missing values. The sample size increases by 85 percent, thus recovering a large number of observations that are dropped in the baseline model. Results for the quake propensity variables in corrupt and non-corrupt

Table 7.4: Multiple Imputation Test

	m1: baseline	m4: missings imputed	ρ
Maximum quake magnitude	0.00577	0.0170***	0.357
	(0.00489)	(0.00445)	
Magnitude population density	3.68e−05**	3.04e−05*	0.955
	(1.72e−05)	(1.56e−05)	
Minimum focal depth	−0.00106	−0.00692	0.961
	(0.00727)	(0.00476)	
Democracy	−2.369***	−1.704***	0.990
	(0.770)	(0.363)	
Per capita income (ln)	−0.595***	−0.499**	0.932
	(0.218)	(0.214)	
Population (ln)	0.547**	0.650***	0.993
	(0.235)	(0.145)	
Lack of corruption	−0.173	0.00237	0.891
	(0.290)	(0.309)	
Quake propensity in more corrupt countries	−0.00318	−0.00423***	0.996
	(0.00195)	(0.00104)	
Quake propensity in less corrupt countries	−0.00770***	−0.00819***	0.912
	(0.00164)	(0.00182)	
p-value χ^2 test propensity corrupt vs non-corrupt	0.008	0.043	
Observations	698	1,288	

Note: Dependent variable is earthquake fatality. Negative binomial estimations. Constant not reported. Standard errors clustered on countries in parentheses. Statistically significant *at 0.1, ** at 0.05, *** at 0.01 level.

countries remain robust. Quake propensity now has a statistically significant effect in non-corrupt countries.

7.6 CONCLUSION

The definition of population and the sampling of cases stand at the heart of the external validity of empirical research. Most, if not all, researchers intend to formulate generalizable findings. However, population definitions that have been determined by data availability rather than theory hamper the validity of causal inferences. Convenience samples inevitably cause selection bias. Selection bias in turn threatens the external validity of empirical research.

In an ideal world, researchers draw a random sample from a given population of cases for which their theory claims validity. This justifies the nice optimality properties of estimators and allows valid generalizations from the sample results to the population. Alas, the real world looks very different. Deductively derived, researchers are uncertain about the set of cases (the population) for which their theory claims validity, which renders drawing a random sample impossible. Inductively derived, researchers are uncertain about the set of cases (the population) to which a result based on a given sample of cases can be generalized.

Deviations from random sampling caused heated debates between those who argue that non-random samples do not allow valid inferences and those who defend inferences from non-random samples. If the former are correct, the majority of studies in the social sciences – those who fail to produce true random samples or who use convenience samples – cannot make inferences and they would at best have a purely historical value. For others, inferences do not require random sampling. For example, Valliant, Dorfman, and Royall (2000: 19) argue that the "claim that (...) probabilistic inferences are not valid when the randomization distribution is not available is simply wrong." This statement is certainly correct for conservative generalization and inductively derived populations. If researchers manage to generalize to cases which have properties sufficiently similar to the cases included in the sample, bias does not need to occur. For every selected sample, there exists at least one population that has identical properties to the sample, so in the worst-case scenario the population and the sample are identical. Yet, the scientific status and the real-world impact of empirical research that does not allow generalization is questionable.

Robustness tests allow researchers to test whether their results are robust and their inferences are upheld if they make alternative plausible assumptions regarding the relevant population or the process of sampling. Robustness tests cannot guarantee unbiased estimates, neither by improving the definition of the population nor by moving the sampling process closer to a true random draw. They can, however, provide evidence on the degree to which estimated effects and inferences depend on the definition of the population and on sampling decisions.

8 Concept Validity and Measurement

Count what is countable, measure what is measurable, and what is not measurable, make measurable.
Attributed to Galileo Galilei

Everything that can be counted does not necessarily count. Everything that counts cannot necessarily be counted.
Attributed to Albert Einstein

8.1 INTRODUCTION

A necessary condition for the success story of scientific research has been the development of measurement units, scales, and instruments. Scientific progress is not only about new ideas and theories, paradigmatic change, and revolutionary findings. Science also progresses by the nitty-gritty scientific work that initiates the development of better measurement units, scales, and instruments, the implementation of global measurement standards, and an ever-improving understanding of how measures relate to reality, and vice versa. Measurement in the natural sciences often is of the ideal type: objects are measured with predefined units of measurement on agreed scales, which exist independently of the measurement instrument. These measures have an inter-subjective validity: they can be replicated within the limits determined by the measurement error.

Social scientists have by and large been bystanders to this success story. Development of agreed measurement scales with predefined units of measurement? Not much comes to mind. Measurement instruments? Same problem. Social scientists prefer a different and broader understanding of measurement, namely one that accepts the assignment of numerals to phenomena as measurement as long as the assignment follows certain rules. Social scientists occasionally use measures such as geographical distance, but we know of no core concept or construct in the social sciences which can be measured on an agreed scale with a predefined measurement unit using a reliable measurement instrument.[1] Power, skills, knowledge, wealth, inequality, happiness, democracy, freedom, and utility are not directly observable. As a consequence, many social science measures fall short of the ideal type of measurement. Put differently, many social science concepts are not *measured* if we apply a narrow definition. Instead, they are either counted or quantified. Counts do come with a unit, typically a definition of what is counted, but require neither scale nor measurement instrument. Quantification explicitly does not employ a measurement instrument; it is a process of assigning numerals to properties of objects without either counting or measurement in the strict sense.

The lack of measurement, narrowly defined, triggers measurement error of two distinct kinds: a) error deriving from the operationalized measure of unobserved concepts – typically called a proxy variable – deviating from the true properties of the concept; and b) error deriving from errors in measuring the chosen proxy variable or variables. When the argument requires, we will refer to the first problem as concept invalidity and to the second problem as measurement error. However, as a shortcut we will often merely speak of measurement error as encompassing both problems. As Wansbeek and Meijer (2000: 1) remark: "Despite these differences, their implied econometric problems are to large extent identical and hence warrant an integrated treatment."

Problems with concept validity and measurement error – the lack of precision in the measurement of social science concepts – stand in remarkable contrast to the attention measurement issues receive in empirical research.[2] Accordingly, this chapter explains where uncertainty about the validity of concepts as well as measurement error come from, why they are omnipresent, and how social scientists can analyze their relevance and study their consequences with robustness tests.

We start by clarifying the distinction between measurement, counting, and quantification. Next, we review the role that proxy variables play in dealing with uncertainty about concept validity. We then discuss and propose robustness tests for uncertainty about concept validity: the problem caused by many social science theoretical concepts being unobserved,

---

1 We use the terms "concept" and "construct" interchangeably.
2 In the scathing verdict by Kennedy (2008: 164): "Econometricians tend to ignore measurement error problems because they cause too much trouble." Yet, methodologists have developed measurement error models for a multitude of estimators. The validity of inferences based on these models depends on strong assumptions about the error term, its distribution and correlation with the dependent or explanatory variables. For the realistic case where researchers are uncertain about the type and extent of measurement error, these models offer nothing useful.

multidimensional and not clearly defined. Finally, we turn to measurement error – the deviation of measured from true values – and robustness tests for it. We distinguish uncertainty about concept validity and measurement error for analytical purposes but the two problems of measurement cannot be neatly separated since uncertainty about concept validity must result in measurement error and measurement error can be so large as to threaten the validity of the measured concept.

8.2 MEASUREMENT, COUNTING, AND QUANTIFICATION

The term "measurement" can have different meanings. In the broadest possible sense, measurement "is defined as the assignment of numerals to objects and events following rules" (Stevens 1946: 677). We prefer a narrower definition. Two conditions need to be satisfied for *measurement* in the narrow sense: first, the property to be measured must in principle be observable via a measurement instrument. Second, the measurement has to be conducted on predefined units of measurement, using an agreed scale, which exists independently of the measurement act.

Counting requires neither a scale nor a measurement instrument, but relies solely on a defined unit. Clearly, the unit matters. 4 pens plus 6 pencils give 10 writing instruments, but only 4 pens. The precision of the count depends on the precision with which the unit can be defined. Imprecision results from objects for which it is unknown whether they belong to the group of counted objects or not. Some definitions of writing instruments combine elements of pens and elements of pencils, others do not. Counting objects using an ill-defined unit brings about lack of precision or measurement error. Additional measurement error may occur because human beings find it difficult to count a large number of objects in a short period of time. Counting requires observability of the objects and a definition of the object, but neither a measurement scale nor a measurement unit.

Quantification, finally, assigns a number (which results from neither measurement nor counting) to an object without employing a measurement instrument. For example, researchers can use a binary variable which equals 1 if an item is blue, 0 otherwise. Or they can code red=1, blue=2, and green=3. This process turns observations into variables, though nothing has been measured in a narrow sense or counted. Values have been assigned numerals in a subjective fashion. Quantification is an important technique because many properties can be neither measured nor counted. And even if properties can be measured in principle, researchers prefer to quantify information because it is easier, cheaper, and faster than measurement. For example, one can measure the wavelengths or the frequency of light rather than merely quantifying colors, but it is more difficult, more expensive, and takes more time and effort.

Quantification and counting can imply large measurement uncertainty and error. The fundamental problem of measurement is that not everything that ought to be measured in the narrow sense can be measured – an issue that presents an under-estimated obstacle to progress in the social sciences. What is the value of developing "unbiased" estimation strategies when the measurement uncertainty and accordingly the error of the data are large? What is the meaning of estimating the determinants of happiness using the latest permutation of an ordered-logit estimator if researchers are not able to tell whether happiness of degree 3 of individual i differs from happiness of degree 4 of individual j?

When social scientists "measure" happiness, results are likely to vary across different "measurement instruments." The number of questions in a happiness survey determines the range and potential categories (or degrees) of happiness. If scholars ask five questions, happiness will usually be measured on a 6-point, 11-point, 16-point, 21-point or 26-point scale, depending on the number of possible answers to each question and assuming that all questions have the same number of answer categories. If we were to take another "measurement instrument," say one with 12 questions that allows only "yes" or "no" as answers, we suddenly measure happiness on a 13-point "scale." Hence, the measurement instrument determines the scale and, to some extent, the measure itself. Given the absence of a measurement unit and an accepted instrument, it cannot be surprising that at least six different measures of happiness exist (Helm 2000; Hills and Argyle 2002; Hsee and Tang 2007; Kammann, Farry, and Herbison 1984; Kozma and Stones 1980).

Nothing can prevent social scientists from using the term "measurement" for any process that assigns numbers to properties of observations if they wish to use a lax definition of measurement. In this sense, the count of correct answers to four questions, where "correct" is defined by the survey researcher, can "measure" political knowledge. Yet, in the narrow definition of measurement proposed above, the political knowledge variables based on the American National Election Study (DeBell 2013; Pietryka and MacIntosh 2013) are far from measured; rather, they are quantified. Assigning values to an observation through a process of quantification, even if rule-guided, has little in common with the measurement of distance, temperature, or even gross domestic product.

8.3 UNCERTAINTY ABOUT CONCEPT VALIDITY: THE ROLE OF PROXY VARIABLES

Concept validity concerns the relationship between concept and its measurement. Operationalization becomes necessary when the concept of interest – the term used in the theory from which testable hypotheses are derived – cannot be observed and thus not measured. At least in quantitative research, some form of counting or quantification is necessary for empirical testing. As Geoffrey Evans has argued, concept validity "is a matter of degree" (Evans 1998: 189). Uncertainty about the concept validity of the operationalization of unobservable concepts has two root causes: multidimensionality and lack of an agreed definition.

That important theoretical concepts are not consensually defined remains a key problem in the social sciences. Power, happiness, utility, welfare, knowledge, skills, justice, fairness, salience, democracy, corruption, and other concepts are abstract and have no meaning without definition. Many social scientists employ these and similar concepts in their research without offering accepted or even their own definitions. Moreover, these concepts carry different meanings in different contexts. The meaning of power, for example, varies depending on whether social scientists analyze wars, parliamentary agenda-setting, or decision-making within families. The problem posed by lack of clear definitions is compounded by the complex nature of abstract social science concepts. Social science concepts are multidimensional with each dimension capturing some partial aspect of the complex concept, and scholars need to employ an algorithm to aggregate these dimensions. Multidimensional concepts, however, cannot be reduced without losing information. This leads to the difficult question as to which of the various dimension reductions works best given the research question.

Consider as an example the research on party positions. In principle, the political sphere has as many dimensions as there are policy dimensions on which parties can have independent preferences. These dimensions are often correlated, but not all political dimensions are perfectly correlated and therefore cannot be reduced to a single dimension without "error." And yet, the "measurement" of political parties explicitly tries to reduce the actual number of political dimensions to a single dimension known as the *left–right scale* (Castles and Mair 1984; Budge 2001). Evidence to suggest otherwise amply exists: the distributions of political preferences on, for example, environmental policies, immigration policies, exchange-rate policies, higher education policies arguably deviate from the simplistic relative placement of political parties on the left–right axis.

Or take as another example the concept of power. Power cannot be observed; it has a different character and different sources in different interactions between agents. How many dimensions of power exist and how do military power and economic power compare to other forms of influence which we may or may not want to include in a broad concept of power? Bachrach and Baratz (1962) argue that there are two faces of power: the ability to influence decisions, and the ability to prevent the making of decisions. Lukes (1974) argues that power has three "faces": the ability to win an argument, the ability to set the agenda, and the ability to influence the preferences of others. Power can have different roots – knowledge and experience can be a source of power, but so too can the number of nuclear missiles. Power can be a stock concept or a relational concept. All these complexities prevent social scientists from directly measuring power. It cannot be measured in the way humans have learned to measure the color and brightness of light, the temperature of air, or the distance between two points in a Euclidian space.

In the absence of an agreed scale, a predefined measurement unit and instrument, social scientists employ various techniques for quantifying unobservable concepts. The first available strategy is the use of a proxy variable. For example, in international relations, power has frequently been approximated by military spending. A second strategy employs multiple proxy variables for capturing multiple dimensions of power. These variables are usually turned into a single variable by one of four different techniques: by taking the sum or mean of normalized raw variables, by some sort of multidimensional scaling (aggregation), by computing the principal component of these variables,[3] or by a latent variable measurement model that produces confidence intervals around the central estimates.[4] A third strategy replaces the measurement of the unobservable concept with subjective measures, for example with expert views on how corrupt countries are on some scale.

All these strategies have specific weaknesses. The proxy variable approach requires the existence of a single variable which sufficiently corresponds to the latent variable that measures the unobservable concept. Necessarily, proxies cannot be perfect and the resulting imperfection will always cause uncertainty about the extent to which any proxy variable validly measures the underlying theoretical concept, i.e. "whether a variable measures what it is supposed to measure" (Bollen 1989: 184). Proxies can be measured with more or with less variation than the latent concept has. In the former (latter) case, the estimate may not just suffer from bias because the properties of the proxy deviate from the properties of the construct, but also from overconfidence (underconfidence). For example, the use of word count data to approximate "political preferences" or

3 For examples, see Falbo (1977) in psychology and Sieberer (2011) in institutional politics.

4 For examples of the latter technique, Pemstein et al. (2010) provide an overall measure of democracy with confidence intervals around central estimates based on 10 existing proxy measures. Kaufman et al. (2010) use an Unobserved Components Model (UCM) to aggregate data from various proxy measures into central estimates with confidence intervals of six governance measures.

"positions" of political parties is likely to generate a proxy variable that has more variation than the true variation of policy positions.

That an unobservable concept is typically complex and multidimensional renders it unlikely that it can be sufficiently captured by a single proxy. Does military spending approximate power well enough? What about scores from an intelligence test and intelligence? Should "per capita income" be accepted as proxy for the wealth of nations? Few doubt that power is more than military spending and intelligence more than the result of a standardized test. However, the question is not whether proxies lose information (we can take that for granted), but whether the correlation between the observed variable and the unobserved latent construct is sufficiently high. Obviously, the latent variable remains unobserved. The question, therefore, cannot be answered: proxy variables are necessarily contestable, and are in fact typically contested.[5]

Lack of observability often leads to more than one proxy. Competing proxies with different operationalizations exist for many concepts. Naturally, scholars will disagree about the "best" proxy. In addition, measurement error necessarily occurs when researchers reduce the dimensionality of a latent construct since information disappears. Dimension reduction demonstrates that uncertainty about concept validity cannot always be distinguished from measurement error.

The most relevant disadvantage of the strategy that employs multiple variables to capture multiple dimensions of the latent variable lies in the arbitrariness of aggregating them into one single variable. Not only is the inclusion and exclusion of constituting variables somewhat arbitrary, so also is the way in which dimensions are reduced. This allows researchers to *engineer* a construct which gives the required result in the final model estimation. In addition, multiple reduction algorithms exist creating multiple competing aggregated variables – a solution that causes uncertainty about which of the variables is best suited.

Finally, the disadvantage of subjective "measures" is, not surprisingly, their subjectivity. The perception of a variable can only be as good as the observability of the original concept or its causes and consequences. If a concept cannot be observed, subjective quantifications will inevitably resort to taking more observable causes or consequences of the concept into subjective account. This creates endogeneity problems if scholars use the variable to analyze a causal effect of the latent variable.

To illustrate the problem of uncertainty about concept validity, take measures of democracy as an example. Theories formulate predictions

---

5 See, for example, Thomas (2010) and Langbein and Knack (2010) on the contestability of proxies of good governance.

about the determinants of democracy or the effects of democracy on other social phenomena. But democracy cannot be directly observed and measured. Accordingly, existing proxy variables for democracy such as the well-known and much-used *polity2* score of the Polity IV project (Marshall and Jaggers 2007) or the political rights and civil liberties measures of Freedom House (2013) not only differ from each other (Munck and Verkuilen 2002) but also from alternative conceptualizations like the ones suggested by Vanhanen (2000), Bueno de Mesquita and Smith (2005), Przeworski et al. (2000) or Cheibub et al. (2010).

Some of the democracy measures use single proxy variables (Vanhanen 2000), others use subjective measures (Freedom House 2013) or aggregate multidimensional data to a single unidimensional proxy variable (e.g., *polity2*). As concerns the latter, not surprisingly there is controversy over how the information from multiple constituent indicators from the Polity IV project should be aggregated to form the composite democracy indicator (Gleditsch and Ward 1997). As Treier and Jackman (2008: 202) point out more generally: "Among scholars who operationalize democracy via multiple indicators, there is no agreement regarding how one should aggregate the information in the indicators, a data reduction task whereby we assign a score to each country-year observation, given the scores on the indicator variables for the country-year." The optimal operationalization of data from a single source is not independent of the amount of measurement error contained in the proxy measures. Given that each constituent indicator is likely to be measured with error, any composite measure based on these constituent indicators must contain error, yet is typically treated as being measured with certainty. As Munck and Verkuilen (2002: 6) lament, researchers using measures of democracy pay too little attention to the "important problems of conceptualization and measurement."

8.4 ROBUSTNESS TESTS FOR PROXY VARIABLES

Lack of observability does not prevent social scientists from quantifying a concept. Indeed, for theories that rely on concepts that cannot be directly observed and measured, researchers need to find one or more proxy variables – or as some prefer to call it: an operationalization. The process of operationalization, somewhat miraculously, turns an unmeasurable concept into a measurable and measured variable.

This solution comes at a price: proxies ought to correspond to the concept of interest, but neither can the correlation be discovered, nor are the properties of the proxy identical to the properties of the original concept, if that was measureable. Thus, it can be taken for granted that proxies deviate from the original latent construct. All proxies have a deviation from the concept and the extent and nature of the deviation from the true values remains unknown. Inevitably, researchers cannot know whether the deviation is systematic or not. Hence, it is impossible to know whether one has obtained an unbiased estimate by using a proxy.

Since the properties of the latent variable remain unknown, the deviation of the properties of the proxy from the properties of the latent construct cannot be known either. In reality, researchers' choice of a proxy is therefore more a matter of personal taste and research tradition in a discipline than a matter of optimizing the model specification. Often, researchers simply do not know enough about competing data sources that provide different proxies to be able to choose the optimal proxy.

Robustness tests can help in dealing with different operationalizations of unobservable theoretical concepts. Though they cannot bridge the gap between the concept and its proxies, they can test whether a theory finds empirical support regardless of the operationalization of the variables and/ or the different sources of data used in the analyses. If researchers do not know which of the various alternative proxy variables offers an undoubtedly superior approximation to the original concept, it seems natural to use two or more proxies interchangeably – one in the baseline model and the other ones in an *alternative proxy test*. As an alternative to a simple comparison of estimation results based on the use of two different proxies, one can compare the baseline model based on the preferred proxy variable to an estimate based on the principal component of the baseline model operationalization and the alternative proxy or proxies. This *principal component test* employs the covariation of two or more proxy variables simultaneously.

Not only are there often competing proxy variables for unobserved theoretical constructs; the construct is also typically multidimensional. Unidimensional proxy variables are thus derived from the underlying latent multiple dimensions according to some dimension reduction formula. Two approaches dominate social scientists' attempts at reducing multidimensional data into a single, unidimensional variable: the first approach assumes that the dimensions are additive in an unweighted or weighted form. The second approach employs principal component techniques, identifies dimensions which are highly collinear, transfers them into a single dimension by using the "factor loads" suggested by the algorithm, and gives the result a fancy name. Since researchers use only the first few principal components, they dismiss a share of the original information and eliminate the multidimensionality of a concept.

Yet, no approach can solve the problem that, in principle, multidimensional data can be reduced in virtually infinite different ways, with no single way dominating all the others. Multiple ways for adding up dimensions exist and a limitless number of potential weights can be used. Likewise, principal component analyses can be tweaked and rotated and engineered to give different principal components – some of which may even give the desired result in the estimation model!

Robustness tests can test whether estimates are robust to changes in the procedure with which dimensions are reduced. Naturally, it is not possible to estimate all possible combinations of information aggregation including all possible functional forms, methods of dimension reduction with and without rotation, and so on. There are simply too many options. Instead, we suggest two randomized permutation robustness tests, depending on the nature of the unidimensional aggregate proxy variable used in the baseline model.

For the first robustness test, the *randomized components test*, if the variable is an additive index such as the democracy score in *polity2*, researchers can use the underlying original data to produce alternative aggregates, where in every iteration each component of the original variable gets a weight that is a random draw from a distribution whose values average to the original weight. The uniform or normal distributions are plausible candidates. For each new composite, the model permutation is estimated.[6]

We illustrate the test based on a re-analysis of Fearon and Laitin (2003), who put forward a large number of hypotheses in their analysis of the determinants of civil and ethnic war onset over the period 1945 to 1999 covering 161 countries that had a population of at least half a million in 1990.[7] We will focus here on a single hypothesis: that "anocracies" – regime types that are neither clearly autocratic nor democratic – are more prone to civil war onset than autocracies, which Fearon and Laitin interpret as an indication of "weak" states – too weak to turn themselves into either clear autocracies or democracies – falling prey to internal violent conflict. In its original coding, *polity2* rests on the sum of five components that reflect the competitiveness and the openness of executive recruitment, constraints on the chief executive, and the regulation and competitiveness of political participation. We conducted 1,000 Monte Carlo simulations in which in

6 As always, we suggest at least 1,000 Monte Carlo iterations if computationally feasible.

7 In many respects, the estimate of the anocracy effect in Fearon and Laitin (2003) appears to be problematic. First, as Vreeland (2008) has observed, the Polity project's definition of anocracies includes political instability and civil war. Hence, the "effect" of anocracy on civil war onset is partly tautological. And second, as we have shown elsewhere (Plümper and Neumayer 2010a), interregnums are assigned a value of 0 and thus automatically coded as anocracy by the Polity project, a coding definition which erroneously inflates the number of anocracies or anocracy years.

each simulation the weights are drawn from a uniform distribution around the mean of 1.0, a simulated *polity2* variable is created and from this simulated *polity2* variable regime type dummies are then derived. The estimated degree of robustness averaged across all 1,000 models without model weighting equals $\rho = 0.90$ (95 percent of simulations have ρ between 0.57 and 0.96).

For the second robustness test, the *principal component jitter test*, if the unidimensional variable has been produced using a principal component technique, we suggest researchers accept the weights for each component, but generate jitter around these weights similar to what we have suggested above. For example, if the original weight of one component in the principal component analysis equals, say, 0.7, analysts can replace this weight by a random draw from a normal distribution with mean 0.7 and standard deviation of 0.35 or from a truncated uniform distribution centered around this mean.

For our illustrative example, the unidimensional variable *polity2* has not been produced via principal component analysis. However, we can create one based on the five individual components. We then conducted 1,000 Monte Carlo simulations in which, in each simulation, the weights are drawn from a uniform distribution around the mean of the weights from the principal component analysis and a simulated *polity2* variable is created based on these simulated weights from which regime type dummies are derived. The degree of robustness averaged across all 1,000 models without model weighting equals $\rho = 0.87$ (95 percent of simulations have ρ between 0.19 and 0.96).

8.5 MEASUREMENT ERROR

Measurement error – the deviation of measured from the true values – is relevant for all variables in an estimation model. For continuous variables, measurement error results in values that are not the true values, whereas for categorical and dichotomous dummy variables[8] the consequence of measurement error is misclassification: observations are attributed to a category to which in truth they do not belong. In small samples even classical[9] measurement error in one variable can bias results of multiple variables that are correlated with each other (Carroll et al. 1995: 26; Wooldridge 2010: 81). If classical measurement error affects multiple explanatory variables, the estimates will be biased in ways that are a priori unknown (Bound

---

8 A categorical variable takes on a limited number of specific values; a dichotomous dummy variable takes on one of two values, e.g. 0 and 1.

9 For error in the measurement of a variable to be classical, the measured values must be a linear combination of their true values and random error, that is, error that is uncorrelated with the true values and with the error term in the estimation equation.

et al. 2001: 3716). The same holds for non-linear estimation models and systematic error. As Bound et al. (2001: 3708f.) summarize the cacophony of consequences of measurement error: "The effect of measurement error can range from the simple attenuation (...) to situations where (i) real effects are hidden; (ii) observed data exhibit relationships that are not present in the error free data; and (iii) even the signs of the estimated coefficients are reversed."[10]

In an optimal world, all properties of objects would be reliably and validly measurable on a continuous scale. In this perfect world, measurement error would be random or unsystematic – that is, uncorrelated with any other property of the data-generating process – with a mean of zero and conveniently distributed. Random error would occur because precise one-off and repeated measurements are difficult or costly or both. Almost all measurements have an unsystematic component. Rounding error, for example, is expected to be unsystematic.

Yet, in the real world systematic measurement error – error that is systematically correlated with at least one of the properties of the data-generating process – dominates. Social science data tends to be more precise for some cases than for others. Per capita income in Germany is measured with higher precision than the per capita income of North Korea. Estimates of the number of people killed by natural disasters can be distorted by political incentives (Keefer et al. 2011). Likewise, survey responses on the extent of marijuana use, even if we assume respondents answer truthfully, will show more measurement error for users than for non-users (Wooldridge 2010: 81f.). Bound et al. (2001: 3708) judge that "in most micro data analyses using survey data," the assumption of classical (random) measurement error reflects "convenience rather than conviction." Stegmüller (2011) argues that cross-national surveys suffer from response heterogeneity, which results in systematic measurement error if not accounted for.

Systematic measurement error has numerous sources. We focus on three here. A first source results from the nature of the measurement process. Large values will be recorded with larger error than small values. For example, the number of fatalities after relatively minor earthquakes is usually known with great precision, but measurement error in earthquake fatalities increases with the true total number of fatalities since larger quakes destroy more infrastructure of a region or even country and thus render

---

10 Any kind of nonlinearities tend to "exacerbate biases introduced by measurement error" (Bound et al. 2001: 3727) as well, be it because of non-linear functional form in linear estimators or nonlinear estimators. In a linear model with quadratic terms included, for example, measurement error will often flatten the curvature of the non-linear functional form (Kuha and Temple 2003).

measurement more difficult and costly. Systematic measurement error can also differ from place to place (e.g., easier to measure and less prone to error in more developed than in developing countries) and depend on the kind of government or institution that takes the measurement (Davidov et al. 2014). Sometimes the dividing line between measurement error and fraud becomes narrow. One does not need to go back to Greece's desire to become a member of the Eurozone to expect systematic under-reporting of public debt, government spending, and inflation, and potential over-reporting of employment and economic growth figures. As another example, affected governments and non-governmental organizations may have an incentive to exaggerate fatalities after disasters or violent conflict in order to prompt faster and larger aid inflows or to promote their campaigns. Conversely, affected governments may instead be tempted to downplay the number of fatalities and suppress measurement attempts by external actors if they fear their political survival is at risk if the true number of fatalities becomes known. In general, sources of information for the measurement of variables have an interest in biasing the data.

A second source of systematic measurement error occurs in the absence of measurement scales and predefined measurement units because the individual who quantifies variables will usually exert an influence on the quantification. This has been frequently discussed in survey research (based on multiple interviewers) and in the context of data gathering that depends on multiple coders, e.g. country experts. The phenomenon of measurement and precision heterogeneity has been discussed under the rubric of "intercoder reliability" in these literatures (Lewis and Cook 1968; Ruggeri et al. 2011), which measures the overlap between the subjective judgements of different individuals.

Even measures of intercoder reliability are subject to uncertainty. It seems at least likely that the influence of coders on results is systematic and likely to be correlated with other variables potentially included in a regression model. Lack of intercoder reliability occurs with higher probability as concepts become increasingly difficult to observe and the more researchers resort to quantification rather than measurement. Systematic measurement error can easily occur when measures are taken with different measurement instruments.

When counting or quantification draws on individuals' survey answers, systematic measurement error is inevitable independently of the number of interviewers. Measurement error creeps in because, due to flawed memory, survey respondents cannot recall the true value at the time when they are surveyed – a measurement error known as recall error which need not be randomly distributed across respondents. A further and under-appreciated source of measurement error is that different subjects might understand different things when asked the same question. Implicit measurement scales for values, perceptions, ideas, and opinions are not necessarily stable over time or across space or across different groups of people. For example, even if survey respondents answer sincerely they may use different thresholds between categories. As a consequence, the chosen answer category of two individuals with the same attitude differs, or two individuals with diverse attitudes select the same answer category. Finally, if respondents give answers that they feel are expected from them or simply lie, then, obviously, they do not reveal true values. These errors are likely to be systematic rather than random because individuals differ in their propensity to be subject to these errors or incentives to misrepresent answers.

A third source of systematic measurement error derives from researchers undertaking non-permissible transformations. As Stevens (1946: 678) has demonstrated, the measurement scales determine permissible transformations of the data. Appendix 8A reproduces his overview of permissible variable transformations depending on the scale of measurement. Many social scientists violate these rules, for example by calculating the mean of ordinal variables. In behavioral political science, researchers use categorical placements on a left–right scale to calculate the position of the mean voter. Yet, all the information the initial survey contained was whether a first respondent was more on the left of the political spectrum than a second respondent, not how much further to the left. When scholars use non-permitted transformations to compute sums and means of categorical variables, measurement error becomes not only inevitable but systematic. The size of the measurement error may vary largely, depending on the distribution of the true underlying scale.

8.6 ROBUSTNESS TESTS FOR MEASUREMENT ERROR

The properties of measurement error and therefore the type of robustness test for measurement error depend on the measurement scale used, which is why it is important to relate measurement error to scales. Measurement scales are usually divided into four groups: nominal, ordinal, interval, and ratio. If a construct is measured on a nominal scale, measurement error triggers misclassification: for example, a color is blue, but it will be categorized as green. If a construct is measured on an ordinal scale, measurement error not only causes misclassification but also distorts the ranking of observations in the entire sample. With interval and ratio scales, measurement error extends to wrong differences to other measured values and, if we have a ratio scale, wrong ratios among measured values.

A first type of robustness test changes the measurement scale of the variable of interest. For example, if researchers use the *polity2* proxy measure of democracy in its linear pseudo-continuous form in the baseline model as if it were measured on an interval or ratio scale, they can test the robustness of estimates toward classifying countries into nominal groups of autocracies, anocracies, and democracies, and vice versa. There can be good reasons for collapsing pseudo-continuous proxy variables into dummy variable categories if variation within the categories represents more measurement error than meaningful variation.[11] The *rescaling test* explores to what extent results depend on a particular operationalization.

In addition, for continuous variables measured on an interval or ratio scale, we have developed a randomized permutation robustness test, which examines the fragility of estimates toward specified amounts and types of measurement error. We have employed this *measurement error injection test* in a number of publications (Plümper and Neumayer 2009; Keefer, Neumayer, and Plümper 2011; Neumayer, Plümper, and Barthel 2014). It works by injecting a specified amount of measurement error of a specified type (for example, random or correlated with a specific variable) into a specified share of observations and running Monte Carlo simulations with these created variables in order to obtain a distribution of estimates.

The robustness test requires four decisions. First, researchers need to determine for which variables measurement error is a serious concern. Second, researchers need to determine the maximum size of the measurement error. Though the measurement error for each observation cannot be known, researchers tend to have information about the maximum extent of measurement error. If competing sources of data exist, differences in their reported values can provide a hint about the extent of measurement error. Third, researchers need to decide on the type of measurement error injected into observations. We can add random error or, for example, impose larger measurement error on observations with larger measured values or let the measurement error be correlated with an explanatory variable. For example, in Keefer et al. (2011) we assume that earthquake mortality is measured with systematically higher error in autocracies since autocratic governments have greater incentives to bias estimates and render measurement by external actors more difficult. Fourth, researchers need to decide onto what share of the observations they add this artificial measurement error.

Once these decisions have been taken, analysts use Monte Carlo techniques to add a random draw from the predefined maximum set of measurement error to the selected variables for the predefined set of observations, repeatedly estimate the model and obtain a distribution of parameter

---

11 For example, Høyland et al. (2012) suggest that given the considerable amount of measurement error likely to be present in international index rankings such as the Human Development Index or the Doing Business Index, countries should be classified into a limited number of groups rather than ranked continuously.

estimates from these models. The mean of the distribution will be close to the estimate of the baseline model if they inject random measurement error to the dependent variable.[12]

We employ the study by Keefer et al. (2011), which we used already in the previous chapter, as our illustrative example. The baseline model tests the hypothesis that countries with larger historical experience of earthquakes experience lower mortality (holding the size of the actual quake constant) and that this effect – we call it quake propensity – is larger in less corrupt than in more corrupt countries. In autocracies, governments might have an incentive to downplay the actual number of deaths, whereas foreign observers might over-estimate fatalities, knowing that domestic sources tend to under-estimate them. In addition, fatalities in richer countries can be measured more easily than in poorer countries. In the Monte Carlo simulation of 1,000 models we multiplied the value of the dependent variable of all observations by a uniform random number. For high-income countries and democracies, the number was drawn from the interval [0.5, 1.5], which mirrors measurement errors of up to 50 percent. For low-income countries and autocracies, it was drawn from the interval [0.25, 2] to reflect the larger degree of measurement error in these countries. This gives us mean estimates across the simulations and mean standard errors of these estimates, to which we add the standard error of the mean standard error estimate to account for the additional source of uncertainty (see table 8.1).

Table 8.1: Measurement Error Injection Test				
	mean	**std. dev.**	**min.**	**max.**
Quake propensity in corrupt countries	−0.0029	0.0012	−0.0056	0.0021
Standard error	0.0022	0.0007	0.0011	0.0047
Quake propensity in non-corrupt countries	−0.0077	0.0008	−0.0103	−0.0054
Standard error	0.0018	0.0003	0.0011	0.0029

Note: Dependent variable is earthquake fatality. Negative binomial estimations.

12 Even with unsystematic measurement error injected into the dependent variable, the measurement error will only be uncorrelated with the explanatory variables on average, but correlated with one or more explanatory variables in almost all individual model iterations. By looking at the extremes of the estimated parameter distribution, one would therefore take some non-random measurement error into account as well even for this case of injecting random error.

For corrupt countries, we get a mean estimate of quake propensity of −0.0029 and standard error 0.0022 compared to the baseline model estimate of −0.0032 and standard error 0.0020 and, for non-corrupt countries, a mean estimate of −0.0077 and standard error 0.0018 compared to baseline model estimate of −0.0077 and standard error 0.0016. Our findings of a larger effect in non-corrupt than in corrupt countries remains robust. The estimated degrees of robustness averaged across all Monte Carlo simulation models without model weighting are $\rho = 0.89$ for the effect in non-corrupt countries (95 percent of simulations have ρ between 0.73 and 0.98) and $\rho = 0.88$ for the effect in corrupt countries (95 percent of simulations have ρ between 0.58 and 0.99).

In figures 8.1 and 8.2 we show the estimated quake propensity effect in, respectively, corrupt and non-corrupt countries across the 1,000 simulations together with the 95-percent confidence interval of the baseline model. The figures thus display the entire distribution of robustness test estimates of this randomized permutation test.

The figures illustrate the relatively small influence measurement error has on the estimated effects. Not a single one of the permutations results in low degrees of robustness, thus signaling that the baseline model estimates are robust to plausibly sized and systematic measurement error in earthquake fatalities. We also find that the baseline model's estimate of quake propensity in non-corrupt countries is slightly more robust than the effect in corrupt countries.

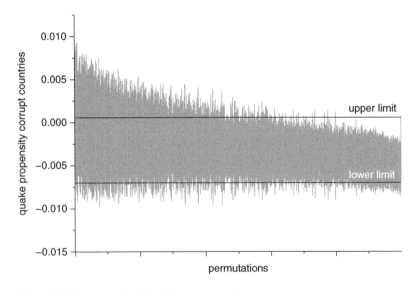

Figure 8.1: Error Injection Test: Corrupt Countries

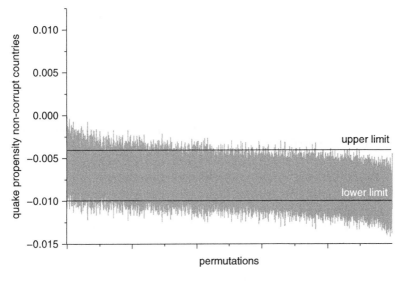

Figure 8.2: Error Injection Test: Non-corrupt Countries

This randomized permutation variant of the *measurement error injection test* can be turned into a robustness limit variant. Rather than injecting measurement error of a specified maximum size and specified type into a specified share of observations in order to test the robustness of estimates, we can turn this task upside down and explore which maximum extent of measurement error, which share of observations inflicted with measurement error, or which type of measurement error would suffice to render the estimates from a baseline model non-robust.

Robustness limit tests allow scholars to discuss whether the required measurement error is likely to exist. In the earthquake mortality example discussed above, a plausible limit for measurement error – at least for contemporary quakes – seems to lie in the range of plus or minus 50 percent (we injected larger measurement error into observations from developing and autocratic candidates for illustrative purposes). If 80-percent measurement error is required to render results non-robust, the odds are that the estimates are robust to measurement error.

Measurement error in categorical data measured on an *ordinal or nominal scale* such as survey research and other forms of quantification materializes as mis-categorization. We suggest two types of re-categorization robustness tests, one for unsystematic mis-categorizations, and one for systematic mis-categorizations. For the *re-categorization test*, researchers draw a random sample of a specified percentage of the answers, and increase the category chosen by the respondent by 1.0 in half of these cases, and reduce the category chosen by the respondent by 1.0 in the other half of the cases. In cases in which the respondents have chosen either of the two extreme categories, the value of the observation remains unchanged. Then the regression model is estimated, saved, and a new set of deviations can be drawn. We suggest at least 1,000 Monte Carlo iterations. Unless selected cases have a large impact on the estimation results, the mean estimate does not change considerably, but the variation of the point estimates around this mean adds to the uncertainty of the point estimate and provides a more realistic picture of the true uncertainty.

When mis-categorizations are systematic, the robustness test will have a larger influence on the point estimates. For example, a systematic mis-categorization occurs if some survey respondents use systematically higher or systematically lower thresholds than another. In this case, a first variant of the *re-categorization test* can randomly lower the answer categories of a share of the respondents who answer systematically higher than average and randomly increase the answer categories of the respondents who give answers systematically lower than the average respondent.

Systematic differences may not only occur in relation to the distribution and frequency of each category, but also according to the probability that a respondent selects an extreme category. If two individuals choose extreme answers with different probabilities, we do not necessarily know whether an extreme answer aversion of the respondent affects her responses or whether she truly has moderate views, preferences or attitudes. Nevertheless, we want to know whether the estimates are robust if systematic differences in the probability of extreme answers are due to extreme value aversion rather than the person truly holding less extreme views. To evaluate this question, in the second variant of the *re-categorization test* scholars can change a specified share of the answers of a respondent with suspected aversion against extreme answers, moving them closer to the extremes. On an agreement scale, this implies changing "agree" to "agree strongly" and "disagree" to "disagree strongly." The specified share can be varied and, unless there is reason to deviate, we suggest evenly changing the responses at both ends.

8.7 CONCLUSION

Over the history of mankind, the development of measurement units, scales and instruments and scientific progress were mutually reinforcing. Unfortunately, the social sciences seem to be lagging behind the development in the natural sciences. This is not surprising: the social sciences grapple with more challenging measurement problems than the natural sciences given that its theoretical constructs are typically latent (unobservable), multidimensional, and based on subjective quantification.

Measurement error hardly ever is unsystematic, and it is unlikely to be unsystematic when the measured property is unobservable or multidimensional. Subjectivity of quantification and multidimensionality of social science concepts pose problems which can be more important than a distinction between different scales or the question whether measurement error can be assumed to be unsystematic.

Given the difficulties and problems in measuring the social world, the case for robustness tests is simple: theoretical concepts used in the social sciences are often unobservable and their best operationalization remains uncertain, and even if they are observable, their measurement suffers from both random and systematic error. At the same time, econometric techniques are least likely to account for this error, unless of course the magnitude, direction, and distribution of the error is known well enough, but then the question emerges why data suffers from measurement error in the first place. If correcting measurement error were simple, social scientists would just do it. Robustness tests explore the potential frailty of estimates to changes in the operationalization and measurement of concepts. They do so in a flexible way suitable to measurements, counts, and quantifications, suitable for both random and systematic error in measurement of any size and any extent.

APPENDIX 8A: SCALES AND PERMISSIBLE VARIABLE TRANSFORMATIONS

According to Stevens (1946: 678)			
Scale	**Basic empirical observation – determination of:**	**Permissible statistics**	**Allowed operations**
nominal	equality	number of cases mode contingency correlation	= ≠
ordinal	greater or less	all the above plus: median percentile	= ≠ > <
interval	equality of intervals or differences	all the above plus: mean standard deviation rank correlation product-moment correlations	= ≠ > < + −
ratio	equality of ratios	all the above plus: coefficient of variation	= ≠ > < + − :

9 Explanatory and Omitted Variables

9.1 INTRODUCTION

No other model misspecification has attracted more attention than the choice of explanatory variables. Beginning with the first researcher who added a control variable to her baseline model and reported both models, scholars have long since argued that the true set of explanatory variables remains unknown and that it is likely that relevant regressors are omitted. Failure to include all relevant confounding variables, i.e. variables that have a causal effect on the dependent variable, results in a biased estimate for the variable of interest if covariance between the vector of omitted variables and the dependent variable is correlated with the variable of interest. Contrary to randomized controlled experiments, which can render the influence of confounding variables (though not of those that condition the treatment effect) irrelevant by increasing sample size to infinity, in observational data with no control over treatment status omitted variable bias does not disappear as sample size grows to infinity.

The potential exclusion of relevant variables has received notably more attention than the potential inclusion of irrelevant variables. However, the erroneous inclusion of irrelevant variables threatens the validity of inferences just as does the omission of variables (Clarke 2005). At the very least, including irrelevant variables will decrease the efficiency of estimations. Some cling to the belief that inefficiency "only" implies inflated standard errors and can therefore be neglected unless sample size is small or the data exhibits little variation. This view ignores the fact that researchers obtain a single point estimate per model. Erroneously included variables increase the sampling variance of the estimates, which implies that the expected deviation of an estimate from the truth increases. In this sense, inefficiency has the same effect as bias. Reducing efficiency means increasing the influence of noise on estimation outcomes. Inefficiency – just like bias – increases the probability of invalid inferences (King, Keohane, and Verba 1994;

Plümper and Troeger 2007, 2011). Accordingly, researchers should worry about erroneously included variables.

In reality, including all relevant confounding variables, but excluding all irrelevant variables, is not merely easier said than done: it is outright impossible with observational data. With limited information, the optimal number of variables to include in an estimation model may fall short of the number of variables contained in the true data-generating process. To make matters worse, even if we ignored the fact that, given limited information, models have to trade off simplicity versus generality, the inclusion of additional variables does not necessarily reduce bias even if the additional variable is part of the data-generating process. It is not difficult to construct a simple data-generating process with more than two omitted variables that results in an increase in bias if we add one omitted variable and a reduction in bias when both omitted variables are added.

We show how robustness tests help researchers uncertain about the choice of regressors by exploring the stability of estimated effects toward plausible changes to the set of explanatory variables. We start by discussing observed control variables, regarding which researchers are uncertain whether to include or exclude them. Both the exclusion of potential confounders and the inclusion of irrelevant variables threaten the validity of inferences on the effect of the variable of interest. We argue that estimation models will never include all the right and exclude all the wrong variables. We suggest that baseline models should contain only control variables known or suspected to exert a strong effect on the dependent variable, accompanied by robustness test models addressing uncertainty about the set of explanatory variables.

We then move to unknown and unobserved omitted variables potentially confounding the effect of the main variable of interest. We argue that the standard solution to "unobserved heterogeneity" in the form of differencing the data or unit fixed effects does not reduce bias if model misspecifications other than the omission of time-invariant unobservables represent a more important inferential threat. We suggest a number of tests that are less costly than differencing or unit fixed effects and at the same time are more flexible since they can also deal with time-varying unobserved confounders.

9.2 INCLUSION AND EXCLUSION OF CONTROL VARIABLES

Theories are typically focused on identifying a single or at most a few causal mechanisms and cannot be expected to provide a full account of the data-generating process. Theories typically aim at simplifying complex relationships instead of seeking to provide a full account of the determinants of a certain phenomenon – and if they do so, they fail. In other words, theories are not intended to guide the selection of explanatory variables. As a consequence, empirical models continue to be chosen in a haphazard way. As Leamer (1983: 34) has observed, the "standard set" of control variables tends to be arbitrary since it is "often based on whatever list the first researcher happened to select." Other variable selection algorithms may even be worse: what gave regression analysis of observational data a bad name is the possibility of selecting variables based on the desired result. Researchers typically provide only limited justification of why they include and why they exclude a variable that other scholars have included. Many right-hand side variables seem to have been selected based on common sense, tradition, or – perhaps – desired results. If common sense were a good scientific adviser, social scientists would be paid considerably less. Tradition – or path-dependence – seems to be a reasonable strategy, but it perpetuates model misspecification and severely reduces competition between models, which likely hampers scientific progress.

The fear of omitted variable bias induces some to include a long list of *potential* determinants as control variables – sometimes called the "kitchen sink" or "garbage can" approach. Some of these variables will be irrelevant and cause inefficiency. Others capture the same or a very similar causal factor, which creates bias and reduces the efficiency of the estimate. For example, political scientists know that the choice of different political institutions is correlated. Therefore, researchers need to be careful not to include institutional variables that are not independent of each other. One of the more blatant examples would be including both the electoral system and the number of parties in government or political fragmentation in the estimation model. Even if the explanatory variables are sufficiently independent of each other, they can still be highly correlated with each other in small to medium-sized samples containing limited information, which will decrease the efficiency of estimations and may result in biased estimates.

Political methodologist Christopher Achen's (in)famous rule of three, which in a nutshell denounces regression analyses with more than three regressors as "meaningless" (Achen 2002: 446), at least when no formal model structures the investigation, stems from these concerns. Achen seems to argue that researchers should construct empirical models that closely resemble the theoretical model – and ignore the data-generating process. However, this in turn downplays the need to control for all potential confounders in regression analysis of observational studies. Including "too many" control variables and including "too few" variables can equally threaten causal inferences (Clarke 2005). Naturally, the same goes for wrongly included explanatory variables.

Control variables bridge the gap between the theoretical model and the true data-generating process. Control variables, in other words, ought to move empirical models closer to the data-generating process and away from the stylized causal effects of theories. Models will nevertheless never match the complexity of the true data-generating process.[1] With limited information to analyze, researchers should not try to exactly model the true data-generating process. Instead, a good empirical model balances omitted variable bias and inefficiency. If researchers are interested in the effect of one or a few variables of interest, controls only need to be included if they are correlated with the variables of interest. The omission of a variable that is not correlated with the variable of interest does not bias the estimate of the effect of the variable of interest – regardless of how strongly it influences the dependent variable. This logic makes clear why two empirical models that explain the same phenomenon should be specified somewhat differently when the variable of interest differs. It also clarifies why researchers have to be reluctant to interpret the effect of control variables: a model that isolates the variable of interest from the influence of confounders does not need to isolate controls from the influence of confounders. However, in non-linear models some bias is inevitable even when omitted determinants of the outcome are uncorrelated with any of the right-hand side variables (Wooldridge 2010: 584f.).

Rather than trying to build all complications into a single model, we suggest that researchers conduct robustness tests to check whether estimates from a relatively simple baseline model are robust to systematically added complications. Following our suggestion, the baseline model would only contain those control variables known or suspected to exert the strongest effect on the dependent variable.

Explanatory variables tests are almost as old as regression analysis: adding or removing explanatory variables checks whether estimates are robust toward changing the covariance structure of the model. Adding or removing variables changes both the efficiency of an estimate and the part of the variance of an explanatory variable that is not correlated with the variance of another explanatory variable included in the model.

As always, any model known to be misspecified cannot function as a robustness test. A consequence of this rule is that researchers must take care not to additionally include variables through which other

1 As Hsiao (2003: 8) explains: "In explaining individual behavior, one may extend the list of factors ad infinitum. It is neither feasible nor desirable to include all factors affecting the outcome of all individuals in a model specification, since the purpose of modelling is not to mimic the reality but to capture the essential forces affecting the outcome. It is typical to leave out those factors that are believed to have insignificant impacts or are peculiar to certain individuals."

explanatory variables exert their impact on the dependent variable (King, Keohane, and Verba 1994: 173). This is not a straightforward rule given that in the social sciences many phenomena co-determine each other or – to exaggerate – everything has an impact on everything else. For example, the level of economic development will partly determine the political regime type, and vice versa, but both economic development and political regime type can be valid determinants of famine mortality (Plümper and Neumayer 2009).

Testing robustness toward dropping some of the regressors contained in the baseline model can provide another robustness test but requires even more thought than adding further control variables. Given that in the social sciences many variables are not entirely independent of each other, the effect of one variable has to be interpreted as conditional on the set of other right-hand side variables included in the model. For example, a civil war increases mortality rates directly and indirectly through increasing food scarcity. Dropping a variable measuring food scarcity from the baseline model can be justified as a robustness test, but researchers must keep in mind that the effect of civil war tested in the baseline and robustness test model differs across the two models. In one model the effect is conditional on food scarcity, in the other model any direct effect of food scarcity is assumed to be absent. This raises the question whether food scarcity should ever have been included in the baseline model if researchers are interested in the total (direct and indirect) effect of civil war on mortality since the estimation will fail to account for civil war partly determining food scarcity, thereby partly affecting mortality through its effect on food scarcity. There is no easy answer to this type of question since social scientists are necessarily uncertain about the correct set of regressors to be included in an estimation model.

9.3 UNKNOWN AND UNOBSERVED OMITTED VARIABLES

The standard econometric argument for the existence of "unobserved heterogeneity" is that some factors influencing the outcome cannot be observed. Unobserved heterogeneity, by definition, is unobserved and can-not be directly captured by control variables. Known unobserved factors can be indirectly and approximately captured by proxy variables. Yet, if a factor cannot be observed, the quality of a proxy cannot be known. Even more challengingly, omitted variables need not be "known unobservables" but can be "unknown observables" and "unknown unobservables." These variables are omitted because scholars do not even know that they are part of the data-generating process.

Econometric theory has developed a simple "solution" to the problem of omitted variables in panel or cross-sectional time-series data: assume that all omitted variables are time-invariant and employ unit fixed-effects or first-differences estimation, which throw away the between-variation of all included variables to isolate their parameter estimate from the bias resulting from omitted time-invariant variables. This provides no alternative to robustness testing. The solution only works if all omitted unobserved variables are indeed time-invariant and not just assumed to be time-invariant. In other words: the apparent solution determines the description of the problem, rather than the problem determining the solution. An undesirable side-effect has been the relative neglect of omitted unobserved *time-varying* variables.

Proponents of fixed-effects or first-differences estimation could argue that the between-variation of omitted unobserved variables tends to be larger than the omitted over-time variation within units. Even if this were true, differencing or unit fixed effects would reduce overall bias only if the existence of omitted time-invariant variables dominated all other model misspecifications. The two techniques are likely to perform worse than a model that ignores the bias from omitted time-invariant variables if other model misspecifications dominate (Plümper and Troeger 2016), most importantly dynamic misspecification. This is not ignorable since dynamic model misspecifications are common (De Boef and Keele 2008). For example, consider a trended dependent variable, trended independent variables, and an omitted trended variable. Differencing and unit fixed-effects estimates will be spurious, because the within-variation of interest is trended and will be correlated with the omitted trended variable. As another example, measurement error may become exacerbated if the between-variation is dropped under the plausible assumption that the true values are highly correlated over time but measurement error is randomly distributed over time in each unit. If so, moving from "levels" to "changes in levels" intensifies measurement error by lowering the signal-to-noise ratio (Bound et al. 2001: 3714).

Given that these techniques mitigate one potential model misspecification at the expense of exacerbating the impact of other potential model misspecifications, the widespread use of fixed-effects models appears problematic and unwarranted. Between-variation is information. Differencing and fixed-effects estimation eliminate valuable information. In fact, both techniques eliminate more information – all the between-variation – than they would do in an optimal world, in which they would merely eliminate the variance of the regressors correlated with the omitted time-invariant variables. This leads to a loss of efficiency, which can be substantial if the within-variation is low and the between-variation high. In addition, both techniques implicitly change the hypotheses tested in subtle ways. For example, the hypothesis that individuals with higher income have a higher propensity to buy certain goods differs from the hypothesis that an increase in income results in a higher propensity to buy certain goods. A theory that makes predictions about the effect of x on the between-variation in y cannot be tested.

Let us not be misunderstood: we are not arguing that differencing or unit fixed effects should be avoided under all circumstances. There will be conditions where they are warranted to make meaningful inferences about short-term adjustments to changes, and we have used them in our own research. For example, Plümper and Neumayer (2013) – aided by substantial within-variation in all variables – take out all level effects to identify the effect of co-payment schemes on changes in mortality rates. Likewise, Gibbons, Neumayer, and Perkins (2015) include year fixed effects and fixed effects for all combinations of subjects, universities, and entry tariffs, without which it would be impossible to identify an effect of student satisfaction on subject-specific student applications to universities. Rather than condemning these techniques per se, we are criticizing the "fixed effects by default" attitude that persists in many research areas of the social sciences – in some more so than in others.

9.4 ROBUSTNESS TESTS FOR POTENTIALLY OMITTED VARIABLES

Depending on the specification of the baseline model, robustness tests for unobserved variables assess whether the baseline model estimates are robust toward either eliminating a part of the variation that might be correlated with the unobserved variables or toward accounting for unobserved variables in a plausible alternative way. We start our discussion with two robustness tests that remain squarely within traditional thinking and that assume, entirely unrealistically, that unobserved variables are strictly time-invariant.

The first test is of the robustness limit type: the *between-variation test* increases the between-variation that is dropped from all variables (including the dependent variable). Researchers start with a pooled-ordinary least squares (OLS) model (or its equivalent), and then eliminate the between-variation in 10-percent steps, where the transformation of a variable x is $x_{it} - \sqrt{\lambda_s}\bar{x}_i$ (and similar for all other variables including the dependent variable), where λ_s $(0.0 \leq \sqrt{\lambda_s} \leq 1.0)$ denotes the degree to which between-variation is eliminated. Thus, in order to eliminate the between-variation in 10-percent steps, we need to successively increase λ_s from 0 to 1, which means increasing $\sqrt{\lambda_s}$ from 0 to 0.316, 0.447, 0.548, 0.632, 0.707, 0.755, 0.837, 0.894, 0.949 and, finally, 1, at which point we have reached the unit fixed-effects specification.

Table 9.1: Between-variation Test			
Degree of de-meaning ($\sqrt{\lambda_s}$)	**Coefficient (s.e.)**	**ρ short term**	**ρ long term**
0.0 (0.000)	0.00960***	baseline	baseline
	(0.00219)		
0.1 (0.316)	0.0108***	0.89	0.87
	(0.00242)		
0.2 (0.447)	0.0112***	0.84	0.80
	(0.00259)		
0.3 (0.548)	0.0113***	0.81	0.76
	(0.00275)		
0.4 (0.632)	0.0110***	0.81	0.74
	(0.00293)		
0.5 (0.707)	0.0103***	0.82	0.74
	(0.00313)		
0.6 (0.775)	0.00904**	0.79	0.74
	(0.00339)		
0.7 (0.837)	0.00694*	0.64	0.68
	(0.00372)		
0.8 (0.894)	0.00406	0.37	0.48
	(0.00406)		
0.9 (0.949)	0.00115	0.17	0.26
	(0.00438)		
1.0 (1.000)	−0.000138	0.11	0.19
	(0.00455)		

Note: Coefficients show the effect of pre-tax income inequality on the Gini coefficient in longevity. All other independent variables of baseline model included but effects not reported.

Statistically significant at *0.1, ** at 0.05, *** at 0.01 level.

In Neumayer and Plümper (2016b) we analyze the effect of pre-tax income inequality as well as income redistribution (the absolute difference between pre-tax and post-tax income inequality) on inequality in longevity, that is, the inequality in the number of years individuals in a country live. We analyze a pooled cross-sectional time-series sample of up to 28 countries over the period 1974 to 2011. The OLS baseline model does not include unit fixed effects. We have two main variables of interest, but, for the purpose of illustrating this robustness test, let us focus on pre-tax income inequality, for which table 9.1 shows estimated coefficients (the robustness analysis is almost identical for the other variable of main interest). Since the baseline model includes the lagged dependent variable, we analyze the degrees of robustness ρ for both short-term and long-term effects. The top of the table starts with the pooled-OLS baseline model (zero degree

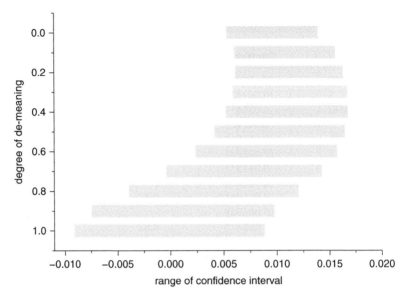

Figure 9.1: Visualization of the Between-variation Test

of de-meaning), increasingly eliminating the between-variation in the data by successively de-meaning all variables in 10-percent steps, arriving eventually at the unit fixed-effects model as variables are completely de-meaned. The estimated effect remains stable until at least 70 percent of between-variation is dropped. Beyond this point, the estimated effect declines and even switches signs with full de-meaning in the unit fixed-effects model. The degrees of robustness decline to 0.11 in the short term and 0.19 in the long term in this model.

In figure 9.1, we display the same information as in table 9.1 to demonstrate the stability of the estimated coefficients. It demonstrates with greater clarity that the estimates remain very stable unless we remove at least two-thirds of the between-variation.

A second test does not drop the between-variation from the estimation, but includes group fixed effects based on a grouping of units. This *group-wise fixed-effects test* eliminates the between-group variation but leaves the between-variation within groups intact. Ideally, the grouping of units is theoretically informed.[2] Where this is not possible, group membership can be simply based on locational or relational information. In comparative cross-country research, for example, a simple proxy for group heterogeneity

2 See for example Cederman, Buhaug, and Rød (2009: 519).

	m1: baseline	m2: group fixed effects	ρ
Table 9.2: Groupwise Fixed-effects Test (replacement type)			
Longevity inequality (t–1)	0.867***	0.853***	0.872
	(0.0305)	(0.0367)	
Life expectancy	−0.000306***	−0.000358**	0.765
	(0.000103)	(0.000162)	
GDP per capita (ln)	0.000234	−0.000253	0.790
	(0.000392)	(0.000349)	
Health expenditure relative to GDP (ln)	0.00124**	0.000548	0.673
	(0.000468)	(0.000503)	
Alcohol consumption per capita (ln)	6.64e−05	0.000113	0.859
	(0.000120)	(0.000153)	
Lung cancer mortality rate	0.000916	0.000983	0.895
	(0.000664)	(0.000802)	
External cause mortality rate	0.00273***	0.00282***	0.923
	(0.000556)	(0.000611)	
Pre-tax income inequality	0.00960***	0.00603***	0.637
	(0.00219)	(0.00207)	
Income redistribution	−0.00940***	−0.00645**	0.782
	(0.00249)	(0.00248)	
Observations	476	476	
Number of countries	28	28	

Note: Dependent variable is the Gini coefficient of longevity. OLS estimation. Year-specific fixed effects included. Standard errors adjusted for clustering on countries in parentheses.
  Statistically significant at * 0.1, ** at 0.05, *** at 0.01 level.

can be based on the World Bank's definition of macro-regions or on Huntington's (1996) definition of civilizations.

For our illustrative example, we rely on Böhm et al.'s (2013) classification, which groups countries into types of healthcare systems according to the private, societal or state organization of the regulation, financing, and provision of health care, giving us seven group dummies in total. Model m1 in table 9.2 presents results for the baseline model and the robustness test model m2 with these group fixed effects included. We only show estimated degrees of robustness for short-term effects. The estimated coefficients of our two main explanatory variables decrease by about 30 percent in size when the group fixed effects are included. Nevertheless, the estimated degrees of robustness are high.

As an alternative, a robustness limit variant of this test stepwise increases the number of exclusive groups and thus the number of group fixed effects. The more exclusive groups are formed, the more the model resembles the unit fixed-effects model, with the latter being reached as the number of exclusive groups reaches $N-1$. If, as will often be the case, the categorization of units into groups is uncertain, researchers can base group membership on a cluster analysis of the *between*-variation in the substantive regressors, thereby ensuring that all units exclusively cluster in one group. Researchers can either vary the specification of the number of groups into which units are clustered or they can vary the specification of the similarity value used in the cluster analysis.

In our illustrative example, we employ a Ward's linkage cluster analysis (1963) to sort countries into increasingly larger number of groups. We decrease the dissimilarity measure starting from 51 in steps of 2 until we reach the unit fixed-effects model at dissimilarity measure 1. Table 9.3 shows results whenever an increase in the number of groups is the consequence of the decrease in dissimilarity measure applied to the cluster analysis. Results are very robust up to and including a dissimilarity value of 5, which sorts the 28 countries into 21 groups. Lower dissimilarity values and consequently more groups result in low degrees of robustness.

As we have argued above, the assumption that all omitted variables are time-invariant is usually not supported in real data. Researchers should therefore explore the robustness of their baseline model to changing assumptions about omitted unobserved variables that can vary over time. We suggest a robustness limit type test which investigates to what extent the omitted variable needs to be correlated with the variable of interest and the dependent variable to render the estimated effect for the variable of interest non-robust. A similar robustness test has been proposed by Frank (2000), who suggests generating a random placeholder for an omitted confounder and stepwise increasing the correlation between the placeholder and the dependent variable.

With panel data, the *correlated artificial variable test* can be specified in three ways. The first variant just uses the time-invariant components of x and y and creates a placebo variable z which has a specified covariance structure with the between-variation of x and y, $\bar{x}_i$ and $\bar{y}_i$. The second variant uses only the overall correlation with the within-variation of x and y, $x_{it} - \bar{x}_i$ and $y_{it} - \bar{y}_i$ (this is a test about omitted common trends), and the third variant uses the correlation with both observed variables x and y. Of course, in cross-sectional data only the first variant and in time-series data only the second variant is possible.

A further robustness test that works for both time-invariant and time-varying unobserved variables can be based on what is known as a spatial-

Table 9.3: Groupwise Fixed-effects Test (robustness limit type)			
Maximum degree of dissimilarity (no. of groups)	**Coefficient (s.e.)**	**ρ short term**	**ρ long term**
51 (4)	0.00960***	0.96	0.96
	(0.00219)		
41 (5)	0.00914***	0.94	0.95
	(0.00220)		
39 (6)	0.00920***	0.95	0.95
	(0.00216)		
35 (7)	0.00916***	0.95	0.95
	(0.00216)		
25 (8)	0.00812***	0.92	0.94
	(0.00196)		
21 (11)	0.00870***	0.93	0.94
	(0.00221)		
15 (13)	0.0103***	0.80	0.83
	(0.00326)		
13 (15)	0.00998***	0.77	0.81
	(0.00352)		
9 (18)	0.0105**	0.67	0.70
	(0.00428)		
7 (19)	0.00776*	0.68	0.70
	(0.00386)		
5 (21)	0.00709*	0.62	0.66
	(0.00411)		
3 (24)	0.00216	0.19	0.29
	(0.00363)		
1 (28)	−0.000138	0.11	0.19
	(0.00470)		

Note: Coefficients show the effect of pre-tax income inequality on the Gini coefficient in longevity. All other independent variables of baseline model included but effects not reported.

Statistically significant at * 0.1, ** at 0.05, *** at 0.01 level.

error model. The *spatial-error test* exploits (and depends on) the fact that in many research designs omitted variables will be spatially correlated. To estimate a spatial-error model, analysts first predict the residuals by estimating the baseline model without spatial-error component. They can then create a spatial-error component by weighting the residuals of other units with a measure of "closeness" between the unit under observation and these other units as weights (see chapter 14 for more details). This could be a measure of geographical contiguity or inverse distance, but it could also be some other measure of connectivity or relatedness. If the assumption that

Table 9.4: Spatial-error Test

	m1: baseline	m3: spatial-error variable included	ρ
Longevity inequality (t–1)	0.867***	0.869***	0.946
	(0.0305)	(0.0310)	
Life expectancy	−0.000306***	−0.000296***	0.947
	(0.000103)	(0.000104)	
GDP per capita (ln)	0.000234	0.000201	0.949
	(0.000392)	(0.000392)	
Health expenditure	0.00124**	0.00125**	0.952
relative to GDP (ln)	(0.000468)	(0.000464)	
Alcohol consumption per	6.64e−05	6.53e−05	0.952
capita (ln)	(0.000120)	(0.000119)	
Lung cancer mortality rate	0.000916	0.000922	0.953
	(0.000664)	(0.000657)	
External cause mortality	0.00273***	0.00270***	0.947
rate	(0.000556)	(0.000562)	
Pre-tax income inequality	0.00960***	0.00956***	0.955
	(0.00219)	(0.00214)	
Income redistribution	−0.00940***	−0.00920***	0.950
	(0.00249)	(0.00248)	
Spatial-error variable		0.214**	
		(0.104)	
Observations	476	476	
Number of countries	28	28	

Note: Dependent variable is the Gini coefficient of longevity. OLS estimation. Year-specific fixed effects included. Standard errors adjusted for clustering on countries in parentheses.
Statistically significant at * 0.1, ** at 0.05, *** at 0.01 level.

omitted variables spatially correlate holds, the spatial-error control variable included in the robustness test model reduces the influence of omitted variables.

Model m3 includes a spatial-error variable based on geographical contiguity as the connectivity variable for the spatial-weights matrix (see table 9.4). The coefficient of the spatial-error variable is positive, as one would expect if residuals are spatially clustered among contiguous countries. The other estimates are very robust, which suggests that the omission of a spatial-error variable, in this case at least, is essentially inconsequential.

In other research projects, the test could affect the estimated degrees of robustness more strongly.

9.5 CONCLUSION

The continuing development of apparent econometric solutions to the problem of variable choice demonstrates that a silver bullet method for selecting all the right and none of the wrong explanatory variables does not exist. Empirical research will therefore continue to omit the right and include the wrong variables. Like any other method, robustness tests will not lead to the correct set of regressors. But that is neither their purpose nor our intention. The main idea of robustness tests is to analyze whether unknown and known but unobservable factors exist which could render estimates non-robust and potentially invalidate inferences.

Due to their strong emphasis on unknown potential confounders, structured permutation and robustness limit type tests are best suited for analyzing the effects of uncertainty about the set of explanatory variables. In other words, many of the robustness tests discussed here stand in the tradition of Leamer's sensitivity testing and Rosenbaum's bounds test. Yet, researchers need to avoid drawing inferences from models which are known to be misspecified. This not only requires care in the selection of substantive variables; it also means that techniques that eliminate a specific kind of variation from the data, like the unit fixed-effects model, should not be employed as the default option. Such models can make sense either as baseline or robustness test models in some limited number of research projects but represent models known to be misspecified in many others.

10 Functional Forms Beyond Default

10.1 INTRODUCTION

In a parametric regression model, the effect of an explanatory variable on the dependent variable follows a functional form. The functional form is jointly determined by the scale of the independent variable, the scale of the dependent variable, the estimator used, and potential transformations the researcher imposes on either independent or dependent variables. In the vast majority of empirical analyses, researchers do not transform the variables they include into their model – they estimate functional forms by default.

Linear estimators impose a linear functional form (given the scales) on the relation between independent and dependent variable. Nonlinear estimators allow a nonlinear functional form and, to some extent, let the data influence the functional form but only within the narrow bands allowed by the estimator's algorithm and parametrization.

Assuming simple functional form relationships of variables "as measured" can be justified on the basis of parsimony. The true data-generating process may well contain complex functional forms, not least because the measurements of variables do not capture the true scale of the latent theoretical concept, but simple functional form assumptions can represent a good modelling choice given that theories rarely predict the functional form of the variable of interest, let alone of control variables. Yet, if the implicitly or explicitly assumed functional form assumption does not closely resemble the true functional form, estimates are biased and inferences potentially wrong.

Researchers receive little help in developing assumptions about or justifying functional forms. Theories rarely make functional form predictions.[1]

---

1 Examples include the theory of the Kuznets curve (Kuznets 1955), which suggests that income inequality rises before it falls with higher per capita income of a country; the theory of the environmental Kuznets curve (Grossman and Krueger 1995), which proposes that a country's pollution rises before it falls as per capita

Most theories will not allow the derivation of predictions other than that x will have a positive or negative effect on y.

In the absence of sufficient theoretical guidance scholars might put their hope in flexible and versatile modelling options, along the lines of "letting the data speak for themselves." This approach too will not necessarily find the true functional form. Most importantly, seemingly complex functional forms can be the consequence of other model misspecifications, for example unaccounted for or wrongly specified causal heterogeneity, omitted variables or unobserved conditionality. The omission of a variable correlated with or even conditioning the variable of interest can appear as complexity in the functional form of the variable. In addition, flexible modelling approaches such as high-degree polynomial or semi-parametric regression run the risk of over-fitting the particular data at hand, capturing random variation in the sample rather than in the data-generating process and, in effect, mining the sample data for a more complex functional form. This is not unproblematic since estimated functional forms can depend on the inclusion or exclusion of few cases with high leverage. Researchers should be cautious and not simply infer a specific complex functional form based on a model that allows for largely unconstrained functional forms.

The next section discusses potential problems with the standard practice, which typically assumes linearity either in the variable's original scale "as measured" or as arbitrarily transformed. We argue in this chapter that the standard practice of making simple functional form assumptions in the baseline model is justifiable if combined with robustness tests that relax these assumptions. We then suggest robustness tests that can be used for both continuous and ordinal variables. Robustness tests explore the stability of baseline estimations to either alternative rigid functional form assumptions or, preferred by us, to more flexible functional form assumptions that contain the baseline model's assumption as a special case, including of course if the baseline model already allows for non-linearity. Addressing the functional form of only the variable of interest is insufficient. Estimates of the parameter of interest are likely to be biased if the functional form assumptions of control variables are wrong. As a consequence, exploring the robustness of the functional form assumption of the variable of interest does not suffice. Robustness tests should also account for the effect of changes in the assumptions about functional forms of control variables.

---

income grows; and the Calmfors-Driffill (1988) model, which predicts an inverse U-shaped relation between centralization of wage bargaining and wage inflation. Other theories do not predict turning points, but diminishing effects of x on y. The Solow growth model (Solow 1956), for example, predicts diminishing returns to investment as countries move closer to the technological frontier.

Partial robustness provides the relevant concept for functional form uncertainty since the baseline model's estimates can be strongly robust in some parts of the variable's distribution and weakly robust or even non-robust in other parts of the distribution. Functional form uncertainty buttresses the argument we made in chapter 3 that robustness needs to be defined in relation to the baseline model's estimated effects, not in terms of inferences, which can be arbitrarily weakly formulated. If researchers are only interested in the direction of an effect and solely make inferences about the direction, the inferences are not invalidated by the demonstration that the predictions of the empirical model depend on the assumed functional form and are therefore not robust. For example, the inference of a positive or negative effect is consistent with any functional form that is monotonically increasing or decreasing, be it a linear, an exponential, a diminishing, a logistic functional form, and so on. A stronger inference is that x affects y according to a *general* functional form. An even stronger inference is that x affects y according to the *specific* functional form of the baseline model. This inference is directly tested by robustness tests. If there is partial robustness, this inference is supported over some parts of the range of a variable but not others.

10.2 STANDARD PRACTICE: BETWEEN "AS MEASURED" AND ARBITRARILY TRANSFORMED

Few social science variables are genuine measures that come with a measurement unit and a predefined scale. When variables are quantifications rather than measures or counts, the scaling of a variable typically becomes rather meaningless. In survey analyses, the difference between category 2 and category 3 is not likely to be equal to the difference between category 4 and category 5, and variables coded on these scales should not enter the estimations in such arbitrary original scales "as measured," requiring the transformation into dummy variables for different categories instead. Likewise, linearity is not meaningful for variables measured on ordinal scales. For example, the *polity2* variable from the Polity project measures democracy on a 21-point additive scale of aspects of executive constraints and competitiveness of the political system, themselves measured on ordinal scales with few categories. This variable tends to enter estimations in a quasi-continuously fashion. The implicit linearity assumptions are that a one-point increase of the variable represents a small move toward a more democratic regime, that a five-point increase on the variable represents an exactly five times larger move toward a more democratic regime, and that it does not matter from which initial level the increase occurs. Implicitly, the operationalization assumes that changes from, say, −10 to −5 represent an equally strong move to a more democratic regime as a move from 5 to 10. None of these implications seem plausible. In fact, most countries cluster toward either end of the range with little variation among them that can be meaningfully inferred from small differences in the *polity2* value toward either extreme end of the range. Clearly, scholars should not include 20 dummy variables for each category of the ordinal scale, so some aggregation needs to take place if they depart from treating the variable quasi-continuously.

Occasionally, scholars depart from the linearity in a variable's original scale assumption and rescale variables in a more or less ad hoc fashion. A different functional form assumption can be imposed by transforming the dependent variable y, or the explanatory variable x, or both. Options include the natural log of a variable or the exponential or the square root or some other transformation such as a Box-Cox transformation. Transformations of a variable replace one rigid functional form with a different rigid functional form. For example, most economic research uses the natural log of variables, sometimes justified on the basis that researchers believe variables ought to be normally distributed. If the dependent variable remains untransformed, the log transformation of, for example, per capita income implies that scholars assume that the effect of an increase in per capita income from USD2,000 to USD3,000 has a larger effect on the dependent variable than an increase in per capita income from USD4,000 to USD5,000. In fact, the logarithmic transformation implies that the former effect is exactly 1.817 times as strong as the latter effect.

Even if researchers transform variables and manipulate the functional form, they cannot guarantee that the resulting functional form resembles the true functional form. For example, researchers often specify the effects of geographical distance on trade volume or on the probability of war to be a linear relation in the logarithm of distance – thereby implying that the marginal effect of distance on outcomes declines as distance increases in a predefined, determined fashion. However, while the assumption of a non-linear relation between distance and trade seems plausible, the much stronger assumption that the functional form of this relation resembles an exact logarithmic function is not likely. In other words: using the log of distance instead of distance replaces one strong and arbitrary assumption by another. Ad hoc transformations of the dependent variable are especially unappealing. A particular alternative rigid functional form will be imposed on the effect of all explanatory variables on the dependent variable. By contrast, transformations of the regressors allow different transformations and ultimately different functional forms for different variables.

Transformations of variables are sometimes theoretically informed. In a study of the effect of the strengths of earthquakes on economic damage (Neumayer, Plümper, and Barthel 2014) we transformed our measure of earthquake strength, the Richter scale. The Richter scale can be transformed in two meaningful ways. For the amplitude of earthquake waves, seismologists use a logarithmic scale with a base of 10: an earthquake of magnitude 6 on the Richter scale has a ten times higher amplitude than an earthquake of magnitude 5. With respect to the released energy, seismologists use a logarithmic scale with a base of 32: a quake of magnitude 6 on the Richter scale unleashes 32 times as much energy as a quake of magnitude 5. Arguably, the amount of energy set free better approximates the destructive force of the hazard event than does the amplitude of earthquake waves. We therefore raised the Richter scale to the power of 32 to estimate earthquake damage as a linear function of the energy unleashed by an earthquake, not as a function of its Richter scale value or as a function of the amplitude of earthquake waves.

There can be theoretical reasons for transforming both the dependent and explanatory variables. For example, Cobb-Douglas production functions and gravity equations in economics are nonlinear equations based on economic theory that can be "linearized" by taking the log of both sides of the equation. Log-log models are popular since they allow an interpretation of estimated parameters as elasticities.[2] Yet, examples of theoretically justified transformations are rare. It remains unsatisfactory to let the implicit functional form be determined by the fact that log-log models allow a convenient interpretation of effects as elasticities.

In sum: in the social sciences, the functional form is typically determined by the variables' original scales "as measured" or ad hoc transformed, and by the estimator's influence on functional form – the link function. Ad hoc variable transformations give researchers a small edge to move parameter estimates over the hurdle of statistical significance, but the "as measured" assumption remains arbitrary, too.

The functional form of the relation between two variables can typically not be known *a priori*. This is exactly the terrain in which robustness tests are most useful. Robustness tests can subject the potentially problematic linear or other functional form assumption to other plausible assumptions.

10.3 POLYNOMIAL ROBUSTNESS TEST MODELS FOR CONTINUOUS VARIABLES

There are two main approaches for testing the robustness of a baseline model's functional form assumption, be it linear or not. On the one hand,

---

2 Lau (1986) and Kennedy (2008: 106–108) provide an overview of production and consumption functions in economic theory that give rise to specific transformations of the dependent variable and/or the explanatory variables.

researchers may replace the specific rigid baseline model assumption with a different rigid assumption in the robustness test model. For example, analysts can replace the variable as measured with its natural log transformation. On the other hand, researchers may relax the baseline model's functional form assumption, allowing greater flexibility and complexity. This approach nests the baseline model in the robustness test model, thus allowing the robustness test to recover the baseline model's functional form as a special case.

We prefer the second approach. Testing the robustness of a parsimonious baseline model functional form assumption can be done by undertaking a *higher-degree polynomial test*.[3] Polynomial models are only suitable for continuous variables measured on an interval or ratio scale. Polynomials of a degree higher than the first polynomial allow for nonlinear effects of x on y by estimating more than one parameter for a variable: they allow the functional form to have inflection and turning points. Usually, scholars use the squared (second-degree polynomial), the cubic (third-degree polynomial) and occasionally higher-degree polynomials of a variable in addition to the "linear term" (first-degree polynomial) to allow for non-linearity. The number of parameters estimated for a single variable determines the maximum number of turning points: with k parameters for one variable, $k-1$ turning and inflection points are possible. It is important to note that the maximum degree of polynomials included merely determines the maximum number of *possible* inflection and turning points estimated. It does not determine the actual number of relevant points since estimated parameters can be close to 0. Thus, a higher-degree polynomial regression model includes the functional form that a lower-degree polynomial regression model can produce as a possibility or special case.[4]

There is no reason why scholars should be restricted to estimating full sets of polynomial models that include all polynomial terms up to the highest degree. For example, the polynomial regression model

$$y = a + b_1 x + b_2 x^2 + b_3 x^9 \qquad (10.1)$$

---

3 See Schleiter and Morgan-Jones (2009: 508) for an example.
4 Instead of including further polynomials of degree higher than 1, it is possible to include further polynomials of degree lower than 1, also called fractional polynomials. Royston and Altman (1994) argue that polynomial models of degree lower than 1 (fractional polynomials) are less prone to fitting badly at the extremes of the observed range of x than are polynomial models of degree higher than 1 and are equally capable of estimating non-linear relationships.

allows the same number of inflection and turning points as

$$y = a + b_1 x + b_2 x^2 + b_3 x^3 \tag{10.2}$$

but more skew of the functional form. It typically remains unclear which of these two similar models approximates the true functional form better and, more importantly, which offers the best robustness test model for the more parsimonious baseline model.

Given that there exist a large number of polynomial models that could in principle qualify for testing robustness, we suggest three rules to guide the selection of polynomials for structured permutation tests, which is the robustness test type most suitable for functional form uncertainty:

1. Polynomial models for robustness testing must be less constrained, thus allowing for a more flexible functional form than the baseline model.
2. Polynomial models for robustness testing should contain both even and odd polynomial terms.
3. The terms contained in the baseline model must always be included in the robustness test model.

As an illustrative example, we use an analysis of the effect of per capita income on carbon dioxide (CO_2) per capita emissions. The theory of the "environmental Kuznets curve" postulates an inverse-U shaped functional form between per capita emissions and per capita income (Grossman and Krueger 1995). It predicts that emissions increase proportionally with economic activities but that demand for environmental quality increases as societies become richer. Governments, thus, increasingly internalize environmental damage, which results in fewer emissions per unit of economic activity. However, since CO_2 emissions damage the environment neither immediately nor locally, the validity of the environmental Kuznets curve for CO_2 emissions has been questioned. Baseline model m1 in table 10.1 regresses CO_2 per capita emissions on per capita income in thousands of 2005 constant dollars in a global sample over the period 1960 to 2012. We use this as an illustrative example only, making no claim that a model without control variables is correctly specified. Models m2 to m4 employ increasingly higher-order polynomial models as robustness tests, namely from the quadratic (2nd-order) baseline model to a 4th-order model.

Higher-order polynomial models make it difficult and at times impossible to identify the functional form from looking at the estimated parameters. We therefore plot the predicted effects of income on emissions over the relevant range of per capita income for the robustness test model versus the baseline model. The point estimates from the second-degree polynomial robustness test model shown in figure 10.1 seemingly

Table 10.1: Higher-degree Polynomials Tests				
	m1	m2	m3	m4
constant	0.990**	0.339	−0.320	−0.569
	(0.403)	(0.368)	(0.433)	(0.449)
x	0.343***	0.548***	0.842***	1.011***
	(0.0497)	(0.0626)	(0.119)	(0.165)
x^2		−0.00452**	−0.0188***	−0.0330**
		(0.00180)	(0.00573)	(0.0141)
x^3			0.000150***	0.000504
			(5.55e−05)	(0.000375)
x^4				−2.56e−06
				(2.78e−06)
RMSE	4.535	4.381	4.295	4.284
R^2	0.472	0.508	0.527	0.530

Note: Dependent variable is CO_2 per capita emissions. OLS estimation. x is per capita income in thousands of USD. Year fixed effects included. Standard errors clustered on countries in parentheses. $N = 7,135$. RMSE = root mean squared error.
Statistically significant * at 0.1, ** at 0.05, *** at 0.01 level.

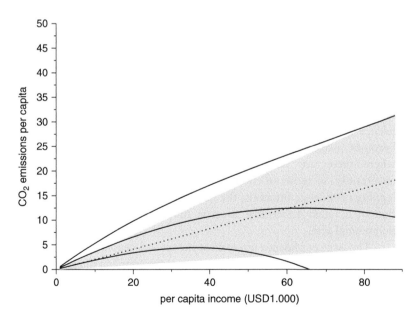

Figure 10.1: Higher-degree Polynomial Test 1
Note: Grey-shaded area represents confidence interval of baseline model.

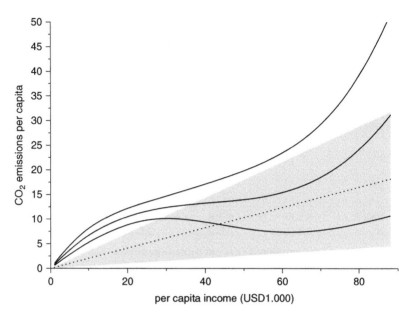

Figure 10.2: Higher-degree Polynomial Test 2
Note: Grey-shaded area represents confidence interval of baseline model.

suggest not only a decreasing positive effect of per capita income but even a turning point after which emissions start to decrease very slowly. Simple algebra allows computing the turning point after which emissions are predicted to decrease: $-0.548/(-0.00452 \cdot 2) = $ USD60,620, a level of per capita income that lies within the sample. However, the calculation ignores uncertainty around the point estimates and the confidence interval for the second-order polynomial robustness test model becomes increasingly large at very high levels of per capita income, where there are relatively few observations and much sampling uncertainty. In terms of robustness analysis, and given the largely overlapping confidence intervals, the baseline model's parsimonious assumption of a linear functional form is fully robust to the second-degree polynomial test.

The large confidence intervals of the second-degree polynomial model at high levels of per capita income suggest large sampling uncertainty about the correct functional form in that area. Not surprisingly, the point estimates for the third-degree polynomial model, shown in figure 10.2, suggest a different functional form, namely an inverted S-shape, in which emissions are growing again after a second turning point has been reached.

Taking into account the confidence intervals, the robustness test offers the new insight that the linearity assumption imposed by the baseline model is not robust at low levels of per capita income, where it seems to under-estimate emissions. The estimated degree of robustness ρ is close to 0 up to a per capita income of around USD20,000, where the majority of observations lie.

The same picture emerges from the fourth-degree polynomial robustness test and indeed higher-degree polynomials that are not shown, which, despite allowing even more flexible forms, do not add any new insight. In sum, the baseline model's assumption of a linear relationship between per capita income and per capita CO_2 emissions appears robust in per capita income ranges where the turning point predicted by the environmental Kuznets curve might set in but it is not robust at levels of per capita income below USD20,000, where it might under-estimate the emission increase related to income increases. Accordingly, the baseline model's linearity assumption is not robust across the entire range of per capita income but neither is the Kuznets curve prediction.

10.4 SEMI-PARAMETRIC ROBUSTNESS TEST MODELS FOR CONTINUOUS AND ORDINAL VARIABLES

Semi-parametric models offer a flexible alternative to any kind of higher-order polynomial model. They can be used for continuous data too but are ideally suited for ordinal data for which higher-order polynomials are no option. The term "semi-parametric regression model" is often used synonymously with "generalized additive model" (GAM), which combines the non-parametric modelling of the effect of variable x on y with the parametric modelling of the effect of other variables z on y (Beck and Jackman 1998; Keele 2008: 10).

We suggest a different type of semi-parametric regression model as a robustness test, which seems equally flexible and easier to handle. In this test, we create dummy variables for various categories over the range of variable x. The estimated parameters from these dummy variables included in an estimation model allow an entirely flexible form. Semi-parametric models can retrieve almost any functional form if the number of categories is sufficiently large. Even structural breaks in the functional form are possible. This flexibility comes with costs. Most importantly, flexibility runs the risk of over-fitting the data. Random variation in the data will exert an influence on the estimated functional form. In addition, the more categories scholars build, the more flexible the functional form estimated. On the other hand, more categories imply fewer observations per category. Particularly in smaller datasets, a trade-off occurs between the number of categories and the number of observations in each category.

The optimal number of categories chosen depends on three factors: the number of observations, the distribution of the variable, and the degree of functional form flexibility the researcher wishes to achieve. As always, flexibility conflicts with parsimony. The higher the degree of flexibility, the more categories are required and the lower the level of parsimony. Another question analysts ought to address is how to group observations into distinct categories. An answer to this question results in two variants of the *semi-parametric test*: for continuous variables one can group observations into either percentiles or categories (bins) of equal width. For ordinal variables, only the latter option is available.

We suggest splitting the variable at least into quintiles, but into smaller percentile categories if the data allow. Percentile categories have an advantage: they estimate each parameter with the same ex-ante efficiency – though de facto the variance may vary largely in each category. Their disadvantage is that, unless x is uniformly distributed, the categories have different widths. This disadvantage can make the use of percentile categories undesirable. For example, in our analysis of per capita CO_2 emissions, the last income decile already starts at approximately USD26,000, with a mean of USD39,000 – too low to make reliable inferences about the existence of a turning point in emissions, which, if it exists, will be somewhere around USD60,500. The estimated degrees of robustness ρ from the percentile category semi-parametric robustness test are around 0.05 for the first five percentiles, close to 0 for the sixth and seventh percentile and above 0.1 only for the last two percentiles. This supports the conclusion from the third- and higher-degree polynomial robustness tests that the linearity assumption of the baseline model is not robust at low levels of per capita income, where the vast majority of observations are, whereas it is robust at high income levels, where any conceivable turning point might lie.

The same test works with a different categorization. Rather than defining groups by an (about) equal number of included observations, researchers can use equally broad categories if the variable is measured on at least an interval scale. Equal width means grouping observations into categories or bins of equal size in terms of the unit of measurement of x, such as, for example, equally wide bands of income (USD1–10,000, USD10,001–20,000, USD20,001–30,000 and so on). Equal width categories seem intuitive, but suffer from the problem that the number of observations in each category varies, unless of course x is uniformly distributed. The differences become evident with a normally distributed variable: using the equal width approach, the middle categories will have many more observations than the extreme categories. In our example, the bottom two categories are heavily populated while the remaining eight categories have far fewer observations. The estimated degrees of robustness ρ from the equal bin width semi-parametric robustness test support the insight that the baseline model's linearity assumption turns out to be not robust below USD20,000 but robust beyond.

For interval variables that are not strictly continuous or not strictly continuously recorded (such as age), splitting the variable's range into percentiles does not make much sense. Observations cannot, unless by chance, be grouped into categories such that each category includes the same number of observations. Variables measured on ordinal scales offer "natural categories," namely the categories in which they are ordered. For example, the *polity2* measure of democracy from the Polity project distinguishes 21 categories. In principle, it is possible to estimate the functional form of democracy by including 20 dummy variables for each of the categories. Yet, many of these categories are scarcely populated. Therefore, researchers usually aggregate *polity2* into three categories of autocracies, anocracies, and democracies or two categories of autocracies and democracies.

As an alternative to semi-parametric robustness tests, one can add an interaction effect between the variable of interest x and a dummy variable that takes the value 1 if a unit of analysis satisfies a certain property. This *functional form break test* assumes there is a break in the functional form of a variable at a certain threshold. The test can be particularly useful for testing whether the model results in robust estimates in areas that have little leverage on the estimate because there are few observations. This could be at the extremes of x, say the 1st and the 10th decentile, but also in the middle of the distribution as in the ordinal *polity2* measure of democracy. Accordingly, scholars would estimate

$$y_i = \alpha + \beta^1 x_i + \beta^2 (x \cdot g_i) + \dots + \varepsilon_i \qquad (10.3)$$

where $g_i = 1$ if $i \in G$, 0 else. The model allows us to test for parameter homogeneity in different parts of the distribution if the group G is defined based on a range of x. In other words, it tests whether the estimated average effect between the range defined by G and the rest of the distribution of variable x is the same. As in all these tests, to allow reliable inferences the minimum number of cases per group should not become too small.

10.5 CONCLUSION

In an optimal world, researchers would derive testable predictions on functional forms from theory and specify the empirical model accordingly. The reality of social science research differs from this optimal world.

Researchers rely on parsimonious, default functional form assumptions in the scales of variables as originally coded or as more or less ad hoc transformed.

The opposite extreme of accepting parsimonious functional forms comes in the form of flexible non-parametric, semi-parametric or high-order polynomial models, which essentially mine the data and run the risk of over-fitting the random variation of a particular sample. Extremes are often not optimal, but it is unclear where the optimal compromise between over-simplifying default functional form assumptions and data-mining approaches lies.

Robustness tests of functional form assumptions offer a solution to this conflict. Researchers can continue to employ a mixture of theory, diagnostic testing, and common sense to specify the functional form of their baseline model. Most scholars know and understand that this strategy will not capture the true data-generating process. The onus is therefore on the researcher to explore whether the estimates are robust to plausible alternative rigid functional form assumptions or, as we prefer, to relaxing the functional form in robustness tests employing higher-order polynomial or semi-parametric regression models.

Our illustrative example demonstrated the value of the concept of partial robustness for functional form uncertainty. As we have seen, the baseline model's estimates can be strongly robust in some parts of the variable's distribution and weakly robust or even non-robust in other parts of the distribution. Ironically, we found that the linearity assumption of the baseline model was robust at high levels of per capita income, where the environmental Kuznets curve might suggest that it over-estimates per capita CO_2 emissions, but was not robust at low levels of per capita income, where the linearity assumption might under-estimate emissions.

11 Causal Heterogeneity and Context Conditionality

11.1 INTRODUCTION

Few effects are homogeneous across units and unconditioned by other factors. At the individual level, people are not identical and they respond differently to the same stimulus. Brand and Simon-Thomas (2013: 190) contend that "causal effects should vary across members of a society; it is implausible to assume that different members of a population respond identically to the same treatment condition." Heterogeneity can easily be observed in experiments which control for "all confounding factors": typically, neither the individuals included in the treatment group nor the individuals included in the control group behave identically. Rather, behavior within each group varies both within a single experiment and between experiments. If anything, these experiments demonstrate that human beings differ and that – apparently – not all confounders are accounted for.

These differences in response to treatment (or non-treatment) occur either because human beings are different in an unobservable way – causal heterogeneity – or because the context they operate in conditions their response – context conditionality. *Causal heterogeneity* implies that different types of human beings exist. Individuals may respond differently to identical stimuli despite holding everything else constant, including all individual and environmental factors. In contrast, individuals may respond differently to an identical stimulus because of intervening factors which are not identical, for example because they differ in age, gender, socialization, experience, intelligence, and individual levels of risk aversion, among other factors. At least some of these factors can be known and observed. Similarly, conditional relationships among explanatory variables likely exist at the macro-level. For example, most effects analyzed in comparative politics are conditioned by institutions. *Context conditionality* implies that units of analysis are homogeneous and vary only according to the context in which a causal stimulus occurs.

The distinction between causal heterogeneity and conditionality is subtle. It may well be that if social scientists had all relevant information, all behavior would be conditional and heterogeneity between actors fully accounted for. Alternatively, it may be that true free will does exist and therefore actors remain heterogeneous even after controlling for all context conditionalities. In this case, behavioral variation would occur even if social scientists knew everything that can be known about human behavior. Mankind may one day know; for the time being, however, the question remains philosophical. Social scientists do not have full knowledge of context conditions and their effects, and for this reason they have to deal with both causal heterogeneity and context conditionality at the same time.

Comprehending the heterogeneity of effects does not tell us anything about the potential conditioning factors and how to measure them. In other words, the factors that drive effect heterogeneity are often unknown or unobservable, or both, and no conditional effects model can capture the heterogeneity. For empirical research, it matters whether conditionalities are modelled or not. If they remain unmodelled we have causal heterogeneity; if they are modelled we are dealing with conditionalities. This simple distinction turns a philosophical question into a matter of research design and model specification.

In standard practice, researchers typically assume effect homogeneity by estimating unconditional mean effects for the treatment variable. Increasingly, though, researchers include one conditional relationship between two explanatory variables, not least because it allows them to claim an original contribution over previous research that presented results as unconditional.[1] The standard practice is not surprising: if the effects of treatment and other variables are heterogeneous and conditioned by a potential multitude of other factors, the true model is complex. Arguably, identifying the true conditioning relationships becomes difficult, if not impossible, given limited information. There is, in other words, a "ceaseless tension between the reality of effect heterogeneity and the practical assumption of effect homogeneity" (Brand and Simon-Thomas 2013: 195). The decision to assume causal homogeneity and *not* model effects as being conditioned by other factors can be justified as a parsimonious approach. Conditional relationships and causal heterogeneity are probably omnipresent, but the principle of parsimony suggests ignoring them whenever simplification matters more than accurate complexity.

---

1 Modelling conditional relationships seems more popular in linear than in non-linear models, perhaps due to the difficulty of interpretation in the latter (Ai and Norton 2003; Berry, DeMeritt, and Esarey 2010), while modelling conditionalities among control variables is practically non-existent.

Yet, simplification threatens the validity of inferences: an over-simplified model may jeopardize internal validity, and lack generalizability, jeopardizing external validity. Unaccounted causal heterogeneity usually implies that the estimated mean effect fails to represent all units in the sample. Social scientists need to care about causal heterogeneity. They ought to know whether the effects of policies or other treatments are uniformly positive or, alternatively, benefit some but harm others. Even if treatment effects are uniformly positive we still may need to know whether they benefit everyone equally. The failure to adequately capture the joint effect of two variables that condition each other can be understood as omitting one or more variables, which will result in omitted variable bias if the omitted term(s) are correlated with any explanatory variable – as they are bound to be, not least with the two variables constituting the joint effect. Simplification is thus a necessary evil that needs to be subjected to careful robustness testing.

The next section distinguishes two types of heterogeneity – causal heterogeneity and context conditionality – and discusses how simplified models that ignore heterogeneity can be useful but potentially misleading and therefore need to be subjected to robustness testing. We then propose suitable tests for, respectively, causal heterogeneity and context conditionality. So-called "unobserved heterogeneity" is just a fancy term for additive omitted variables; it does not vary the effect strength across units and is therefore not part of this chapter.

11.2 HETEROGENEITY AND THE LOGIC OF MODEL SIMPLIFICATION

A population, or a sample drawn from it, is homogeneous if the data-generating process is identical for all units. Any two units can be homogeneous for one research question but heterogeneous for another. Both "context conditionality" and "causal heterogeneity" result in variation in effect strengths. With the former, third factors influence the effect strength of the variable of interest. In other words, the context conditions how units react to an exogenous stimulus. With the latter, causal heterogeneity exists *sui generis*. No known conditioning variable determines the heterogeneity in effect strengths. This closely resembles what Judea Pearl (2015: 1) calls "the presence of idiosyncratic groups that react differently to treatment or policies."

The above definition allows for two sources of heterogeneity: model and nature. If nature generates heterogeneity, then for a given population researchers cannot eliminate heterogeneity. If the model produces heterogeneity through misspecification, researchers can increase the model's complexity up to the point where heterogeneity disappears. In addition, given our definition of homogeneity, population and sample size may influence heterogeneity: it is possible to eliminate heterogeneity within a sample by selecting a homogeneous sample (as in matching and small-N designs). However, heterogeneity is ultimately a property of the population. By eliminating heterogeneity in the sample, the sample is no longer representative of the population. As a consequence, sample size and model complexity are necessarily related. For any given population heterogeneity, a larger sample is likely to have more causal heterogeneity and context conditionality. Put differently, heterogeneity and sample size determine how complex a model specification has to be in order to capture the data-generating process.

Nevertheless, the quest for homogeneity may tempt researchers into adopting a narrow sampling strategy (Davidsson and Delmar 2012: 20) in order to avoid complex model specifications. If researchers select cases to minimize heterogeneity, they produce selection bias and their sample no longer represents the population. Narrow sampling also reduces efficiency if data-generating processes are not entirely different from each other but partly overlapping. In this case, it is possible to model the data-generating process in a way that allows for heterogeneity across groups in the sample, either in the baseline model or as a robustness test. Therefore, narrow sampling runs the risk of gaining internal validity (a homogeneous causal effect is estimated) at the expense of external validity (a loss of generalizability). Witness for example what Davidsson and Delmar (2012) offer as a success of narrow sampling: Baum and Locke's (2004) study of the effect of individual psychological traits on the growth of young firms, for which the authors narrowly sampled north American architectural woodwork firms – a narrow sample for which the assumption of causal homogeneity seems plausible. This raises the question then whether and to what extent their inferences are generalizable. For Davidsson and Delmar (2012: 22), "it is difficult to see why this type of variables would have completely different effects in other industries, countries or periods." But Davidsson and Delmar cannot have their cake and eat it: it is not consistent to justify narrow sampling because of causal heterogeneity of the population *and* at the same time generalize findings from a narrow sample to the population as if heterogeneity did not exist. In other words, if homogeneity is assumed, the rationale for narrow sampling is already defeated. More importantly, narrow sampling presupposes that the causes of heterogeneity and context conditionalities are understood. If that is not the case, narrow sampling reduces efficiency with certainty, but does not necessarily guarantee causal homogeneity.

Social scientists do not always struggle with unknown sources of heterogeneity. In many cases, conditioning factors are known. At least scholars can formulate theories about conditioning factors, which can be modelled. Uncertainty results from the existence of many more possible conditionalities than can be included in the baseline model. Though more and more empirical studies now acknowledge that effects are unlikely to be unconditional and model a conditional effect in their baseline model, they typically only do so for their central explanatory variable, which is conditioned by one factor. Yet, conditionality can be multifaceted and multidimensional: neither is conditionality limited to a single conditioning factor nor necessarily is it only the variable of central interest that is conditioned by other factors.

Researchers may be uncertain about the functional form of conditionalities. The vast majority of studies employing conditional effects (our own included) model the conditional relationship between x, the variable of interest, and some variable z with a multiplicative term $x \cdot z$, which implies a "bi-linear" (Jaccard and Turisi 2003: 21) fully symmetric interaction effect (we call it linear-symmetric for short). Symmetry cannot be taken for granted, though. For example, the most famous equation in the history of science, $E = mc^2$, demonstrates that interactive relationships do not need to be linear and they do not need to be symmetric in their functional form.

In sum, simplification and other strategies of dealing with causal heterogeneity and context conditionality cause model uncertainty, as researchers cannot know a priori whether their simplifications remain neutral in terms of estimation results and inferences. Accordingly, if researchers decide to rely on a model of homogeneous effects without conditionalities, it is possible that they over-simplify the model and that the true data-generating process contains heterogeneous types and/or includes conditional effects. By contrast, if they model conditionalities, researchers may model the wrong ones or model them wrongly.

11.3 ROBUSTNESS TESTS FOR CAUSAL HETEROGENEITY

Robustness tests for causal heterogeneity assess whether estimates based on a model that assumes homogeneity and thus estimates mean effects are robust toward relaxing the causal homogeneity assumption.[2] Alternatively, if the

2 Given the book's focus on regression analysis based on observational data, we ignore designs and techniques that specifically address causal heterogeneity issues in experiments and quasi-experiments. For this rapidly evolving literature see, for example, Brand and Simon-Thomas (2013), Heckman and Vytlacil (2005), Heckman, Urzua, and Vytlacil (2006), Morgan and Todd (2008), and Rosenbaum (2010).

baseline model already allows for some form of causal heterogeneity, robustness test models ought to specify causal heterogeneity differently. We start with robustness tests that deal with unspecified heterogeneity in the effect of all variables, then discuss tests for uncertainty about causal heterogeneity in the effect of specific variables.

Tests that allow conclusions about the existence of unknown or unobserved causal heterogeneity draw on a simple property: if a sample results from a random draw from a homogeneous population, neither randomly adding nor subtracting units from the sample will have a systematic effect on the estimates. Obviously, removing observations from the sample can be more easily done than adding new ones. A first robustness test is the well-known *bootstrap test*, which redraws samples of the same size as the original sample with replacement of drawn units. As a consequence, the bootstrapped sample will include doublets or "multilets" of observations included in the original sample, but will exclude other observations from the original sample (Efron 1979; Efron and Gong 1983). The bootstrap is often used to compute alternative standard errors. However, the difference between "normal" and "bootstrapped" standard errors can be interpreted as information about the degree of heterogeneity within the sample. The larger the difference between bootstrapped and normal standard errors, the larger the heterogeneity within the sample given the model.

A second randomized permutation test addressing the existence of unknown or unobserved causal heterogeneity is the *split sample test*. This test splits the sample randomly in two halves, duplicates each observation in each half-sample (to maintain identical degrees of freedom and therefore identical expected standard errors[3] as the original estimate), and estimates the same specification as the baseline model for these newly created samples. We suggest repeating the procedure 1,000 times. Sample split and duplication can be considered a special case of the bootstrap.

As an illustrative example, we use our analysis of foreign terror on Americans (Neumayer and Plümper 2011). More terrorism on American victims originates from nationals of countries whose governments are relatively more dependent on United States (US) troops being stationed in these countries, defined as the share of US to domestic military personnel. The dependent variable is the number of US citizens killed by terrorists of a certain nationality, which we estimate using a negative binomial

---

3 Standard errors are ex ante identical if the two halves have identical properties. If ex post the two halves of the sample have different properties, the standard errors will ex post not be identical. The variation in the standard errors and in the estimated coefficients can therefore provide insights into the heterogeneity of the sample.

estimator. Coefficients can be interpreted as semi-elasticities, which allows us to use estimated coefficients for the robustness analysis. The degree of robustness of the *dependence on US military* variable for this randomized permutation test averaged across the 1,000 models without model weighting was $\rho = 0.60$ (95 percent of simulations have ρ between 0.16 and 0.83). This result points to some mild causal heterogeneity, which we will explore further with other robustness tests below.

The two tests introduced above reveal whether unknown heterogeneity exists and whether the baseline model is robust to the possibility of causal heterogeneity. However, they do not say much about which units or groups of units drive the heterogeneity. This question can be tackled by a third test, the *groupwise jackknife test*, which tests whether the estimates from the baseline model are robust to excluding one set of observations grouped together at a time.

All three robustness tests discussed so far deal with uncertainty about the possibility that units are causally heterogeneous in entirely unknown or unobserved ways and for all explanatory variables. We now move to tests for uncertainty about causal heterogeneity for specific variables as well as causal heterogeneity that is known or suspected to take a particular form.

Whenever researchers estimate a single coefficient for all units, they implicitly assume homogeneity. The extreme opposite is a model which estimates $N-1$ parameters for the variable of interest:

$$y_{it} = \alpha + \beta_i x_{it} + \gamma z_{it} + \varepsilon_{it} \tag{11.1}$$

This *unit-specific effect test* demonstrates that allowing for causal heterogeneity in the effect of a variable merely relaxes one constraint imposed on the baseline estimation model. Yet, these unit-specific parameters can be estimated with substantial sampling uncertainty, particularly if the time dimension T is small. A *group-specific effect test*, in which coefficients are constrained to be identical for all units of a group, offers a compromise option between the homogeneous causal effect model and the unit-specific varying coefficients model.

Model m1 in table 11.1 shows results for the baseline model that assumes a homogeneous effect of the *dependence on US military* variable. Model m2 displays the results from a group-specific varying coefficients model, in which we allow the effect of our central explanatory variable to differ across income groups as defined by the World Bank.[4] The estimated effect is 20 times larger for the group of low-income countries than the

4 The results are qualitatively similar in terms of suggesting large effect heterogeneity if we additionally include income group dummy variables in the estimation model.

	m1: baseline	m2: group-specific effects	ρ
Table 11.1: Group-specific Effect Test			
Population (ln)	0.645***	0.689***	0.912
	(0.155)	(0.173)	
Distance from US (ln)	−0.0345	−0.0292	0.935
	(0.361)	(0.384)	
GDP per capita (ln)	0.112	0.210	0.919
	(0.167)	(0.161)	
Democracy	−0.0710**	−0.0644**	0.954
	(0.0314)	(0.0301)	
Dependence on US military in:	0.0285***		
	(0.00877)		
Low-income countries		4.389	0.001
		(2.707)	
Lower-middle-income countries		0.222***	0.000
		(0.0468)	
Upper-middle-income countries		0.0292***	0.967
		(0.00803)	
High-income non-OECD countries		0.199	0.044
		(0.249)	
High-income OECD countries		−0.00698	0.116
		(0.0154)	
Observations	3,483	3,483	

Note: Dependent variable is number of US citizens killed. Negative binomial estimations. Constant not reported. Standard errors clustered on countries in parentheses.
  Statistically significant * at 0.1, ** at 0.05, *** at 0.01 level.

baseline model's effect based on the causal homogeneity assumption. Yet, the standard errors are large, rendering the estimate statistically indistinguishable from 0 at conventional levels. The estimated degree of robustness compared to the baseline model homogeneous effect equals $\rho = 0$. In lower-middle-income countries, the effect size is almost eight times larger than the baseline model homogeneous effect with small standard error and, again not surprisingly, the estimated degree of robustness equals $\rho = 0$ for this effect too. In upper-middle-income countries, the effect size and standard error are practically the same as in the baseline model. In high-income countries, the degrees of robustness are very low again and standard errors large. In sum, while the baseline model that assumes homogeneity correctly finds the direction of an effect, the estimates by construction overlook the large and important effect size variations across groups of units. As a consequence, the baseline model correctly identifies an effect, but the estimated coefficient is not internally valid. The robustness test suggests that due to causal heterogeneity the findings of the baseline model can only be generalized to upper-middle-income countries. The baseline model seems to under-estimate the effect of US military support, in the case of low- and lower-middle-income countries, on terrorist attacks killing US citizens. At the same time, military cooperation with other high-income countries does not seem to stimulate terrorist attacks on Americans.

In addition to the group-specific varying coefficients model test, the *random coefficients test* offers another compromise between the homogeneous causal effect model and the fully flexible unit-specific varying coefficients model test. Random coefficient models assume that the coefficients β_{it} are drawn from a probability distribution with a fixed number of parameters that do not vary with N and T (Hsiao and Pesaran 2004). They usually impose the assumption that the coefficients are normally distributed with a constant variance–covariance structure (Swamy 1970; Western 1998; Hsiao and Pesaran 2008). The coefficients can be made a function of variables that vary across units, but not over time. This leads to a complicated error term (Beck and Katz 2007). Varying coefficients and random coefficient model tests can be combined so that some variables are estimated with fixed and others with random coefficients (Hsiao et al. 1989). A generalization of the random coefficient model test is the *multilevel test*, which additionally allows explanatory variables at the higher level (here: the units) to enter the estimation model (Steenbergen and Jones 2002). All these models can function as robustness tests for baseline homogeneous causal effect models.[5]

Finally, a set of tests based on the Chow test (Chow 1960) can assess potential causal heterogeneity in groups across units and over time. For simplicity, assume analysts wish to test for causal heterogeneity in one variable across two groups – the test can easily be generalized to more groups or more variables or to varying effect strength over time in groups. Specifically, the first variant of the *Chow test of group heterogeneity* estimates

$$y_{it} = \alpha + \beta^1 x_{it} + \beta^2 (x_{it} d_i) + \beta^3 d_i + \gamma z_{it} + \varepsilon_{it} \tag{11.2}$$

5 While additional techniques have been suggested – see, for example, Bartels (1996) for "fractional pooling" and Kyung, Gill, and Casella (2010) for Dirichlet process random-effects models – these have not (yet) been taken on board by empirical social scientists. There is also a significant lack of understanding of the finite sample properties of these techniques.

Table 11.2: Chow Test of Group Heterogeneity

	m1: baseline	m3: group heterogeneity	ρ
Population (ln)	0.645***	0.580***	0.939
	(0.155)	(0.149)	
Distance from US (ln)	−0.0345	−0.152	0.862
	(0.361)	(0.463)	
GDP per capita (ln)	0.112	−0.0272	0.874
	(0.167)	(0.163)	
Democracy	−0.0710**	−0.0257	0.723
	(0.0314)	(0.0276)	
Dependence on US military	0.0285***		
	(0.00877)		
Dependence on US military		0.0288***	0.946
(non-Muslim majority country)		(0.00893)	
Dependence on US military		0.259	0.029
(Muslim majority country)		(0.3978)	
Muslim majority country		0.998**	
		(0.474)	
Observations	3,483	3,483	

Note: Dependent variable is number of US citizens killed. Negative binomial estimations. Constant not reported. Standard errors clustered on countries in parentheses.

Statistically significant * at 0.1, ** at 0.05, *** at 0.01 level.

where d_i is a dummy variable coded 0 for group 1 and 1 for group 2. Alternatively, one can set up the test with two group dummies d_i^1 and d_i^2, one for each group, and estimate

$$y_{it} = \alpha + \beta^1 (x_{it}d_i^1) + \beta^2 (x_{it}d_i^2) + \beta^3 d_i^1 + \gamma z_{it} + \varepsilon_{it} \qquad (11.3)$$

The two models give identical estimated effects.

Model m3 (table 11.2) applies this test to our illustrative example. Based on Samuel Huntington's (1996) *Clash of Civilizations* hypothesis, which suggests violent conflict between the Islamic and the Western civilizations, we may expect that countries with a majority Muslim population are different and that their terrorists react more strongly to the dependence of their own government on US military personnel than do terrorists from countries that do not have majority Muslim populations.

Results from model m3, presented in table 11.2, point again toward causal heterogeneity. The point estimate for *dependence on US military* is much larger in Muslim majority countries compared to the baseline model estimate, which assumes causal homogeneity, and the degree of robustness is very low at 0.03. However, the standard error of the point estimate is very large. To us, this suggests causal heterogeneity not only between Muslim majority and other countries but also very substantial causal heterogeneity within Muslim majority countries. This is a good example where a robustness test that finds the baseline model estimate to be non-robust opens very interesting research questions. In this case, the question is, what explains the apparently strong causal heterogeneity within Muslim majority countries?

The second variant of the *Chow test of group heterogeneity* follows the same logic, but generalizes the test toward uncertainty about classifying units in distinct groups. There are numerous sub-variants of this test. For simplicity, assume again that two groups g^1 and g^2 can be identified and each unit $i = (1, 2, ..., N)$ can be assigned a probability that it belongs to g^1 such that $p(g^1) + p(g^2) = 1$. For a first variant of this test, define a dummy variable g_i that equals 1 if $p(g^1) > 0.7$ and 0 if $p(g^1) < 0.3$ and leave the dummy as missing if units have probabilities between 0.3 and 0.7.[6] Randomly draw additional units from both groups into the sample so that the number of observations that have no missing in the dummy variable is identical to the number of observations in the original sample. Define

$$v^1_{it} = \left\{ \begin{array}{l} x_{it} \ \textit{if} \ g_i = 1 \\ 0 \ \textit{if} \ g_i = 0 \end{array} \right\}$$

and

$$v^2_{it} = \left\{ \begin{array}{l} x_{it} \ \textit{if} \ g_i = 0 \\ 0 \ \textit{if} \ g_i = 1 \end{array} \right\}$$

Then we can estimate the following robustness test model

$$y_{it} = \alpha + \beta^1 v^1_{it} + \beta^2 v^2_{it} + \beta^3 g_i + \gamma z_{it} + \varepsilon_{it} \tag{11.4}$$

Due to the exclusion of units that are unallocated, this test may over-rate the true differences between groups. A second variant of the test therefore takes the units in the middle category and randomizes each case to either of the two groups and then estimates equation 11.4 again. We should repeat each random draw at least 1,000 times, so that we get a distribution

---

6 These probabilities can be varied and themselves made subject to robustness tests.

of test results. The third variant of this test assigns each unit to either group with the expected probability and then estimates equation 11.4.

11.4 ROBUSTNESS TESTS FOR CONTEXT CONDITIONALITY

Robustness tests for context conditionality assess whether estimates from baseline models without conditionalities are robust to including conditionalities of various forms or, where baseline models already include conditionalities, are robust to modelling these conditionalities differently, e.g. by changing the functional form of the conditionality. For simplicity, we focus on the conditional relationship between two explanatory variables, x and z. This can be generalized to more complicated conditionalities among three or more variables with multiple conditional effects. Non-linear estimators automatically estimate all effects as conditional on the values of all other right-hand side variables. The implicit conditionality is enforced by the estimator, but not explicitly modelled (Berry, DeMeritt, and Esarey 2010). Conditional relationships between two variables are therefore understood here as explicitly modelled conditional relationships.

Researchers do not necessarily know whether conditional effects exist and which are the variables that condition each other. Lack of certainty does not mean lack of knowledge altogether. Often, theory or common sense can suggest suspected potential conditional effects. The *conditionality test* introduces conditional effects into the model. The baseline model is nested within the robustness test model as a special case. If estimates are robust, one cannot reject the simplifying assumption of an unconditional effect taken in the specification of the baseline model.

Even if conditionalities were known, a follow-on modelling uncertainty stems from uncertainty about how to model this conditionality. Two main modelling decisions need to be taken that can be subjected to robustness testing: firstly with respect to whether one or more of the interacting variables can have an effect in the absence of the other variable or variables, and secondly with respect to the functional form of the modelled conditionality.

With respect to the first decision, interaction effects can exist between variables in cases where the effect of one or both (or more) of the variables equals zero if the conditioning factor takes on the value of zero. Despite this possibility, Brambor, Clark, and Golder (2006) recommend always including the constituent terms even if theory predicts that x cannot have an effect on y if z equals zero (and vice versa for leaving out x) because the theory may be wrong. Kam and Franzese (2009) suggest excluding the constituent terms if two conditions hold: theory predicts the unconditional effects of the variables to be zero and their estimated coefficients are close to zero with small standard errors (but not if they are merely statistically insignificant due to large standard errors). Researchers may leave out the constituent terms if they believe that the ensuing inefficiency of including both terms threatens the validity of inferences more than the potential bias resulting from excluding both terms (Kam and Franzese 2009: 102). In our view, these uncertainties should be dealt with by two variants of the *conditionality test* rather than by rules of thumb. In the first variant, if the constituent terms are excluded in the baseline model, the robustness test model with the constituent terms included should find the baseline model to be robust if the assumption of no unconditional effects holds true. In the second variant, if the constituent terms are included in the baseline model, the robustness test model excludes these.

As concerns the second decision, more complex robustness tests deal with uncertainty about the functional form of the modelled conditionality. Uncertainty about context conditionality and uncertainty about functional forms are closely interlinked because estimates of interaction effects tend to be biased by functional form misspecification of the constituent terms of the interaction (Ganzach 1997, 1998). As appendix 11A demonstrates, if the true functional form relationship of x and z is non-linear, failure to model this non-linearity but erroneously modelling an interactive relationship between x and z will result in spurious evidence for a conditioning relationship between the two variables.[7] The opposite also holds: misspecified or ignored conditionality can cause wrong inferences about functional form relationships. If z conditions x, failure to model the conditioning relationship, but erroneously modelling a non-linear functional form of x and z instead, will almost certainly produce spurious evidence for this non-linear unconditional relationship (see appendix 11A).[8] In conclusion, functional form uncertainty exacerbates uncertainty with respect to conditionalities, and vice versa. As a corollary, researchers cannot be entirely certain whether empirically observed data has been produced in the data-generating process by non-linearity or conditionality or both.

Interaction effects are almost exclusively modelled as linear-symmetric. Yet, no theory suggests this has to be the case. The "symmetry by default" assumption is simply brought about by the standard way of modelling and estimating interaction effects by multiplying two (or more) constituent terms by each other.

7 Some of the effect of x is unexplained by the imposed linear functional form of x and some of this unexplained effect will spuriously suggest an effect of the interaction term $x \cdot z$ due to its correlation with x.
8 Some of the variation that is due to the conditional relationship will be spuriously picked up as a non-linear effect of x and z due to the correlation of the omitted interaction effect term with higher-degree polynomials of x and z.

A higher-degree polynomial model allows one to employ a *non-linear conditionality test*. In this model, the symmetry assumption implicit in interaction models is relaxed. Given that the complexity of high-order polynomial models becomes compounded when applied to interaction effect models, researchers should stick to second- or third-degree polynomial models. For example, instead of modelling the standard linear-symmetric interaction between x and z, one can estimate a second-degree polynomial interaction effects model as follows:

$$y = \beta_1 x + \beta_2 x^2 + \beta_3 z + \beta_4 z^2 + \beta_5 xz + \beta_6 x^2 z + \beta_7 xz^2 + \beta_8 x^2 z^2 + \varepsilon$$
(11.5)

To assess robustness quantitatively, with both constituent variables of the interaction effect entering the estimation model in non-linear form, plotting ρ against the values of one variable is no longer possible since the degree of robustness now varies with the varying values of both one and the other variable. We therefore need to present partial robustness in the form of a carpet plot or a heat contour plot. Alternatively, the overlap in confidence intervals between predicted effects from the linear-symmetric baseline model and the second-order polynomial robustness test model will allow a qualitative assessment of robustness, which will often suffice.

Alternative robustness tests that allow for asymmetric and non-linear interaction are semi-parametric for one of the two conditioning variables or both. Assume the interaction effect consists of the two continuous variables x and z. There are three variants of the semi-parametric approach to the *non-linear conditionality test*. In the first variant of the test, one keeps one variable in its continuous form and interacts it with percentile category dummy variables of the other variable. In the second variant, each of the variables of a conditional relationship is split into different categorical dummy variables. Researchers should generate, for each variable, at least three categorical dummy variables for low, medium, and high categories with each one containing a third of the observations. Multiplying the three dummy variables x_l, x_m, and x_h for x with the three dummy variables z_l, z_m, and z_h for z gives nine categories. Excluding a base category, researchers estimate eight parameters of interest, namely

$$
\begin{aligned}
y = {}& a + \beta^1 x_l z_m + \beta^2 x_l z_h + \beta^3 x_m z_l + \beta^4 x_m z_m + \beta^5 x_m z_h \\
& + \beta^6 x_h z_l + \beta^7 x_h z_m + \beta^8 x_h z_h + \varepsilon
\end{aligned}
$$
(11.6)

The first two variants are robustness tests of the model variation type. Alternatively, researchers can use a structured permutation variant of the above tests and vary the number of categories as well as the thresholds between categories.

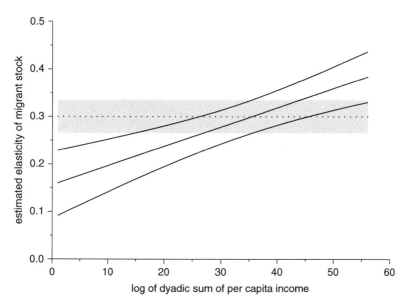

Figure 11.1: Conditionality Test
Note: Grey-shaded area represents confidence interval of baseline model.

As an illustrative example, we use data from Perkins and Neumayer (2013), who analyze the effect of foreign migrants residing in a country on bilateral international telephone traffic (measured in duration of telephone calls) between the host and the resident country in a global sample of undirected country dyads. Nowadays telephone over internet and Skype have rendered this analysis pointless, but during the sample period of 2001 to 2006 telephone was the predominant, almost the only, way for migrants to communicate verbally with their friends, relatives, and business partners back home. Perkins and Neumayer (2013) estimate a gravity-type log-log model. A simple baseline model would estimate the migrant effect as being unconditional. The estimated elasticity equals 0.3. A 10-percent increase in the combined migrant stock increases bilateral telephony by 3 percent. Assessing whether the assumption of an unconditional effect appears to be robust, we include an interaction effect between the dyadic sum of migrants and the dyadic sum of per capita incomes. In other words, we test whether the migrant effect is conditioned by the combined per capita income in both countries since migrants residing in relatively richer countries might face lower opportunity costs for calling back home. Figure 11.1 suggests that the unconditional effect from the baseline model is not robust at either low or high levels of the sum of average incomes in a country dyad. Instead, the

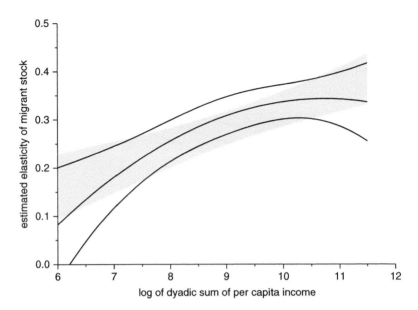

Figure 11.2: Non-linear Conditionality Test
Note: Grey-shaded area represents confidence interval of baseline model.

migrant effect is clearly conditional, with the estimated elasticity rising from around 0.17 at low levels of combined average income to around 0.38 at high levels of combined average income.

A second test explores the robustness of the linearity assumption of the conditional effect by estimating a second-degree polynomial of the conditional relationship. It seems plausible to argue that the conditioning effect becomes smaller as per capita income increases. Figure 11.2 suggests that this is indeed the case. However, the 95-percent confidence intervals are sufficiently overlapping; the simplification of a bi-linear interaction effect is at least weakly robust.

11.5 CONCLUSION

For a social science that wishes to inform real-world actors, the analysis of causal heterogeneity and context conditionality provide important insights. Causal heterogeneity robustness tests have a simple purpose: to figure out whether the estimated mean effect is representative for the entire sample. The same holds for context conditionality robustness tests: they assess whether the estimated treatment effect is approximately constant across the range of the conditioning variable. Our illustrative examples showed that our baseline models' assumptions of a homogeneous effect and of an unconditional effect were not robust. We performed similar tests in other research projects and regularly found evidence for causal heterogeneity and context conditionality. Social scientists do not study homogeneous cases, and this often shows in quantitative analyses that allow for causal heterogeneity or context conditionality.

For reasons of parsimony, social scientists should not and will not give up the assumption of homogeneous and unconditional effects and, while they should allow for context conditionality more often than is standard practice, limited information prevents researchers from estimating complex models. Yet, social scientists need to acquire a better understanding of the limits of inferences. Statistical significance of an effect does not mean that the estimated coefficient represents the entire sample, let alone that it can be generalized to the population researchers have in mind.

Largely ignoring causal heterogeneity and context conditionalities represents simplifications that conflict with the likely complexity of the true data-generating process; but this can be justified, we have argued, on the basis of the principle of parsimony. Researchers face a trade-off between keeping the baseline model as simple as possible on the one hand and as complex as necessary on the other hand. Robustness tests can alleviate the tension. They do not aim at recovering the true model, but bring back some of the heterogeneity or conditionalities in a systematic way. This allows researchers to observe whether their results and inferences depend on the imposition of causal homogeneity, on the exclusion of a conditional effect, or on a particular functional form of any modelled conditional effect. Even if estimates are found to be robust to the specific changes in model specification tested, nothing guarantees that this carries over to a fully complex true model. But with limited information, researchers will not be able to achieve full certainty of estimates and inferences based upon these estimates; they can merely improve the imperfect confidence one has in them.

APPENDIX 11A: A GENERATED EXAMPLE DEMONSTRATING THE CLOSE LINK BETWEEN FUNCTIONAL FORM AND CONDITIONAL EFFECT UNCERTAINTY

Section 11.4 noted how estimates of conditional effects tend to be biased by functional form misspecification of the constituent terms of the interaction, while the functional forms of estimates tend to be biased by conditional effect misspecification. To demonstrate this point, we employ an artificially generated dataset of size 1,000, in which two variables x and z are drawn from a normal distribution of mean 0 with an imposed average correlation of 0.5. Assume the true data-generating process to be

Table 11A.1: Functional Form Test: Quadratic Relationship

	m1	m2
x	0.923***	0.984***
	(0.242)	(0.0351)
x^2		1.030***
		(0.0281)
z	1.084***	0.993***
	(0.192)	(0.0172)
z^2		1.008***
		(0.00596)
$x \cdot z$	1.924***	−0.0138
	(0.126)	(0.0210)
constant	3.024***	−0.0399
	(0.203)	(0.0447)
Observations	1,000	1,000
R^2	0.539	0.978

Note: Statistically significant *** at 0.01 level.

Table 11A.2: Functional Form Test: Bi-Linear Conditional Relationship

	m1	m2
x	0.912***	0.984***
	(0.0981)	(0.0351)
x^2	0.846***	0.0298
	(0.0645)	(0.0281)
z	0.999***	0.993***
	(0.0539)	(0.0172)
z^2	0.186***	0.00758
	(0.0167)	(0.00596)
$x \cdot z$		0.986***
		(0.0210)
constant	−0.596***	−0.0399
	(0.0699)	(0.0447)
Observations	1,000	1,000
R^2	0.772	0.920

Note: Statistically significant *** at 0.01 level.

$y = x + x^2 + z + z^2 + \varepsilon$, where ε is a normally distributed error term. Estimating a model that does not account for the non-linear functional form of x and z and instead includes an interaction term between the two variables results in spurious evidence for a conditional relationship between

x and z (see table 11A.1, model 1). In contrast, if we allow for non-linear effects of x and z, then the coefficient of the interaction term becomes indistinguishable from zero (model 2).

The opposite also holds: if the true data-generating process includes an interaction term not included in the model, researchers may find evidence for a non-linear functional form where the data-generating process is linear. In other words, misspecified or ignored conditionality can lead to wrong inferences about linearity. To demonstrate this, we now specify the true relationship of x and z on y to be: $y = x + x \cdot z + z + \varepsilon$. Model 3 reported in table 11A.2 erroneously suggests a non-linear relationship of x on y and of z on y, respectively, due to the failure of accounting for the conditional relationship of x and z. When the conditional relationship is adequately accounted for in model 4, the "evidence" for a non-linear effect of x on y and of z on y disappears.

12 Structural Change as Temporal Heterogeneity

12.1 INTRODUCTION

Social scientists have long debated the extent to which findings can be generalized across time. The evolutionary logic of social interaction implies why there is no definitive answer: causal mechanisms may exist for a long period of time but their effect strengths may vary depending on other social conditions, which evolve over time, a process we call structural change for short. Evolutionary processes in the social world crucially limit the generalizability of causal mechanisms and causal effect strengths over time. This problem relates to what Larry Bartels (1996: 906) calls the "fundamental problem of induction":

... what, if anything, entitles us to make inferences about the behavior of an individual, nation, or other unit on the basis of the observed behavior of (...) the same unit at some different point in time or in some different context (...)? The answer can only be, a prior belief in the similarity of the bases of behavior across (...) time periods or contexts.

Over the last decades, modern econometric theory has become more flexible. Rather than assuming causal and parameter stability over time, econometricians have developed dynamic models – estimation strategies that allow effect strengths to vary over time. Often, these techniques remain confined to time-series analyses – a limitation that we find unnecessarily restrictive, though we admit that it is difficult to allow for changing effect strengths over time and heterogeneity within these processes between units of analysis.

In addition to slowly evolving changes over time, there can also be temporary shocks and structural breaks – shocks that are persistent rather than temporary. Historical events that many would regard as likely candidates for structural breaks include the French and Russian revolutions (Davies 1962), the World Wars (Ben-David et al. 2003), the end of the Cold War (Hogan 1992), and the 9/11 terrorist attacks (Enders and Sandler 2005). Whether other potential candidates, such as fundamental abrupt changes in a country's regime type, as well as other forms of relevant institutional change in a jurisdiction constitute structural breaks remains more contested. Uncertainty dominates the debate whether the consequences of a shock are persistent or whether the change does not last and a return to the status quo ante will occur within a short time. The financial crisis that started in 2007/8 may well be identified by future social scientists as having permanently changed the effect of monetary, fiscal, and other policies on macro-economic variables. But right now it remains too early to call. Examples of temporary exogenous shocks are provided by the various oil crises. Usually, these begin with a sudden and sharp increase in the price of crude oil, often caused by a militarized conflict in the Middle East. The shock is over when actors have adjusted or the oil price falls back to initial levels (Hamilton 2003).

Structural change can be of interest to social scientists as an object of study. We distinguish between three types of structural change: common trends, common shocks, and structural breaks (shocks with persistent effects). As objects of study, trends are directional movements, either increasing or decreasing, in variables over an extended, and identifiable, period of time. Shocks are temporary perturbations while structural breaks are persistent perturbations to variables. What causes the trend in certain variables, what determines a particular structural break or a temporary shock?

There exists, however, a more fundamental way in which structural change matters, which makes it relevant for the vast majority of social scientists: structural change may change the cause–effect relationship of variables over time. In this sense, structural change results in *temporal heterogeneity of causal effects*. Thus, as triggers of temporal heterogeneity, trends are systematic increases or decreases in the strength of the effect of x on y; shocks occur if the effect of x on y changes rapidly at an identifiable period and if the effect strength returns to pre-shock levels after some time; and structural breaks are shocks with persistent changes to the effect of x on y.

Structural change – defined as systematic variation in the strengths of an effect over time – causes inferential problems to all model specifications that assume effects are stable over time. Inadequately modelled temporal heterogeneity can produce both bias, thus threatening internal validity, and lack of generalizability beyond the sample, thus threatening the external validity of causal inferences. Social scientists need to know whether the estimate of an average effect across the entire time period of the sample hides systematic variation within this time period.

The specification of dynamics complicates the estimation of structural change, and vice versa. Dynamic effect specifications will often capture common trends at the observable level. Moreover, if a model misspecifies structural changes, the residuals tend to be serially correlated, which for many observers implies a dynamic misspecification, though it can also be caused by other model misspecifications. Depending on the research project, robustness tests for temporal heterogeneity may have to be combined with robustness tests for dynamics.

Contrary to effect dynamics, the modelling of which has become more common though frequently employed as a quick apparent fix for dealing with serially correlated residuals, the vast majority of empirical studies impose the assumption of temporal homogeneity.[1] The argument for time-invariant parameter estimates cannot be that causal mechanisms and treatment effects do not change over time. In a social world that evolves over time, this is unlikely to be true (Maddala 1998). Instead, researchers have to simplify the data-generating process of reality and therefore have to accept model misspecifications that result from these simplifications. The assumption of time-invariant parameter estimates, while wrong, can be a useful and to some extent even a necessary modelling choice.

We start this chapter by distinguishing two meanings of structural change. The meaning of interest to us understands structural change as change in causal mechanisms and change in effect strengths. We call this "temporal heterogeneity." Just as causal heterogeneity challenges the assumption of a constant effect across units, so does structural change challenge the assumption of a constant effect over time. The other meaning of structural change relates to such changes as an object of study. If the number of democratic countries in the world doubles, then structural change occurs even if the effect of democracy on outcome variables such as peace and economic growth does not change. We then propose robustness tests that relax the assumption of effect strength homogeneity. These tests can allow for common or group-specific trends, shocks, and structural breaks in cause–effect relationships.

12.2 FROM STRUCTURAL CHANGE TO TEMPORAL HETEROGENEITY

Social systems change over time. Even relatively stable societies look different when we revisit them after a period of, say, 40, 50, or 60 years. In the 1960s, some US states still insisted on different compartments for white and black bus passengers; in the 2010s, the US had its first black president.

---

1 Econometrics also does not pay much attention to bias caused by misspecified or overlooked structural changes in model specification, focusing instead on forecasting (Granger 1996; Pesaran et al. 2006).

Leading positions in business and society were almost exclusively held by men, while the Nordic countries will probably be the first to reach gender parity in a few years. In 1954 Germany won the football world championship, while in 2014 ... Well, some things never change.

Change happens continuously most of the time, with variables trending over time in a particular direction. Populations and economies tend to grow, prices tend to inflate, life expectancy tends to rise; there are periods of welfare state expansion and periods of welfare state contraction, and so on. There can be shocks to these trends, for example, when populations and economies temporarily decrease during perturbations caused by natural disasters or violent conflict or when life expectancy temporarily decreases during periods of extreme mortality of the relatively young, as happened during the HIV/AIDS crisis in many sub-Saharan African countries.

From the start, social scientists have been interested in structural change. They have studied why shocks and breaks such as financial crises or deep recessions happen, why no one anticipated them and what their consequences are. They have been interested in the factors that drive, more generally and more fundamentally, the evolution of culture, society, the economy, and the organization of social interactions, the polity. Technological progress plays as important a role in economics as does secularization in sociology and democratization in political science.

Theories of structural change have relied on cultural, religious, economic, scientific, and technological forces, and on ideas. Heracletian theories suggest that change is endemic. Societies can only prevail by changing all the time. Hegelian and Marxist theories suggest that change occurs in response to a "conflict" between antagonistic factors: ideas in Hegel's understanding, social classes in Marx's perspective. Evolutionary theories suggest that change occurs randomly (like mutations) and succeeds only if it proves to be advantageous. With the exception of Marxist and Hegelian theories which predict sudden abrupt and comprehensive changes, most theories perceive change as the rule and an ongoing process. Changes are frequent, evolutionary, and slow rather than revolutionary. Innovations on the social, economic, political, and institutional level compete with old structures for "survival." Naturally, not every innovation will survive. Many, perhaps the vast majority, lead to inferior outcomes for pivotal powerful actors. However, enough innovations survive to result in permanent structural change.

Importantly, social evolution is more dynamic than biological evolution because individuals can actively develop a response to change. Human beings confronted with an innovation can proactively adjust to change and deliberately modify goals, strategies, and behavior. Agents may copy successful strategies from others and update common behavioral norms in cooperative or competitive ways. The success of each individual, group, organization, country and, ultimately mankind, depends on the interaction between actors in the social world and on interactions between the social and the physical world.

Social scientists are most familiar with describing structural change as occurring at the observational level. This type of change can be observed, described, and often enough even measured. Yet, from the perspective of causal inference, the meaning of structural change differs. It may well be that structural changes in causal effect strength or even in causal mechanisms also cause important changes on the observational level, but they do not have to. Conversely, structural change at the observational level tells us nothing about whether cause–effect relationships have changed.

For example, international relations scholars have argued that the end of the Cold War increased the global system's propensity for militarized conflict, which had previously been kept in check by the existence of two opposing superpowers (Baldwin 1995). As time goes by, the rules of the game, the logic of individual and collective behavior change slowly but surely.

Arguments like this can have many different meanings in the language of causal inference. It could be that the causal effect strengths of conventional risk factors for the emergence of militarized disputes have increased or that the end of the Cold War has introduced new cause–effect relationships. It could also be the case that the model that explains militarized conflict remains intact, including the effect of superpower involvement on the emergence of militarized conflict, and that any change in outcomes can be satisfactorily explained by a reduction in superpower involvement. Hence, to the extent that one can measure superpower involvement, the model and its core parameters may remain constant despite the observable change in outcomes.

In other words, temporal heterogeneity in cause–effect relationships cannot be observed; it needs to be inferred and, crucially, depends on the estimation model and not on observable changes in outcomes. Even the set of causal mechanisms may change. As society evolves, some causal mechanisms may disappear while others are born. The various "logics of social interaction" do not persist forever, at least not with the same strengths. The possibility and likelihood of change in causal mechanisms is one of the fundamental differences between the social and the physical world.[2] While natural scientists typically believe that causal mechanisms are approximately or fully time-invariant, social scientists may make the same assumption but

---

2 The other fundamental difference is the ability of agents to anticipate or delay responses to stimulus, which we discuss in the next chapter.

only to simplify the model, not because there is any evidence that causal effects in the social world are constants.

Slow-moving structural changes that occur continuously add up to fundamental alterations, changing the context and setting in which causes have effects. Over any sufficiently long period of time, social systems tend to be unstable and subject to large changes. In terms of institutional stability, for example, 30, 40, 50 years are long periods of time. Contemporary empirical analyses in the social sciences increasingly cover time periods that are this long or even longer. For these datasets, a period of more than 50 years can be analyzed – in other words, we can study periods of time for which structural stability is unlikely.

Structural change as effect strength heterogeneity over time is likely to result from changes in unknown, unobservable, or unmodelled conditionality. The effect of schooling on lifetime income changes as the sectoral structure of the economy changes, if the unemployment rate changes, if institutions of wage negotiations change. In addition, the effect of schooling on lifetime income may change along with cultural changes such as increases in women's rights, with immigration, and with millions of other factors that influence the functioning of the labor market and individual preferences and incentives. The belief that there is a single causal effect of education is, well, absurd. Social scientists should not even be interested in the unconditional effect of schooling on income, simply because in reality an unconditional effect does not exist. An "identified" causal effect of schooling is thus irrelevant for individual and political decision-making.

Temporal parameter heterogeneity can in principle occur in two variants: first, the effect of a variable included in the model changes, and second, a variable enters into the model which previously was not included (which is identical to a change in its effect strength from zero to not zero). The following section focuses on robustness tests for variables already included in the model. A natural robustness test for the second variant of temporal parameter heterogeneity is to include a variable from a particular point in time that was not previously included.

12.3 ROBUSTNESS TESTS FOR EFFECT STRENGTH HETEROGENEITY OVER TIME

It has become so common in the social sciences to assume structural homogeneity across time that researchers find it a stretch to allow for a variation in parameters. Yet, with data that often cover several decades, the constraint of time-invariant parameter estimates becomes questionable. Models that do not allow for temporal heterogeneity are nested within models that allow for heterogeneity. Finite information, however, means that researchers cannot set parameters entirely free. But they can relax, to a greater or lesser extent, one or more of the homogeneity constraints imposed on the baseline model.

Robustness tests for structural change do not aim at testing whether temporal heterogeneity exists. They either test whether estimates from a baseline model based on the assumption of temporal homogeneity are robust when we allow for temporal heterogeneity or whether, if the baseline model already assumes some form of temporal heterogeneity, findings are robust to making different assumptions regarding structural change. We focus on the former given that few analyses assume the existence of structural change.

Robustness test models that account for temporal heterogeneity allow the parameter of at least one variable to vary over time, either commonly for all units of observation together or differentially across groups of observations. This variation can take various forms – we distinguish trends, shocks, and breaks. In the *trended effect test* researchers can interact one or more variables with time. In the simplest version of this robustness test, the variable of interest is interacted with a variable measuring the running periods from $t_1=1$ to $t_T=T$ and estimating the baseline model with this additional variable so that

$$y_{it} = \alpha + \beta^1 x_{it} + \beta^2 x_{it} \cdot r_t + \ldots + \varepsilon_{it} \tag{12.1}$$

where r is a variable counting the number of periods from 1 to T. One may, of course, allow for group-specific trended effects rather than common trends. In this case, researchers estimate separate parameters of $x_{it} \cdot r_t$ for different groups of units and include group-specific dummy variables.

There is no guarantee that the trend of effect strengths must be linear. In fact, linearity appears to be unlikely as the number of periods increases. However, for a robustness test, assuming linearity of effect strengths might well suffice. More complex functional forms of temporal heterogeneity can be modelled by interacting one or more variables with higher-degree polynomials of time. Alternatively, the most flexible but very inefficient form of trend test interacts one or more variables with period dummies. The results will to some extent reflect the temporal heterogeneity of the parameters. However, keep in mind that the best-fitting model is neither the true model nor necessarily the best possible model.

Observable structural change in the dependent variable over time might not be caused by structural change in cause–effect relationships but by other factors not captured in the estimation model. Unfortunately, it is usually not possible with observational data to establish whether the trend, shocks, and breaks were caused by omitted variables. To ensure that the common or group-specific structural change in cause–effect relationships does not spuriously pick up common or group-specific unexplained exogenous structural change, scholars can either add the running period variable to the estimation model or, in our preference, control for period fixed effects. There will almost always be omitted variables that have some impact on structural change. At the same time, some of the regressors in the model are likely to influence structural change. Robustness tests can explore the robustness of estimates toward different ways of accounting for exogenous structural change. Accordingly, the *period fixed-effects test* either includes or drops these fixed effects in the robustness test model, depending on whether the baseline model includes or excludes them. An alternative is the *temporal splines test*, though note that even the inclusion of as few as three temporal splines often renders this specification so flexible in its modelling of exogenous structural change that this test becomes almost identical to the period fixed-effects test.

As an example to illustrate our robustness tests, we analyze the effect of per capita income on life expectancy. We employ a sample of 23 western developed countries (including Israel) and 11 eastern European countries over the period 1961 to 2012. Per capita income and life expectancy are strongly correlated, with a bivariate correlation coefficient of 0.72. There are strong reasons to presume a causal effect of income on life expectancy – richer countries are more technically advanced, spend more money on public health care, and its people have more disposable income to spend on private health care. Equally, however, it appears possible that over such a long period the strength of the effect of income on life expectancy diminishes over time. Plausible candidates for this temporal heterogeneity are the spread of medical technology to poorer countries and an associated decrease in the gap to the technological frontier or diminishing returns of wealth and its indirect effects on longevity as the effect of exogenous trends increases. Since omitted variables such as medical progress almost certainly exist and cause exogenous structural change in life expectancy, we include year fixed effects into the estimation model without subjecting this modelling choice to a robustness test.

Life expectancy data are from the World Bank's World Development Indicators. We control for life style choices that impact life expectancy by including average alcohol per capita consumption in liters of pure alcohol. Since we have no data with comprehensive coverage on tobacco consumption, lifestyle choices, and health and safety regulations that result in death due to external causes, we account instead for the mortality consequences of these by including mortality rates from lung cancer and from external causes per 1,000 inhabitants (data sourced from the World Bank, the OECD, and

Table 12.1: Trended Effect Test			
	m1: baseline	m2: trended effect of GDP p.c.	p
Alcohol consumption	−0.117*	−0.109*	0.926
	(0.0139)	(0.0131)	
Lung cancer mortality	−1.785*	−1.856*	0.954
	(0.316)	(0.303)	
External cause mortality	−5.153*	−5.250*	0.920
	(0.255)	(0.269)	
GDP per capita	0.103*	0.167*	
	(0.00571)	(0.0143)	
(GDP per capita) · (year trend)		−0.00167*	
		(0.000409)	
Constant	75.28*	74.54*	
	(0.411)	(0.382)	
R^2	0.853	0.857	
Period fixed effects	yes	yes	

Note: Dependent variable is life expectancy at birth. $N = 1,328$. Robust standard errors in parentheses.
  Statistically significant * at 0.01 level.

the WHO). Table 12.1 reports the results of the baseline model to an alternative robustness test model, which allows the effect of per capita income to linearly change over time.

The robustness test model suggests that the strength of the effect of per capita income on life expectancy declines over time. Figure 12.1 plots the predicted marginal effect of per capita income of the baseline model against the robustness test model as a function of the year count variable, which allows us to assess partial robustness. In the baseline model, every USD10,000 increase in per capita income increases average life expectancy by slightly more than one year. In the robustness test model, the estimated effect of per capita income on life expectancy is about 60 percent larger in the beginning if we allow for temporal heterogeneity, and the baseline model estimate does not seem robust for at least the first 20 years. Our robustness test suggests that the restriction to estimate a single, homogeneous effect for the entire period leads to a severe under-estimation of the effect strengths of per capita income in the initial periods and a slight over-estimation in the end periods, though not so strong as to render the baseline model estimate non-robust toward the end of our sample period.

In addition to or instead of common trends, the effect of income on life expectancy may have been subject to a shock or structural break.

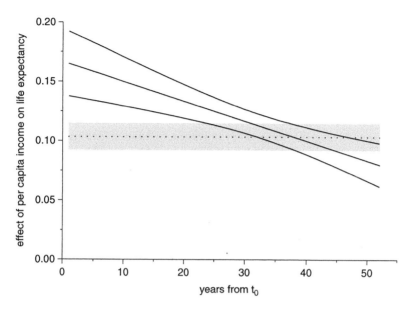

Figure 12.1: Trended Effect Test
Note: Grey-shaded area represents confidence interval of baseline model.

Robustness tests for shocks and breaks allow the effect of one or more variables to vary after the event for a temporary period (shocks) or for the entire remaining period of the sample (structural break). Depending on whether the shock affects all or just selected cases, researchers might restrict the effect of the shock or structural break to potentially affected cases. In addition, the shock or structural break need not start (or, for shocks, end) at the same time for all affected cases. Lastly, the strength of the causal effect can differ across groups even if they experience a structural break with the same start date or a temporary shock with the same start and end dates.

A *Chow test of temporal heterogeneity* interacts the variable(s) of interest with the product of a dummy variable coded as 1 if a case is potentially affected and 0 otherwise. Since, for temporary shocks, the effect strength of the variable of interest is presumed to return to pre-shock levels after the end of the shock, the dummy variable takes the value of 1 only for the number of periods the shock lasts. This test can also account for structural breaks if the dummy variable has the value 1 until the end period T.

In most empirical applications, the onset of a shock or break and the duration of a shock remain unknown. Instead of employing model variation type tests, we can therefore use structured permutation variants of these tests by systematically varying the onset and, for shocks, the duration of the shock.

In our example, the collapse of the communist autocracies of eastern Europe likely resulted in a temporary shock or structural break. Evidence for this assumption clearly exists at the observational level in life expectancy. The drop was most pronounced in countries of the former Soviet Union. Average life expectancy in Russia, Lithuania, Estonia, and Belarus dropped between 3 and 5.4 years between 1990 and 1995 and only slowly recovered after 1995. In contrast, life expectancy in western countries increased in this period by between 0.5 and 1.0 years. A different question is whether the collapse of eastern European communist regimes also resulted in a temporary shock or even structural break for the cause–effect relationship of per capita income. Our baseline model assumes that the drop in life expectancy can be explained by changes in the values of the explanatory variables, predominantly by the dramatic collapse of per capita income, rather than by changes in its causal effect strength.

Allowing for a structural break can be done by interacting the per capita income variable with a dummy variable which takes the value 1 if the country is an eastern European transition country and if the year is 1990 or later (0 else). Allowing for a temporary shock means restricting the dummy variable to some defined period after 1990. One can be fairly certain that a shock or structural break, if existent, started in 1990 but, given the uncertainty until when it lasted, we employ a structured permutation test in which we extend the final year of the presumed structural change by steps of three years, starting in 1996. Results presented in table 12.2 suggest that whatever the end date of the temporary shock, which eventually turns into a structural break in the last robustness test model specification, the baseline model's estimate is not robust for transition countries after the end of the Cold War.

Instead, the estimated effect of per capita income is substantially larger in this group of countries after the fall of the Berlin wall. Apparently, these countries do not only fall behind in life expectancy because of the spectacular collapse of per capita income in these countries in the 1990s; the collapse had a larger impact on life expectancy than we have inferred from the baseline model's assumption of temporal homogeneity, because it apparently also resulted in a larger cause–effect relationship. Whether the size of the effect has been influenced by conditioning factors or by non-linearities in the effects remains an open question that we cannot pursue here.

Table 12.2: Chow Test of Temporal Heterogeneity			
	m1: **baseline**	**m3: shock or structural break in eastern Europe**	ρ
GDP per capita	0.103*		
	(0.00571)		
GDP p.c.		0.102*	0.950
(in other observations)		(0.00562)	
GDP p.c.		0.792*	0.000
(in 1990–1996 post-Soviet obs.)		(0.220)	
1990–1996 post-Soviet dummy		−2.784*	
		(0.601)	
GDP p.c.		0.102*	0.950
(in other observations)		(0.00564)	
GDP p.c.		0.734*	0.000
(in 1990–1999 post-Soviet obs.)		(0.114)	
1990–1999 post-Soviet dummy		−2.757*	
		(0.417)	
GDP p.c.		0.102*	0.950
(in other observations)		(0.00563)	
GDP p.c.		0.673*	0.000
(in 1990–2002 post-Soviet obs.)		(0.0701)	
1990–2002 post-Soviet dummy		−2.914*	
		(0.381)	
GDP p.c.		0.101*	0.940
(in other observations)		(0.00561)	
GDP p.c.		0.558*	0.000
(in 1990–2005 post-Soviet obs.)		(0.0545)	
1990–2005 post-Soviet dummy		−3.265*	
		(0.403)	
GDP p.c.		0.0988*	0.893
(in other observations)		(0.00557)	
GDP p.c.		0.454*	0.000
(in 1990–2009 post-Soviet obs.)		(0.0429)	
1990–2009 post-Soviet dummy		−3.851*	
		(0.404)	
GDP p.c.		0.0970*	0.824
(in other observations)		(0.00556)	
GDP p.c.		0.448*	0.000
(in 1990–2011 post-Soviet obs.)		(0.0385)	
1990–2011 post-Soviet dummy		−4.311*	
		(0.391)	

Note: Dependent variable is life expectancy at birth. $N = 1,328$. Same control variables as in table 12.1 (coefficients not shown). Robust standard errors in parentheses.

Statistically significant * at 0.01 level.

12.4 CONCLUSION

Temporal heterogeneity is omnipresent – especially if we analyze a sufficiently long period of time. The social world does not stand still. The analysis of observational data is often obfuscated by common and heterogeneous trends, common or heterogeneous shocks, and synchronous and asynchronous structural breaks, which can all occur concurrently.

There are, however, two fundamentally different understandings of structural change. One prompts some social scientists to explicitly study the determinants of change. The other understanding of structural change looks at changes in causal mechanisms and at changes in cause–effect strengths over time. Explicitly modelling temporal heterogeneity allows researchers to gain a deeper understanding of structural change, an important question for research that is not genuinely interested in the structural change as an object of study.

Most analyses in the social sciences assume that causal mechanisms and cause–effect strengths stay constant. Should we really believe that the influence of central bank independence on inflation has not changed as governments have learned that inflation is not a reasonable instrument for curbing unemployment? Should we assume that the effect of capital investment on economic growth remains, say, 0.4 before and after the digital revolution?

Over a sufficiently long period of time, structural change will influence cause–effect relationships. And yet, most empirical models hold parameters constant. As with all aspects of model specification, temporal homogeneity is a simplifying virtue that can be justified on the basis of parsimony but that equally needs to be put to test to ensure it does not threaten the validity of inferences.

Robustness tests that allow for temporal heterogeneity are seemingly easy to do since they merely involve allowing parameter estimates to differ across different periods of time. Structural change will not start everywhere at the same time nor occur with the same speed and dynamics. Robustness tests allow structural change to affect groups of units differentially and will employ structured permutation tests to account for uncertainty about start and potential end periods of structural change.

Structural change understood as temporal heterogeneity cannot be observed; it can only be inferred. Its analysis crucially depends on the model specification. Researchers frequently treat structural change as nuisance and push its consequences into the residuals or some catch-all variables such as the lagged dependent variable and period fixed effects. These apparent fixes ignore the fact that there can be structural change in causal effects without any observable structural change in outcome variables. More importantly, they threaten to create type II inferential errors (falsely rejecting a true hypothesis) if some of the structural change is in fact due to temporal heterogeneity in the effect of some of the explanatory variables. Conversely, the absence of these catch-all fixes threatens to create type I errors (falsely failing to reject a wrong hypothesis) if omitted variables influence or cause structural changes. Temporal heterogeneity and its analysis are therefore intricately linked to the modelling of effect dynamics.

13 Effect Dynamics

INTRODUCTION

Effect dynamics refers to all model aspects which specify the temporal particulars of the effect that a cause (or treatment) has on the outcome. Effects have a beginning (onset), which may set in contemporaneously with the treatment or with a delay,[1] and often an end. Effect strength may evolve over several periods and therefore follows a "temporal functional form."

How researchers model effect dynamics crucially depends on the definition of a time period in their data. In the simplest case of pure cross-sectional data, dynamics cannot be modelled. With two periods, research can distinguish the pre-treatment stage and post-treatment stage and compute the treatment effect as the difference between the pre- and the post-treatment level. The effect is still not dynamic. In other words, the requirement for a dynamic model is that the effect can be observed over at least two periods after treatment. The "dynamics" of an effect is then the difference in the outcome of the treatment between the two post-treatment periods.

If researchers are predominantly interested in effect dynamics, the number of periods during which effects are observed will have to be much larger. The shorter the lengths of a period relative to the duration of an effect, the more detailed it is possible to model the dynamics of an effect. Of course, some researchers have little to no influence on the length of a period in the data they analyze. For example, governments and international organizations collect and publish information on a bi-annual, annual or at best monthly basis. Many public surveys are conducted annually, while census data in many countries are gathered only once in a decade or even less frequently. In contrast, stock exchange and other financial information can

---

1 In rare cases, effects can even set in in anticipation of treatment, for example, if actors have rational expectations.

be collected as high-frequency data – if necessary, it is possible to collect the value of a share every minute.

This explains why some research areas mostly neglect dynamics, while in other areas the methods for analyzing dynamics have become sophisticated. For example, most research areas in political science pay little attention to the dynamics of an effect. Theories usually do not predict the lag between cause and effect, how long an effect lasts, and the evolution of an effect's strength throughout an effect's duration. As De Boef and Keele (2008: 186) have put it: "Theories about politics typically tell us only generally how inputs relate to processes we care about. They are nearly always silent on which lags matter, (...) what characterizes equilibrium behavior, or what effects are likely to be biggest in the long run." Political science is not alone: the same holds in many other social sciences disciplines.

Accordingly, researchers remain uncertain about how dynamics in their estimation models should be specified. Left with little or no theoretical guidance, they either ignore dynamics or regard it as a nuisance to be eliminated rather than modelled. To a large extent, the lack of attention results from uncertainty about how best to model dynamics. As Wilson and Butler have put it (2007: 120): "When we leave the confines of the simple static model and enter into the dynamic world, a Pandora's box of alternative models and approaches presents itself."

If researchers model dynamics, they tend to choose simple and restrictive specifications that represent a small subset of the available dynamic specifications, thus ignoring the vast majority of possibilities.[2] Dynamic specifications in empirical models tend to be mere patches for problems such as serially correlated errors – not careful attempts to approximate the data-generating process. In other words, dynamics are not modelled because of and according to theoretical predictions, but because some dynamic specification may eliminate the serial correlation of residuals. Often, these dynamic specifications will reduce the bias from serially correlated errors, while at the same time potentially increasing bias due to a dynamic misspecification. To quote again from De Boef and Keele (2008: 184): "Analysts tend to adopt restrictive dynamic specifications on the basis of limited theoretical guidance and without empirical evidence that restrictions are valid, potentially biasing inferences and invalidating hypothesis tests."

In this chapter, we will first clarify the meaning and decomposition of "dynamics," namely into temporal aggregation (the temporal unit of analysis), the onset and duration of effects, the evolution of effect strength over several periods, and the heterogeneity of dynamic effects across units. We then discuss the causes of dynamic specification uncertainty and suggest

---

2 We briefly review dynamic specifications in appendix 13A.

robustness tests for the multiple, but inter-connected, aspects of dynamics. These tests either relax the constraints on the dynamics imposed by the baseline model or model the baseline model dynamics in a different way. Ultra-flexible dynamic models cannot be the answer to dynamic specification uncertainty. Given limited information in datasets of finite size it is not only highly inefficient but in fact impossible to allow for fully flexible onset, duration, and evolution of effect strengths, let alone heterogeneity in these across units.

13.2 THE MEANING OF "DYNAMICS": A CLASSIFICATION

Dynamics exist in all data-generating processes. That does not mean, though, that all datasets allow the modelling of dynamics. At the very least, a dataset needs to have more than one temporally distinguishable observation per unit of analysis to allow for a dynamic specification. While the real data-generating process nearly always has a dynamic structure, available data and the temporal aggregation of data do not necessarily allow researchers to model and analyze these dynamic processes.

Outside time-series econometrics, which by definition cares about specifying dynamics,[3] social scientists show little interest in modelling dynamics in a complex fashion. Most social scientists seem to be agnostic or uncertain about the dynamic specification of their empirical models and predominantly interested in a simple remedy for the problem of serially correlated residuals.

Researchers need to think about the following specification choices in the modelling of dynamics:

1. Determine the temporal unit (period) of analysis.
2. Determine whether the cause (treatment) resembles an "impulse" or a "process." A cause is best modelled as an impulse if it starts and stops in the same period. A cause should be modelled as a process if the beginning and the end of treatment occur in different periods.
3. Effects can be "immediate," "delayed" or "anticipated." An effect is immediate if and only if it occurs in the same period as the cause. An effect is delayed if it does not occur in the same period as the cause but in later periods. In the social sciences, actors can also anticipate the occurrence of a cause and respond before the cause occurs. Hence, effects can occur in periods before the cause.

---

3 We do not discuss this highly specialized sub-field of empirical analysis here. For textbook-length treatments of time-series econometrics, see Hamilton (1994) and Enders (2008).

4. Similarly to causes, effects too can be like an impulse or a process. An effect is like an impulse if the beginning and end of the effect happen in the same period, whereas an effect is a process if the end is in a later period than the start.
5. If effects are processes, the strength of the effect can evolve over several periods.
6. Any of the dynamic properties of effects can be heterogeneous across units.

Even assuming that the above distinctions are exhaustive, which may not be true, the specification of dynamics can be exceedingly challenging. Of course, not all causes have complicated dynamic effects. However, many causes of interest to social scientists have unknown and potentially non-trivial dynamic effects. The fact that the dynamic specification choices are interdependent exacerbates the challenge of modelling dynamics. For example, the chosen temporal aggregation influences the temporal onset of effects. An effect which seems to be contemporaneous with annual data might well begin with a delay of several periods with monthly or weekly data.

13.3 UNCERTAINTY ABOUT DYNAMIC SPECIFICATION

Temporal aggregation is usually determined outside the researcher's choice, if others decide how frequently data are collected. But even in this case, the researcher can at least aggregate periods into lower frequency than the original data – for example, by averaging data into yearly or quarterly instead of monthly observations.

Collecting data does not solve all problems. Regardless of whether researchers collect and use their own data or secondary data, they often do not know what the optimal temporal aggregation of data is. Many social scientists believe that high-frequency data is superior to low-frequency data. True, ceteris paribus higher-frequency data has more data points and thus more variation. But this advantage may come at a high price: as the number of periods increases, it becomes at the same time more important to model the dynamics of effects appropriately. Having more frequent data can make the "correct" specification of dynamics more difficult and the bias from incorrectly specified dynamics can be larger than that in data with lower frequency. Since effect dynamics can only be specified and modelled relative to the temporal unit of analysis, researchers are uncertain about the optimal temporal aggregation of their data.

Whether causes are of the impulse or process type should in principle be observable. However, the temporal distribution of treatments in general tells us nothing about the onset, duration, and evolution of effect strength over periods. Treatment can be limited to a single period (an impulse), can be repeated over several consecutive periods and either vary in strength (repeated unstable impulses) or not (repeated stable impulses), can be continuous and constant in treatment size (permanent stable treatment) or continuous and varying in treatment size (permanent unstable treatment). Each of these treatment types can occur with an immediate, delayed or anticipated effect of short or long duration and with multiple "temporal functional forms." In contrast, permanent treatments can have quickly vanishing effects or even impulse-type effects.

Thus, researchers are uncertain about the timing of the effect onset even if the specifics of treatment are observable. Human beings are most accustomed to think about effects as occurring more or less immediately after a cause or, given temporal aggregation, contemporaneously with a cause. Inability to directly observe cause–effect relationships triggers the reflex of attributing effects that occur more or less immediately after a perceived cause to the perceived cause, even if this may be erroneous. For example, patients tend to believe that a medication improved their condition, because they have taken it shortly before they noticed improvements, even though in many cases improvements have occurred as a natural response of the human body to the disease.

Effects may take time before they kick in. For example, investments into public education may take decades until they have an effect on economic growth and income inequality. That, conversely, effects can *precede* causes may appear surprising given that generations of scholars have argued that effects temporally follow causes. However, in the social sciences subjects have expectations. They may respond to an expected cause before they or anybody else can observe the cause. As an example, consider a subject who expects a promotion and increases his or her spending in anticipation of it.[4] Game theory and the economic theory of rational expectations provide many more examples of effects pre-dating their causes. Financial market actors may adjust their positions in expectation of a change in monetary policy, investors may shift capital from one currency to another because they anticipate a devaluation, armies may invade another country's territory because the government expects an attack by the other country, and so on.

---

4 One could save the "all effects temporally follow causes" dogma by declaring the expectations to be the cause, but since expectations are unobserved, doing so would prevent us from formulating structural models, posing a great obstacle to our ability to test social science theories.

Since cause–effect relationships cannot be directly observed and instead need to be inferred, researchers are uncertain about the duration of the effect and the evolution of effect strength over several periods. Effects can be limited to a single observed period, they can stretch over many periods, or they can be permanent; and researchers are typically uncertain about which holds. Effects that are limited to one time period are not truly dynamic. They can be fully modelled with a static model, the only question being when the effect sets in, which may require the specification of a certain lag of variable x. Whenever the effect stretches over more than one period, the evolution of effect strength over these periods becomes an issue. For simplicity, researchers like to think about the evolution of effect strength as smoothly decreasing over periods or increasing over periods, and the most commonly used models for dynamic estimation impose smooth functional temporal forms (see appendix 13A). In actual reality the change in effect strength from period to period may be "erratic" with scant resemblance to any smoothly decreasing or increasing effect.

Effects of both short and long duration can exhibit varying effect strengths over time. The Phillips curve (Fisher 1973) provides a good example of an effect of short duration with varying effect strength. Politicians aim to exploit the short-run trade-off between inflation and the unemployment rate, particularly so before elections, if opportunistic theories of monetary policies are correct (Alesina and Rosenthal 1995). As the government manages to trigger an unexpected rise in inflation, the unemployment rate will decline. However, subjects adjust their expectations to the inflationary push quickly. As they do so, the employment effect begins to decline and eventually it will vanish (Nordhaus 1975). A good example of an effect of long duration for which the effect evolves over many periods is the return on investment in university education. As individuals go to university, their income drops relative to subjects who leave school and start working. Yet, once they finish university, they are likely to start with a higher initial salary and, more importantly, receive larger pay rises. As time goes by, the initial income disadvantage disappears and eventually becomes an advantage that has the tendency to grow over time. The treatment "university education" has a long-lasting effect if all goes well.

A related reason for uncertainty about the specificities of effects is heterogeneity in the dynamics of effects across units of analysis. Clearly, individuals have different response functions, different levels of patience, different response thresholds, and often even different response preferences when making decisions. Even if receiving the same treatment at the same time and over the same time period, the effect can have later onset in some cases and earlier onset in others, the effect can be of shorter or longer duration in some cases, and the variation of effect strength can differ over time across cases. Needless to say, social scientists face formidable doubt regarding the modelling of heterogeneity in the dynamics of effects across cases.

Econometric tests may help in specifying models. For example, F-tests and tests based on the Akaike Information Criterion (AIC) or the Bayesian Information Criterion (BIC) can help in testing for lag length and the like, but these inevitably look for the best fit with the given data, not with either theory or the real data-generating process. They do not provide conclusive evidence on which of the models with which exact specification performs best. For example, tests for serial correlation can help in avoiding clearly misspecified models, but the absence of serially correlated residuals does not, in turn, indicate a correctly specified dynamic model.

13.4   TEMPORAL AGGREGATION TESTS

Franzese (1999) and Schmitt (2016) provide examples for how the choice of temporal aggregation can affect the results. Franzese (1999) demonstrates that evidence for an opportunistic business cycle before and after elections depends on a precise modelling of the timing of elections. If scholars merely estimate monetary policy and its consequences in the calendar year in which the elections occur, they will not find a statistically significant result. If, however, scholars consider the exact timing of elections, results become statistically significant. Franzese's analysis pleads for shortening the period under observation.

Schmitt (2016) argues the opposite, namely that periods should become longer, for her particular research question. Specifically, she provides some indication that the effect of political institutions on welfare spending is under-estimated in annual data. Once she switches to a specification in which the units of analysis are cabinets – which normally last for a period of around four years – partisan effects, which tend to be insignificant in annual data, become larger and statistically significant. While the author suggests that misplaced short-termism of annual data causes the difference, we believe that the effect is caused by (a) a delay between treatment (elections) and outcomes (welfare spending) and (b) heterogeneity in the adjustment process across countries. Modelling this adequately in higher-frequency data certainly proves difficult and misspecified dynamics might hide the real effect, which can be recovered in data of lower frequency.

If researchers are uncertain about the optimal temporal aggregation, the *temporal aggregation test* allows them to estimate an alternative to the baseline model with either higher- or lower-frequency data, i.e. shorter or longer temporal units of analysis. Of course, while reducing the number of periods is always possible, an increase in the number of periods will prove impossible if scholars already use the highest frequency that the data allow.

Changing temporal aggregation for robustness testing has to go hand in hand with changes in modelling the dynamics, because all dynamic specification depends on the temporal unit of analysis. For example, the question of lags is closely related to the problem of temporal unit of analysis. The shorter a period becomes, the more difficult does it get to model the lag correctly, the more likely does it become that the correct lag exceeds one period, and the more likely are heterogeneous lag structures across cases.

13.5 ALTERNATIVE DYNAMIC MODEL SPECIFICATION TESTS

Most effects analyzed in the social sciences are dynamic and should not be analyzed by static models. If, however, for some reason a researcher believes that a static model is plausible as the baseline model but uncertain whether a dynamic specification might be more appropriate, they can employ a *dynamic specification test* and employ one or more of the dynamic models discussed in the appendix as a robustness test specification. We stress that dynamic models should only be regarded as a robustness test for static models if researchers believe that the static model is justified as the baseline model and if the dynamic specification is a plausible alternative. This does not seem likely. If the static model is strongly suspected to misrepresent the dynamic structure in the data-generating process, the baseline model has to allow for dynamics. Robustness tests are only informative in the presence of model uncertainty, not in the presence of known model misspecification.

However, researchers may in fact believe the static model to be a plausible choice given the need to simplify, even if there remains evidence of serial correlation in the residuals, which they try to deal with by, say, clustered standard errors at the unit level in the baseline model. With model uncertainty in multiple dimensions, serial correlation does not prove that the dynamics is misspecified. Dynamic misspecification results in serial correlation in the error term, but serial correlation does not conclusively demonstrate dynamic misspecification. To provide examples, functional form misspecification and failure to model heterogeneity or conditionality in trends can produce serially correlated residuals. This in turn implies that there can be uncertainty over whether the baseline model is static or dynamic. Hence, dynamic models can represent a robustness test for a static model.

Dynamic models can be interpreted as more or less constrained variants of the same dynamic hyper-specification, which would be a model with very short periods that allows for separate dynamics for each explanatory variable and includes sufficient lags for each variable to allow for flexible effect onset, duration, and variation in effect strength of each variable over time. Researchers can even allow for flexible heterogeneity in dynamics across cases. The main reasons that nobody estimates such a model are that no theoretical interest in this model exists, too much heterogeneity causes theoretical implausibility, there are insufficient degrees of freedom, and estimates suffer from huge inefficiency due to strong correlations between the regressors. Consequently, the estimation of such a supermodel with finite amounts of data would not be sensible.

As a consequence, any dynamic empirical model will always be a simplification of the true dynamics. Robustness tests can explore whether results are robust toward relaxing one or more of the simplifying assumptions made in the baseline model. Accordingly, the *dynamic constraints test* imposes fewer constraints than the baseline dynamic model. It follows that a finite distributed lag model with a larger number of lags included can function as a robustness test for a baseline model with fewer lags, while an autoregressive distributed lag model can function as a robustness test for both a finite distributed lag model and a lagged dependent variable model without distributed lags. The key is that the robustness test model must allow retrieving the dynamic specification of the baseline model in order to represent a less constrained specification.

In the *alternative dynamic specification test*, researchers model the dynamics differently from the baseline model, rather than relaxing one of the dynamic constraints of the same dynamic modelling specification as in the previous test. For example, instead of relaxing the constraints imposed by the baseline model scholars can employ a different set of constraints in the robustness test model. Even more drastically, they can switch to another type of dynamic model for robustness test purposes. For example, researchers may employ an error correction model as a robustness test for a lagged dependent variable baseline model. Whilst we accept that these model variation robustness tests can make sense in some research designs, analysts have to be careful in replacing a dynamic model specification with an alternative. Dynamic specification can vary largely and effectively test different predictions. Yet, two models that test different predictions cannot serve as robustness tests for each other.

13.6   TESTS FOR ALTERNATIVE EFFECT ONSET, DURATION, AND STRENGTH OVER TIME

By default most researchers assume that effects are contemporaneous, and if the effect does not occur contemporaneously, then the second-best default option relies on lagging the treatment variable by one period, thus delaying effect onset by one period. All deviations from a correct specification bias the estimated effect towards zero.[5] Researchers uncertain about the timing of an effect onset can employ the *effect onset test*, in which they let the effect start with a lag of one or more periods or, if effects might be anticipated, with a lead instead.

In thinking about testing the robustness of results to changes in effect onset, researchers need to keep in mind that the likely duration of effects impacts on the potential bias that results from misspecifying the correct effect onset in the baseline model. If effects are of the impulse type, mistakes in getting the lag structure correct strongly bias the results. In other words, getting the time lag right matters most when the effect is short-lived, in which case, however, one would *not* expect that changes in the lag structure give the same result. If, on the other hand, effects resemble the process type and linger on, a misspecified lag structure usually has a small effect on estimates. This holds especially for long time series and when the stimulus does not occur at the very end.

In the *effect duration test*, researchers change the specified duration that an effect has compared to the baseline model. The modelled duration of an effect can easily be changed in a finite distributed lag model and in the semi-parametric approach presented in appendix 13A. Researchers can test the robustness of the baseline model toward allowing for a longer duration by including further lags into the estimation model. Duration cannot be directly controlled and therefore not easily changed with any model that includes lags of the dependent variable, which comprises all autoregressive distributed lag and error correction models. In these models, the effects of explanatory variables are distributed over time as a function of the estimated coefficients of the lags of the dependent variables.

Finite distributed lag and semi-parametric models allow flexibility in the evolution of an effect's strength over periods, essentially allowing the data to determine the temporal functional form. They can serve as a *temporal functional form test* for baseline models that impose a more rigid temporal functional form. Other dynamic models implicitly impose a specific temporal functional form without researchers being directly able to control or change this form. For example, models with the lagged dependent variable included impose a smoothly increasing effect over time. Another complication is that the modelling of the duration and temporal functional form of an effect are interconnected in many dynamic models. For example, by adding a further lag to a distributed lag model, analysts potentially change the estimate of the temporal functional form. Duration and temporal functional form are best regarded as two dimensions of dynamics changed together in a robustness test.

---

5 First-differencing the data, not uncommon in parts of the social sciences and economics particularly, potentially severely downward biases estimated effect strengths unless the lag structure is correctly specified.

Table 13.1: Effect Onset Test

	m1: baseline (LDV)	m2: LDV and optimized onset	ρ
Spending$_{t-1}$	0.914***	0.861***	0.435
	(0.0240)	(0.0421)	
Left$_t$	−0.00225		
	(0.00204)		
Right$_t$	−0.00416		
	(0.00373)		
Left (best-fit onset)		0.00376	0.194
		(0.00233)	
Right (best-fit onset)		0.00140	0.679
		(0.00378)	
Observations	529	529	
No. of countries	17	17	

Note: Dependent variable is domestic welfare spending as percentage of GDP. Panel-corrected standard errors in parentheses. Coefficients for other variables not reported. Country and year fixed effects included. Model m2 additionally includes country-specific linear year trends. LDV = lagged dependent variable.
Statistically significant ***at 0.01 level.

As an example to illustrate some of the robustness tests discussed in this chapter, we take Garrett and Mitchell's (2001) study of government social welfare spending as a percentage of GDP in 17 OECD countries over the period 1962 to 1993. While Garrett and Mitchell are interested in the effects of numerous regressors, we single out the percentage of cabinet portfolios held by left- and right-wing (predominantly Christian Democrat) parties, respectively. Political science theories tend to predict that left-dominated governments increase welfare spending, whilst right-dominated governments either have no effect or decrease welfare spending. For our robustness analysis we focus on the "left" variable, for which a straightforward theoretical expectation exists. Garrett and Mitchell estimate their model with a lagged dependent variable, country and year fixed effects, and panel-corrected standard errors.

Model m1 in table 13.1, where we report coefficients only for our variables of interest, as good as replicates the first model in table 5 of Garrett and Mitchell (2001).[6] Neither left- nor right-wing governments

6 For reasons we do not understand we cannot exactly replicate Garrett and Mitchell (2001) despite using their dataset. However, the reported coefficients are sufficiently close to the ones published in their article for us to claim "as-good-as" replication.

Table 13.2: Effect Onset Test with Alternative Dynamic Specification Test

	m1: baseline (LDV)	m3: AR1 and optimized onset	ρ	m2: new baseline (LDV and optimized onset)	ρ	m3: AR1 and optimized onset	ρ
Spending$_{t-1}$	0.914*** (0.0240)			0.861*** (0.0421)			
Left$_t$	-0.00225 (0.00204)						
Right$_t$	-0.00416 (0.00373)						
Left (best-fit onset)		0.00776** (0.00328)	0.033	0.00376 (0.00233)		0.00776** (0.00328)	0.565
Right (best-fit onset)		-0.0120* (0.00614)	0.459	0.00140 (0.00378)		-0.0120* (0.00614)	0.165
Observations	529	529		529		529	
Countries	17	17		17		17	

Note: Dependent variable is domestic welfare spending as percentage of GDP. Panel-corrected standard errors in parentheses. Coefficients for other variables not reported. Country and year fixed effects included. Models m2 and m3 additionally include country-specific linear year trends. LDV = lagged dependent variable; AR1 = autoregressive error term of order 1. Statistically signifcant * at 0.1, ** at 0.05, *** at 0.01 level.

have a substantively relevant effect. In fact, the "left" variable turns out "wrongly signed," given that a negative coefficient contradicts the theory. A problem Garrett and Mitchell neglect is caused by the lag between a change in government and the implementation of political reforms. Hence, no new government can change the level and direction of welfare spending on day one in office. In addition, the time between elections and policy reforms starting to show some effects likely varies across countries. With no theory at hand as to how onset might differ across countries, we let R^2 model fit determine the optimal onset for each country chosen from between a contemporaneous effect and a lag of up to three years.[7] Model m2 uses these optimized onset variables with a lagged dependent variable specification, similar to the baseline model. The coefficient of the left-wing government composition variable now switches from being negative. Not surprisingly, given the drastic change in results compared to the baseline model, the estimated degree of short-run effect robustness is low at $\rho = 0.19$.

We next employ a model variation test in that we switch the modelling of dynamics from lagged dependent variable to Prais-Winsten transformation. The "left" variable becomes substantively much larger in model m3, where, instead of the lagged dependent variable specification, we use a Prais-Winsten (autoregressive error term of order 1, AR1) specification with the optimized onset variables (see table 13.2). An additional 10 percentage points of cabinet portfolios held by left-wing parties increases social welfare spending per unit of GDP by 0.78 percentage points. The estimated degree of robustness equals $\rho = 0.03$ compared to the baseline model, but $\rho = 0.57$ if model m2 were the new baseline model.

13.7 DYNAMIC HETEROGENEITY

Practically all dynamic models assume homogeneity across units in the dynamic effect. As always, while convenient, the assumption is unlikely to be a correct specification of the true data-generating process. In order to test the robustness of the baseline model toward allowing for dynamic heterogeneity, researchers can allow one or more of the aspects of effect onset, effect duration or variation of effect strength over time to differ across units of analysis.

For example, heterogeneity of the lag structure is likely. In an early robustness test of Garrett and Mitchell's (2001) study of the effect of party

---

7 To ensure that these optimized onset variables do not spuriously pick up country-specific trends, we additionally include country-specific linear year trends as controls in the models that follow.

composition of governments on government spending, Plümper et al. (2005) demonstrated that the delay between the inauguration of a new government and changes in government spending may depend on the institutional properties of countries – properties that determine the political autonomy of governments. The more veto-players influence the decision-making and policy implementation processes, the longer a new government needs to change the level and structure of government spending. Political scientists should therefore not expect uniform reaction functions of governments in countries with different institutional settings (Döring 1995). As Plümper et al. (2005: 343) put it:

In panel data analyses, the additional difficulty emerges that the correct lag structure can be unit and/or time dependent. Especially in estimating the effect of institutional changes on a dependent variable, lags may seriously differ from country to country. Hence, whenever a research agenda addresses the impact of institutional factors on policies or on social and economic outcomes, researchers should take into account the possibility that lags are not identical across units.

The *random coefficients dynamics test* offers the easiest way to model heterogeneous dynamics. The random coefficient model (Western 1998) allows for a random (normal) distribution of dynamic processes and – while not theory-guided – provides a robustness test for a baseline model that imposes the assumption of homogeneous dynamics on parameter estimates. The *unit-specific dynamics test* is an alternative that fixes the coefficient for each case, while the *group-specific dynamics test* allows for dynamic heterogeneity only between groups of cases. These tests are conducted by interacting the "dynamic specification" of the model with either $n-1$ unit dummies or with $k-1$ group dummies.

For our illustrative example, model m4 allows for some heterogeneity in the explanatory variables by estimating a random coefficient model (see table 13.3). It confirms the finding of a positive effect of left-wing governmental composition on government social welfare spending. The estimated degree of short-run effect robustness equals $\rho = 0.05$ compared to the original baseline model 12.1, but $\rho = 0.97$ in reference to model 12.5. For the long-run effect, these are $\rho = 0.19$ and $\rho = 1$, respectively.[8]

A further robustness test relies on an interaction between the lags of a variable and a substantive variable whose conditioning effect on the dynamic lags can explain heterogeneity in the dynamic effect. Note that this *dynamic interaction effects test* for dynamic heterogeneity may result in unit heterogeneity if the interacting variable is time-invariant, but it could be

---

8 An additional 10 percentage points in left-wing cabinet portfolios increases government spending per unit of GDP by 0.048 percentage points in the short run and by 0.3 percentage points in the long run.

Table 13.3: Effect Onset and Random Coefficients Dynamics Tests

	m1: baseline (LDV)	m4: RCM and optimized onset	ρ	m2: new baseline (LDV and optimized onset)	m4: RCM and optimized onset	ρ
Spending$_{t-1}$	0.914*** (0.0240)	0.837*** (0.0310)	0.167	0.861*** (0.0421)	0.837*** (0.0310)	0.970
Left$_t$	-0.00225 (0.00204)					
Right$_t$	-0.00416 (0.00373)					
Left (best-fit onset)		0.00484** (0.00160)	0.027	0.00376 (0.00233)	0.00484** (0.00160)	0.985
Right (best-fit onset)		0.00187 (0.00277)	0.679	0.00140 (0.00378)	0.00187 (0.00277)	0.992
Observations	529	529		529	529	
Countries	17	17		17	17	

Note: Dependent variable is domestic welfare spending as percentage of GDP. Panel-corrected standard errors in parentheses. Coefficients for other variables not reported. Country and year fixed effects included. Models m2 and m4 additionally include country-specific linear year trends. LDV = lagged dependent variable; RCM = random coefficient model. Statistically significant ** at 0.05, *** at 0.01 level.

a variable that has some variation over time, which would allow for more general heterogeneity in the dynamic effect, not just across units.

CONCLUSION

Effects of interest to social scientists typically follow complex dynamics. Baseline model specifications have to abstract from some if not most of this complexity. Simplifying models are necessary, yet can result in biased results. Specifications of dynamics such as the lagged dependent variable or the Prais-Winsten transformation assume that each explanatory variable has the same dynamic function. For this reason alone, these dynamic specifications are not likely to closely approximate the true data-generating process.

We have suggested that robustness test models relax one or more of the constraints imposed on the specified dynamics in the baseline model. Alternatively, robustness test models can specify dynamics differently from the baseline model, with different constraints or a different type of dynamic model. Researchers can employ tests to explore the robustness of results toward changing the temporal aggregation (the temporal unit of analysis), the onset and duration of effects, and the variation of effect strengths over time, and toward allowing for heterogeneity in any of these dynamics across units of analysis. As always, researchers must be careful not to employ implausible models in robustness tests. For example, models that only allow effects of short duration are simply inappropriate for testing effects that are predicted to be of long duration. Without doubt, finding the optimal baseline dynamic specification poses a great challenge, as does finding appropriate robustness test models.

APPENDIX 13A: A BRIEF SUMMARY OF DYNAMIC MODELLING OPTIONS

In this appendix, we provide a brief overview of some of the commonly used ways of modelling dynamics in linear models. For expositional simplicity, let us assume that there are only two explanatory variables, x and z.

One of the most popular ways of "dealing" with dynamics essentially ignores the dynamics and adjusts standard errors for any serial correlation in the errors that will be the consequence of failing to model any existing dynamics. This results in the following static model specification:

$$y_{it} = \alpha + \beta^1 x_{it} + \beta^2 z_{it} + \varepsilon_{it} \qquad (13A.1)$$

Static models are appropriate for effects that occur immediately and are short-lived – that only have an effect in the period in which they occur – which is why the question of variation of effect strength over time is irrelevant.

Onset in any other time period can simply be modelled by specifying a specific lag or lead, but that does not render a static model dynamic. If the static model does not sufficiently capture the true dynamics contained in the data-generating process, the error term will exhibit serial correlation. The simplest and crudest way of dealing with serial correlation is to cluster standard errors at the unit i level, which allows for unrestricted correlations of errors within clusters (Arellano 1987). This modelling choice is unsatisfactory in many ways. Not only does it fail to take dynamics seriously, it also runs into problems if the number of clusters is not large, which can result in biased standard errors and misleading inferences.

Another approach that treats dynamics as nuisance rather than as something requiring explicit modelling is a model that relegates the dynamics to the error term. This can be done via specifying an otherwise static model with an autoregressive error term of order 1 (AR1) – a model that is typically estimated after a Prais-Winsten transformation of all variables as in:

$$y_{it} - \lambda y_{it-1} = a(1 - \lambda) + \beta^1(x_{it} - \lambda x_{it-1}) + \beta^2(z_{it} - \lambda z_{it-1}) + \eta_{it}$$

$$(13A.2)$$

which shows that, contrary to the static model, some dynamic relationship between x and y and z and y is in fact implicitly estimated.

Probably the most popular way of reducing the nuisance of dynamics is to throw the lagged dependent variable (LDV) into the static model, making it inherently dynamic with a specific dynamic structure:

$$y_{it} = a + \lambda y_{it-1} + \beta^1 x_{it} + \beta^2 z_{it} + \varepsilon_{it} \qquad (13A.3)$$

It is with good reason that we say "throw" the LDV into the static model, because LDV models are often estimated without much thought spent on modelling dynamics. LDV models also impose a specific temporal functional form on the effect that x and z have on y. As long as $\lambda < 1$, it imposes a smoothly decaying marginal effect of x and z on y that converges to 0 after some time period (depending on the magnitude of λ), which implies a smoothly increasing total effect growing, by time T, to $\beta + \lambda\beta + \lambda^2\beta + \lambda^3\beta + ... + \lambda^{T-1}\beta$, or $\beta/(1 - \lambda)$. This equation makes clear why λ has to be smaller than 1, as otherwise the total effect asymptotically grows to infinity as T approaches infinity.[9] Many researchers do not believe

---

9 Yet, a λ close to but smaller than 1 does not render the effect "explosive." For example, with $\beta = 0.5$ and $\lambda = 0.999$, the long-run effect is 500 and not infinity.

that asymptotics in T make sense given the finite nature of everything including the strengths of a dynamic effect. Be that as it may, once we conduct an analysis of a historical process of limited duration λ can obviously exceed 1, because in the short run "explosive processes" do not reach infinity.

Importantly, the long-term effect can be statistically significant even though the immediate or short-run effect is not (Plümper et al. 2005). The standard errors of the short-term effects are simply the standard errors of coefficients in a dynamic model with a lagged dependent variable. See De Boef and Keele (2008: 192) for the computation of the standard error of the long-term effect.[10]

The LDV model thus implicitly models dynamics, but in a peculiar way. In terms of our analytical decomposition, it models dynamics as an effect that starts contemporaneously with the treatment, that is in principle of infinite duration (even if it dies off in the sense that its marginal effect converges to 0 at some point) and that follows the geometric temporal functional form according to the total effect formula listed above. Moreover, while the total effects of different variables will differ, as in general $\beta^1 \neq \beta^2$, the temporal "functional form" imposed is the same for all explanatory variables, as it is dictated by, the estimated coefficient of the LDV.

Whilst it is possible that an LDV model provides a sufficient approximation for the actual dynamics contained in a data-generating process – see Hendry et al. (1984: 1037–1040) for theoretical foundations of these models – the odds that such a model represents a close approximation to the dynamics in the data-generating process are small. For this, we have to turn to models that do not treat dynamics as nuisance, but explicitly try to model it. Before we do so, let us briefly discuss why treating dynamics as nuisance and why the LDV model in particular are so popular. The answer is that treating dynamics as nuisance is easier to apply than modelling dynamics explicitly. Beck and Katz (1995, 1996) primarily deal with panel heteroscedasticity and discuss dynamics on an ad-hoc basis. Nevertheless, their advice of including the LDV in order to purge the data from serial correlation so that the model can be estimated with OLS and panel-corrected standard errors has tempted a large number of empirical researchers, political scientists in particular, into dealing with dynamics via the LDV model.

Applied researchers should keep in mind that "explosive processes" are possible when time series are not infinitely long.

10 In Stata, the *nlcom* command provides a good approximation.

All models reviewed so far face serious constraints. Most importantly, they are either static or allow for only a single type of dynamic process for all independent variables and they do not allow for effects that are strictly only temporary. We therefore now turn to models that model dynamics explicitly rather than treating it as nuisance. We follow De Boef and Keele (2008) and discuss the three most relevant dynamic models: the finite distributed lag model, the autoregressive distributed lag model and the error correction model.

Finite distributed lag models seek to follow the effect of an independent variable on the dependent variable over time. In its general form, the model is specified as

$$y_{it} = a + \sum_{n=a}^{b} \beta^n x_{it-n} + \sum_{m=c}^{d} \beta^n z_{it-m} + \varepsilon_{it} \tag{13A.4}$$

where a determines the onset of the effect that variable x has on y (0 would imply contemporaneous onset) and b determines the number of lags included. These two parameters may or may not differ from c and d, which similarly determine onset and lag structure for the effect of variable z. Finite distributed lag models assume that the effects of explanatory variables dissipate completely in finite time, as modelled by the lag structure. The temporal functional form is determined by the estimated coefficients of the distributed lags. The over-time correlation in many variables limits the number of lags that can usefully be included. Note that researchers should only interpret the overall dynamics and not try to interpret single coefficients of the dynamic specification. However, strongly correlated distributed lags can result in biased coefficients for the individual lag terms, which causes problems for the estimation of effect duration and variation of effect strength over time.

The finite distributed lag model can be combined with the lagged dependent variable plus, potentially, further lags of the dependent variable, making it an *autoregressive distributed lag model*. A commonly used model is:

$$y_{it} = a + \lambda y_{it-1} + \beta^1 x_{it} + \beta^2 x_{it-1} + \beta^3 z_{it} + \beta^4 z_{it-1} + \varepsilon_{it} \tag{13A.5}$$

where the long-run effects of variables x and z are now

$$\frac{(\beta^1 + \beta^2)}{(1 - \lambda)}$$

and

$$\frac{(\beta^3 + \beta^4)}{(1 - \lambda)}$$

Though the autoregressive distributed lag model appears more flexible than the model with only a lagged dependent variable, the long-run effects are similar in their duration and temporal "functional form."

The *error correction model* is an alternative way of explicitly modelling dynamics:

$$\Delta y_{it} = \alpha + \lambda^* y_{it-1} + \beta^{*1} \Delta x_{it} + \beta^{*2} x_{it-1} + \beta^{*3} \Delta z_{it} + \beta^{*4} z_{it-1} + \varepsilon_{it},$$
(13A.6)

where Δ represents the first difference of a variable. By first-differencing the dependent and explanatory variables, this model is suitable for research designs in which there is reason to suspect that some of the effects are non-stationary, but of course only if first-differencing the data allows scholars to test the theoretical predictions.[11] These models assume that the dependent and explanatory variables have a stable equilibrium relationship. In addition, scholars should keep in mind that these models explain not the dynamics in the data, but the deviation from the equilibrium (co-)dynamics.[12]

These dynamic models are flexible. However, they continue to impose a somewhat rigid temporal "functional form" on the effect. A semi-parametric approach can be adopted for modelling flexibly the variation of an effect's strength over time. Assume, for example, that we had reason to believe that the effect of x on y set in one year after a treatment came to an end, that we suspected the effect to last for approximately five years and then terminate, but that we had little idea of the temporal functional form. As an example, assume we wanted to estimate the dynamics of so-called replacement fertility after a genocide. Genocides kill many people and seem to trigger a higher post-genocide fertility rate, but the functional form of replacement fertility remains unknown (Schindler and Brück 2011). The following semi-parametric model provides a flexible way of modelling these kinds of uncertain dynamics:

11 We justifiably say "reason to suspect" since, despite an explosion of research on tests for non-stationarity in cross-sectional time-series or panel data, there does not exist much agreement on which test to use, and different tests often result in opposite conclusions (Baltagi 2008; Breitung and Pesaran 2008).
12 However, the difference between autoregressive distributed lag models and error correction models is merely only apparent, since ADL models can be rewritten as ECMs (Davidson and MacKinnon 2004: 579; De Boef and Keele 2008). ADL models thus also implicitly assume a long-run equilibrium relationship among the dependent and explanatory variables.

$$y_{it} = \alpha + \beta^1 t_{it-1} + \beta^2 t_{it-2} + \beta^3 t_{it-3} + \beta^4 t_{it-4} + \beta^5 t_{it-5} + \beta^6 z_{it} + \varepsilon_{it}$$

$$(13A.7)$$

where the $t_{it-1}\ldots t_{it-5}$ variables are either dummy variables for years 1 to 5 after the "treatment" has taken place, or these variables take on the value of treatment strength that occurred during the treatment event. Naturally, a semi-parametric approach lends itself only to regressors that capture discrete treatment effects, not to variables that are continuously changing over the entire estimation period. But for these discrete treatment effect variables, the semi-parametric approach offers an attractive alternative.

14 Spatial Correlation and Dependence

14.1 INTRODUCTION

Until the beginnings of spatial econometrics some thirty-odd years ago, social scientists assumed that units of analysis were independent of each other. Strictly speaking, the independence assumption has to be wrong. The social sciences come with the "social" adjective for a reason. Almost by definition, the units of analysis in social science research do not act independently of one another: they learn from each other, and – perhaps more often – their preferences, options, and decisions are affected by the outcomes of other actors' behavior.

The learning process on how to account for social interactions in empirical analyses originated in "spatial" econometrics. In its early days, spatial econometrics was "spatial," i.e. geographical in the sense that dependencies between agents were conceived as a function of geographical distance.[1] This logic can be traced back to Tobler's (1970: 236) first "law" of geography, according to which "everything is related to everything else, but near things are more related than distant things."

Modern spatial analysis has moved on. Though geographical proximity and contiguity dominate even where their use as a proxy connectivity variable seems questionable or inappropriate (Neumayer and Plümper 2016a), the recognition that "space is more than geography" (Beck et al. 2006) has gained attention and momentum. Today, few spatial methodologists would disagree with the claim that the *causal mechanism of spatial dependence* operates through the connectivity variable in the form of contact, transactions, interactions, and relations. Inverse distance and proximity may but need not be correlated with the true causal mechanism of spatial dependence and should rarely be considered the mechanism itself.

---

1 Just as the specification of temporal dynamics is a function of the definition of a period, the definition of the unit of analysis exerts a strong influence on the empirical specification of spatial dependence.

Many causes are spatially correlated across units, either because units cluster in certain dimensions (similar culture, customs, preferences, perceptions, constitutions, institutions etc.) or because units experience spatially correlated common shocks. As a caveat to Tobler's first law one can formulate a second law as: "everything resembles everything else, but closer things are more similar." If so, then any omitted variables will result in spatially correlated residuals, while any estimated causal effect might spuriously pick up spatially correlated common shocks.

Similarly to the study of dynamics, there are two main approaches to the study of spatial dependence.[2] One approach treats it as a nuisance to be controlled for or eliminated in a way that does not bias estimated effects of other explanatory variables. A second, entirely different, approach tests theories of spatial dependence and tries to identify the causes for dependence. Rather than a nuisance, spatial dependence lies at the heart of the analysis. This second approach represents greater challenges to researchers. First, the identification of true spatial dependence is occasionally hampered by spatial clustering and unobserved spatial heterogeneity. Second, empirical models of theories of spatial dependence require a weighting matrix that connects units of analysis with each other. The weighting matrix $\mathbf{W}$ needs to adequately capture the causal mechanism of spatial dependence. Third, the specification of $\mathbf{W}$ strongly influences the tested hypothesis. Standard modelling conventions for specifying $\mathbf{W}$ are often at odds with theories of spatial dependence (Neumayer and Plümper 2016a).

For robustness testing, both approaches have their relevance. The likely presence of spatial dependence in the data does not mean that all baseline models have to control for spatial dependence. Readers will be familiar by now with our standard argument that estimation models have to simplify. The most obvious but also the most radical simplification ignores the potential for spatial dependence. Yet, even if researchers adhere to the "spatial dependence as nuisance" approach and ignore potential spatial dependencies, they ought to conduct robustness tests that analyze whether results of the baseline model are robust to allowing for spatial clustering and spatial dependence. In this sense, robustness tests explore whether estimates and inferences change if researchers relax the spatial independence assumption.

By contrast, the "testing causal mechanisms of spatial dependence" approach employs tests exploring the robustness of estimates toward plausible alternative spatial specifications. Given the large leeway researchers

---

2 Spatial dependence is sometimes, explicitly or implicitly, implied by different terms used such as spatial interaction, social interaction, social dependence, diffusion, neighborhood, network, spill-over or peer effects.

have over the specification of spatial models, estimates frequently inspire little confidence. In this sense, robustness tests help in demonstrating that results do not depend on the specification of spatial dependence in the baseline model.

We start by reviewing theories of spatial dependence before suggesting robustness tests for the "spatial dependence as nuisance" and the "testing causal mechanisms of spatial dependence" approaches. In the following, we will refer to spatial-lag, spatial-x, and spatial-error models as well as senders and recipients of a spatial stimulus. Readers unfamiliar with this terminology should read appendix 14A first, which provides a concise overview of models of spatial dependence.

14.2 THEORIES OF SPATIAL DEPENDENCE

Spatial dependence is likely to exist in most phenomena of interest to social scientists because human beings are unlike atoms. They observe each other's behavior and learn from these observations, they seek to maximize their utility function which is influenced by decisions and actions of others, and they are sometimes explicitly targeted by other actors who want to change the former's behavior. Accordingly, there are three main types of theories of spatial dependence: learning-, externality-, and coercion-based theories (Boehmke and Witmer 2004; Neumayer and Plümper 2012).

Learning can be intentional or unintentional, conscious or unconscious. Intentional and conscious learning occurs if actors are not at ease with the outcome of their own behavior and do not know their optimal choice. They observe others, either more successful actors, in order to copy or adopt their behavior, or less successful actors, in order to steer clear of their behavior. At least in principle intentional learning can have subconscious consequences. Learning does not need to be intentional and conscious at all. Actors can also learn from others by merely observing or by interacting with them – and again, they may know or not know that they have learned something.

In contrast to learning, externalities stimulate spatial dependence in ways intended neither by the source nor the target of the dependence (Katz and Shapiro 1985). Tax competition does not occur because one government seeks to reduce the tax revenues of other countries. While tax competition offers the textbook example of negative externalities, spatial externalities need not be detrimental to the receiver. They may be beneficial (Granovetter 1978) or have different effects on different receivers. Externalities occur whenever the behavior of others changes the relative attractiveness of available options for an agent. For example, the choice of a means of transportation undeniably depends on the choices taken by other travelers.

Coercion works by other actors directly or indirectly (via third parties) exerting coercive pressure on agents to change their behavior. Pressure need not work through threats of physical force; it can equally work through economic incentives or disincentives and the manipulation of information. It always presupposes an unequal power relationship between senders and receivers of spatial stimulus. Since these relationships are context-dependent, the likelihood of coercion-based spatial dependence changes with changing contexts. For example, a government may be fairly immune to coercion during normal times but might fall prey to outside pressure in times of severe economic or political crisis.

14.3 SPATIAL DEPENDENCE AS NUISANCE

The main uncertainty for the "spatial dependence as nuisance" approach results from whether spatial patterns in the data are the consequence of spatial dependence or of other model misspecifications. A misspecified functional form of a spatially correlated variable, an omitted spatially correlated variable, an ignored spatially correlated conditionality or simply misspecified dynamics can also cause spatial structure in the errors. If one of these other model misspecifications creates spatial patterns in residuals, then models of spatial dependence may result in more rather than less biased estimates.

Researchers can employ any of the spatial models in a *spatial specification test* for a baseline model that has no spatial component. Moran's I or similar tests can provide evidence on whether robustness tests are likely to be needed.[3] If spatial dependence is of no theoretical interest, the spatial-error model seems superior to the spatial-y and spatial-x models. The spatial-error model does not try to reduce the model misspecification that results from un-modelled spatial dependence. It merely pushes the spatial variation into an uninformative spatial residual variable.

Geographical proximity is typically used as connectivity in the weighting matrix in cases where researchers have no theoretical interest in spatial dependence. This specification seems useful if substantial transaction costs that increase with distance discourage agents from interacting with other agents who are located far away.

If distance is irrelevant for the probability of social interactions, geographical proximity as connectivity in the weighting matrix becomes problematic even for the "spatial dependence as nuisance" approach. For example, the costs of financial transactions are largely independent of distance. The exchange of funds from one currency into another may incur

---

3 Darmofal (2006; 2015) provides an overview of tests.

a fee but, again, this fee is independent of distance. As other examples, interactions may depend on a common language or common regulatory framework. While the probability of a common spoken language is correlated with geographical proximity, the association remains weak for most languages used in more than one country. Countries as distant as the UK, the USA, and Australia speak English as common language, for example. In the absence of theoretical guidance on the connectivity variable researchers can employ multiple potentially plausible connectivity variables.

14.4 SPATIAL DEPENDENCE AS RESEARCH INTEREST

The existence of genuine spatial dependence cannot be inferred from observation alone. In a classic example, it starts raining and someone in the crowd opens their umbrella. Immediately after, a number of other individuals also open their umbrellas. Are these followers spatially dependent on the leader? Or do laggards open their umbrellas because they react to the same common "shock" of the start of rain? When governments all over the world reacted to the world financial crisis of 2007/8 with enhanced financial market regulations, they may have learned from each other or they may have independently come to the conclusion that unregulated finance threatens macroeconomic stability, or both. The observational similarity between the consequences of spatially correlated common trends and shocks on the one hand and the consequences of true spatial dependence on the other is known as Galton's (1889) problem.

Another inferential problem results from the fact that whilst spatial dependence might be present, social science data is often spatially clustered: close units are likely to be more similar than more distant units and consequently most variables used in the social sciences exhibit some spatial correlation. This implies that virtually all model misspecifications will bring about a spatial correlation of residuals. In other words, spatial patterns are likely to result from both the data-generating process and from model misspecification. Accordingly, researchers do not necessarily know whether spatial patterns can be attributed to spatial dependence or to other sources of model misspecification.

In order to deal with the uncertainty over whether true spatial dependence exists, we suggest a set of previously introduced robustness tests. Researchers can vary how they model dynamics, common trends, and common shocks as well as spatial clustering. In time-series cross-sectional data, a stringent specification will include the lagged dependent variable as well as period and unit fixed effects.[4] This specification will shield the

---

4 We are aware that the combination of fixed effects and lagged dependent variable causes Nickell (1981) bias – so that econometric textbooks recommend Arellano-

spatial-effect variable from spuriously picking up the effect of spatially correlated common shocks and trends as well as the confounding effect of spatial clustering in the *level* of the spatial-effect variable (Plümper and Neumayer 2010b).[5] However, spatial clustering in *changes* of the spatial-effect variables may nevertheless result in biased estimates.

A stringent model specification is conservative but potentially problematic and therefore can warrant robustness testing. The lagged dependent variable and period fixed effects can indeed shield the estimates of the spatial-effect variable from being biased if the common trends and shocks are independent of the spatial dependence. Yet, if the common trends and shocks are in part caused by spatial dependence, the stringent specification will bias results in the opposite direction.

Researchers can employ the *groupwise fixed-effects test*, the *between-variation test* or the *correlated artificial variable test*, all introduced in chapter 9 on explanatory and omitted variables, as an alternative to a baseline model specification that includes unit fixed effects. Similarly, they can use the *temporal splines test* from chapter 12 on structural change as an alternative specification to the period fixed effects. Lastly, the *alternative dynamic specification test* from chapter 13 on effect dynamics can substitute for the lagged dependent variable specification.

As an illustrative example, we employ our own analysis of spatial dependence in counter-terrorist policies. Neumayer, Plümper, and Epifanio (2014) argue that the spatial stimulus for counterterrorist policies only stems from other countries that are exposed to a similar level of threat from international terrorism as the country under observation. Countries strongly differ in their propensity to be targeted by international terrorists and governments can safely ignore counterterrorist policies enacted by countries outside their "peer group," but must pay attention to measures undertaken by their peers. We test the theory for a sample of 20 western developed-country democracies over the period 2001 to 2008 with the count of up to 30 potential counterterrorist policies in place as the dependent variable. We use a Poisson estimator with standard errors clustered on countries for which estimated coefficients can be interpreted as semi-elasticities. For this reason, the robustness analysis refers to estimated coefficients.

Bond (1991) or similar models. However, the size of this bias declines sharply with the number of periods. If T exceeds 30, the combination of fixed effects and lagged dependent variables is usually superior to the "consistent" estimation strategy suggested by Arellano and Bond.

5 In dyadic data further controls such as source- and destination-specific fixed effects should be considered (see Neumayer and Plümper 2010).

Model m1 in table 14.1 replicates model 1 of table 3 in Neumayer, Plümper, and Epifanio (2014). Predicted terrorist incidents derived from a theoretically-informed estimation model of terrorist incidents suggests that the 20 western countries group into three clusters: those of low, medium, and high levels of threat from international terrorism.[6] Countries in the same cluster form peers, whereas those outside are called non-peers.

Row-standardized spatial-lag variables are then created based on peer- and non-peer membership.[7] Results from the baseline model suggest that spatial dependence stems only from members of one's peer group, not from countries outside this group. The spatial lag of peer countries is positive and large, whereas the coefficient of the spatial lag of non-peer countries is practically zero.[8]

The baseline model contains a number of control variables, including the initial level of counterterrorist policies in 2000, i.e. before the start of the sample period. But it does not include unit fixed effects, the lagged dependent variable or period fixed effects. Model m2 therefore explores whether the baseline model results are robust toward including unit fixed effects. Since, with fixed effects, the time-invariant initial level of counterterrorist policies drops from the estimation model, we include the lagged dependent variable instead.

The point estimate of the peer-group spatial-lag variable stays almost the same while its standard error more than doubles. The estimated degree of robustness equals $\rho = 0.61$. Model m3 replaces the linear year variable of the baseline model with year fixed effects that account more flexibly for any common trends and shocks. The point estimate goes down and its standard error increases. Not surprisingly, the estimated degree of robustness is relatively low at $\rho = 0.27$.

6 Low category: Austria, Belgium, Canada, Denmark, Finland, Greece, Ireland, New Zealand, Norway, Portugal, Sweden, and Switzerland. Medium category: Australia, France, Germany, Italy, Netherlands, and Spain. High category: UK and USA.
7 We follow Hays and Franzese's (2009) methodological advice for spatial-lag count models and use $\ln(y+1)$ rather than y in the generation of the spatial-lag variables.
8 As with all non-linear models, substantive effects can be expressed in a multitude of ways. Expressed as semi-elasticity, one more policy in the peer group is predicted to increase the count of policies by 76 percent. Given that a percentage increase in policies is not the most intuitive way of interpreting substantive results, as an alternative evaluation of the substantive importance of this variable, holding all other variables at mean values and moving the peer-group-specific spatial-lag variable from its 25th to its 75th percentile value increases the predicted count of counterterrorist policies in place by slightly more than seven policies.

Table 14.1: Spatial Specification Tests

	m1: baseline	m2: unit FE and LDV	ρ	m3: year FE	ρ	m4: unit and year FE and LDV	ρ
Spatial lag (peers)	0.762*** (0.0726)	0.793*** (0.163)	0.609	0.524* (0.306)	0.271	0.0740 (0.363)	0.055
Spatial lag (non-peers)	0.0160 (0.163)	−0.0285 (0.208)	0.867	−0.328 (0.445)	0.410	−1.294** (0.603)	0.047
Policy level in 2000	0.0201*** (0.00735)			0.0164** (0.00822)	0.890		
Policy level (t−1)		0.0116 (0.00965)				0.00494 (0.0106)	
GDP per capita	−0.0181*** (0.00539)	0.0610 (0.0459)	0.042	−0.0171*** (0.00532)	0.949	0.0252 (0.0534)	0.113
% Gov_Left[a]	−0.00188 (0.00150)	−0.00156 (0.00124)	0.979	−0.00127 (0.00163)	0.909	−0.000950 (0.00128)	0.941
% Gov_Right[a]	−0.00108 (0.00154)	−0.00281** (0.00135)	0.830	−0.000860 (0.00153)	0.949	−0.00226 (0.00138)	0.908
International terrorist threat	0.00167*** (0.000246)			0.00190*** (0.000388)	0.709		
Year	0.0312* (0.0190)	−0.0174 (0.0352)	0.367				

Note: Dependent variable is number of counterterrorist policies. Standard errors clustered on countries in parentheses. $N = 160$.
FE = fixed effects; LDV = lagged dependent variable.
Statistically significant * at 0.1, ** at 0.05, *** at 0.01 level.
[a] Percentage of government portfolios held by left- and right-wing parties, respectively.

Table 14.2: Spatial-error Tests

Connectivity for spatial-error component	m1: baseline	m5a: spatial error included contiguity	ρ	m5b: spatial error included inverse distance	ρ	m5c: spatial error included common region	ρ	m5d: spatial error included common language	ρ
Spatial lag (peers)	0.762***	0.702***	0.848	0.674***	0.726	0.767***	0.929	0.662***	0.677
	(0.0726)	(0.0785)		(0.0886)		(0.0787)		(0.0904)	
Spatial lag (non-peers)	0.0160	−0.140	0.785	−0.127	0.820	0.0268	0.900	−0.0799	0.875
	(0.163)	(0.200)		(0.188)		(0.194)		(0.185)	
Spatial error		0.0308**		0.0473***		−0.00241		0.0315**	
		(0.0132)		(0.0166)		(0.0159)		(0.0154)	

Note: Dependent variable is number of counterterrorist policies. Results of control variables not reported. Standard errors clustered on countries in parentheses. $N = 160$.

Statistically significant * at 0.1, ** at 0.05, *** at 0.01 level.

Model m4 combines the previous two models by including unit fixed effects, lagged dependent variable, and year fixed effects. The effect of both spatial-lag variables changes considerably, with the effect that the robustness of these variables declines sharply in comparison to the baseline model and other robustness tests. A likely explanation for this result is the sharp decline in efficiency, which not only increases standard errors but also the influence of random deviations in error processes from the assumed standard normal distributions on point estimates. Moreover, if some of the spatial clustering in the level of counterterrorist policies and some of the common trends and shocks in these policies are due to spatial dependence, then robustness test model m4 will be misspecified.

Even if one knew that true spatial dependence existed, the next uncertainty involves how units spatially depend on each other. At the most fundamental level, the outcome in units could depend on the causes of outcomes in other units (the explanatory variables x) or on the outcomes in other units directly (the dependent variable y). At the observational level, it is difficult to analytically distinguish between the two cases and to disentangle their effects (Gibbons and Overman 2012). In most applications only theory can tell researchers whether outcomes in the receiver depend on the same outcome in sender units or on the causes of outcomes in the sender units. The first mechanism requires a spatial-lag model, the second a spatial-x model.

A concern with the "testing theories of spatial dependence" approach is that the spatial-lag or spatial-x variable might spuriously pick up spatial patterns in the residuals. If baseline models do not yet include a spatial-error term in addition to the spatial-lag or spatial-x variables, researchers can include this term in the *spatial-error test*. Even if the baseline model contains a spatial-error component, researchers can employ different connectivity variables for this component if theory does not clearly suggest a single optimal connectivity variable.

For our illustrative example, models m5a to m5d, reported in table 14.2, add a spatial-error component based on, respectively, geographical contiguity, the inverse of geographical distance, co-location in the same macro region, and sharing the same language as connectivity variable. Three of these spatial-error components are statistically significant with a positive coefficient, but residuals do not seem to be correlated among countries of the same macro region. The estimated degrees of robustness are generally high.

14.5 THE SPECIFICATION OF THE WEIGHTING MATRIX

Even if theory favors a spatial-lag specification over a spatial-x specification, or vice versa, the most challenging uncertainty requires an answer to the question as to how to model connectivity among units. As we have argued above, the specification of the connectivity variable in the weighting matrix models the causal mechanism of spatial dependence. As discussed at greater length in Neumayer and Plümper (2012, 2016a), the modelling choice consists of six dimensions, four of which are most relevant for robustness tests.

First, there is uncertainty over which connectivity variable best captures the causal mechanism through which spatial dependence works. Contact, transactions, interactions, or relations between agents cause spatial dependence. Yet, the variable that best captures the connectivity often remains unclear. And if the "true" connection cannot be measured, measurement uncertainty creeps in and researchers need to find a good proxy for the true connectivity variable. As with all causal mechanisms, the causes of spatial dependence cannot be directly observed. Consider a classical example, spatial dependence in corporate tax rates set by national governments. Tax competition occurs when governments adjust their tax policies in response to (or sometimes in anticipation of) changes in tax policies in other countries to stimulate capital inflows and deter capital outflows. While political economists hardly doubt that a country's choice of tax rate is affected by rates in other countries, they are uncertain about the causal channels through which spatial dependence operates and competing theories postulate different mechanisms (Plümper et al. 2009). Whereas in nonspatial models competing theories can in principle be controlled for, the spatial-effect variables of competing causal mechanisms will be highly correlated with each other rendering it problematic to control for competing causal mechanisms.

If uncertainty about the optimal connectivity variable exists, scholars can use alternative variables for the construction of the spatial-effect variable in the *alternative connectivity test*. This can also be a robustness test for controlling for alternative theories of spatial dependence. For our illustrative example, in model m6 (see table 14.3) we add two further spatial-lag variables to the baseline specification. One uses the Composite Index of National Capability (CINC), taken from the Correlates of War project,[9] as weights. Many researchers use the CINC as proxy for the power of a country. The spatial-lag variable attempts to capture any pressure that more powerful states might exert on other countries to bring their policies more into line with their own. The other additional spatial-lag variable can capture learning effects. Some countries share similar policy cultures and might learn from these policy culture peer groups rather than from peer groups defined according to the level of their exposure to the threat from international terrorism. Accordingly, we created a spatial-lag variable based

9 www.correlatesofwar.org/

Table 14.3: Alternative Connectivity Test	m1: baseline	m6: alternative spatial lags	ρ
Spatial lag (peers)	0.762***	0.459***	0.147
	(0.0726)	(0.154)	
Spatial lag (non-peers)	0.0160	−0.264	0.553
	(0.163)	(0.254)	
Spatial lag (policy culture peers)		0.374**	
		(0.183)	
Spatial lag weighted) (CINC-weighted)		0.773	
		(0.818)	
Policy level in 2000	0.0201***	0.0297***	0.709
	(0.00735)	(0.00865)	
GDP per capita	−0.0181***	−0.0120***	0.846
	(0.00539)	(0.00438)	
% Gov_Left[a]	−0.00188	−0.00147	0.967
	(0.00150)	(0.00132)	
% Gov_Right[a]	−0.00108	−0.00129	0.957
	(0.00154)	(0.00148)	
International terrorist threat	0.00167***	0.00531	0.064
	(0.000246)	(0.00399)	
Year	0.0312*	0.0157	0.874
	(0.0190)	(0.0188)	

Note: Dependent variable is number of counterterrorist policies. Standard errors clustered on countries in parentheses. $N = 160$.
Statistically significant * at 0.1, ** at 0.05, *** at 0.01 level.
[a] Percentage of government portfolios held by left- and right-wing parties, respectively.

on grouping countries into Anglo-Saxon (Australia, Canada, Ireland, New Zealand, United Kingdom, United States), Scandinavian (Denmark, Finland, Norway, Sweden), central continental European (Austria, Belgium, France, Germany, Netherlands, Switzerland), and southern European (Greece, Italy, Portugal, Spain). We find no evidence for pressure as a cause for spatial policy dependence (see table 14.3). The coefficient of the spatial lag based on shared policy culture is positive and relevantly sized, potentially suggesting the existence of learning effects. Apparently, being peers is not independent of shared cultural identity. Therefore, both spatial lags are correlated at $\rho = 0.58$. The point estimate for the peer spatial-lag variable is about 40 percent smaller compared to the baseline model and with a standard error about double its size. Consequently, the estimated degree of robustness is low and equals $\rho = 0.15$.

Second, uncertainty about the specification of the relative relevance of other units may exist. Which other units, if any, exert no spatial stimulus and, for the remaining relevant other units, how quickly does the strength of spatial stimulus decay the more removed other units are? For all non-binary connectivity variables (e.g. contiguity), results can strongly depend on the functional form imposed on the connectivity variable (Plümper and Neumayer 2010b). The *connectivity functional form test* allows scholars to explore whether this is indeed the case. Since functional form transformations such as taking the logarithm of the connectivity variable are often hard to justify theoretically, a semi-parametric approach becomes attractive. Here, analysts divide the connectivity variable into three to five categories of equal width or into percentiles and then create separate spatial-effect variables, one for each category. The semi-parametric approach lets the data determine the functional form of connectivity rather than imposing a specific functional form. Given that the spatial-lag variables in Neumayer, Plümper, and Epifanio (2014) are based on dichotomous peer-group membership, we cannot illustrate the test for our example.

Third, researchers may be uncertain whether units are homogeneously or heterogeneously exposed to the spatial stimulus from other units and, if the latter, what determines heterogeneity in exposure. Standard modelling convention assumes homogeneous exposure by row-standardizing the weighting matrix. This is convenient but typically wrong. Externality-based spatial effects should be experienced more strongly the more exposed recipients are to the flow of capital, goods, services, persons, or pollutants from senders, or whatever else causes the externality. Learning-based spatial effects should be stronger the more intensively recipients interact with those they learn from and possibly also the more actors there are from whom one can learn. Coercion-based spatial effects should be stronger the weaker recipients are relative to senders.

Robustness tests can change assumptions about the exposure of recipients to spatial stimulus. In Neumayer and Plümper (2012, 2016a) we have argued against row-standardizing W, which implicitly imposes the assumption that all recipients are homogeneously exposed to the spatial stimulus from senders. Convenient properties such as matrix non-singularity can be achieved by other matrix normalizations that do not impose the homogeneous exposure assumption and instead allow exposure to be heterogeneous under the assumption that total exposure is the larger the higher is overall connectivity. Those wishing to cling to the row-standardization practice can test the robustness of the homogeneous exposure assumption in their baseline model with the *heterogeneous exposure test*, which interacts the row-standardized spatial-effect variable with a measure of exposure.

Table 14.4: Heterogeneous Exposure Test			
	m1: baseline	m7: heterogeneous exposure	ρ
Spatial lag (peers)	0.762*** (0.0726)		
Spatial lag (peers low exposure)		0.693*** (0.161)	0.581
Spatial lag (peers medium exposure)		0.744*** (0.130)	0.722
Spatial lag (peers high exposure)		1.428*** (0.182)	0.002
Spatial lag (non-peers)	0.0160 (0.163)	−0.0368 (0.160)	0.942
Policy level in 2000	0.0201*** (0.00735)	0.0226*** (0.00707)	0.946
GDP per capita	−0.0181*** (0.00539)	−0.0188*** (0.00545)	0.946
% Gov_Left[a]	−0.00188 (0.00150)	−0.00259 (0.00163)	0.902
% Gov_Right[a]	−0.00108 (0.00154)	−0.00124 (0.00154)	0.949
International terrorist threat	0.00167*** (0.000246)	0.00108*** (0.000302)	0.361
Year	0.0312* (0.0190)	0.0513** (0.0227)	0.770

Note: Dependent variable is number of counterterrorist policies. Standard errors clustered on countries in parentheses. $N = 160$.
Statistically significant * at 0.1, ** at 0.05, *** at 0.01 level.
[a] Percentage of government portfolios held by left- and right-wing parties, respectively.

For our illustrative example, row standardization of the spatial-lag variables seems reasonably justifiable. It should not matter much for countries how many other countries are in their respective peer group, so the average level of policies in the peer groups – this is what the row-standardized spatial lags represent – seems to be the correct operationalization. Nevertheless, allowing the estimated spatial effect to differ across the three groups of countries, namely those with low, those with medium, and those with high exposure to the threat of international terrorism, explores heterogeneity in exposure. Model m7 presents relevant results, reported in table 14.4. Those at low and medium levels of threat have estimated degrees

Table 14.5: Heterogeneous Responsiveness Test

	m1: baseline	m8: heterogeneous responsiveness	ρ
Spatial lag (peers)	0.762***		
	(0.0726)		
Spatial lag (peers) at above group mean		0.625***	0.534
		(0.0643)	
Spatial lag (peers) at below group mean		1.149***	0.001
		(0.0810)	
Below group mean dummy		−1.864***	
		(0.357)	
Spatial lag (non-peers)	0.0160	−0.0770	0.996
	(0.163)	(0.0858)	
Policy level in 2000	0.0201***	0.00781**	0.708
	(0.00735)	(0.00389)	
GDP per capita	−0.0181***	−0.00271	0.014
	(0.00539)	(0.00218)	
% Gov_Left[a]	−0.00188	−0.000701	0.989
	(0.00150)	(0.000769)	
% Gov_Right[a]	−0.00108	−0.000190	0.996
	(0.00154)	(0.000793)	
International terrorist threat	0.00167***	0.000647***	0.000
	(0.000246)	(0.000112)	
Year	0.0312*	0.0271**	0.996
	(0.0190)	(0.0123)	

Note: Dependent variable is number of counterterrorist policies. Standard errors clustered on countries in parentheses. $N = 160$.
 Statistically significant * at 0.1, ** at 0.05, *** at 0.01 level.
[a] Percentage of government portfolios held by left- and right-wing parties, respectively.

of spatial dependence similar to the baseline model, but with higher standard errors, and the estimated degrees of robustness are $\rho = 0.58$ and $\rho = 0.72$, respectively. The estimated degree of spatial dependence increases substantially in the two countries at high levels of threat, however. Not surprisingly, the degree of robustness declines to virtually nil with $\rho = 0.002$ thus casting serious doubts on the baseline model specification of homogeneous exposure.

Fourth, there could be uncertainty over whether recipients respond homogeneously or heterogeneously to any given spatial stimulus by senders and, if the latter, what determines heterogeneity in responsiveness.

Recipients will often differ in their capacity or willingness to respond to or withstand any given spatial stimulus from senders. For example, spatial dependence in policies may depend on a government's accountability, political strength, partisan composition, re-election prospects, constraints on its decision-making, the influence of lobby groups, the state of the economy etc. Where baseline models assume homogeneous responsiveness, researchers can employ the *heterogeneous responsiveness test* (see table 14.5), which allows for heterogeneity by interacting the spatial-effect variable with a measure of responsiveness (Neumayer and Plümper 2012).

For our example, model m8, reported in table 14.5, interacts the peer-specific spatial-lag variable with a dummy variable that equals 1 if a country's counterterrorist regulation falls behind its peers. The estimated degrees of spatial dependence are slightly below the baseline model effect for countries above the group mean and much higher for countries below the group mean. The estimated degrees of robustness are $\rho = 0.53$ and $\rho = 0.001$, respectively. In other words, model m8 rejects the baseline model assumption of homogeneous responsiveness.

As a final robustness test, researchers can generate placebo spatial-effect variables with randomly generated weights. Like other placebo type tests, this *spatial placebo variable test* also requires randomized permutation – here of the weight used in the construction of the spatial-effect variable.

14.6 CONCLUSION

Social scientists are not primarily interested in individual behavior. They are interested in how social interactions shape individual preferences, strategies, and choices. And yet, the nature of regression analysis requires cases to be independent of each other. The development of spatial regression models allows social scientists to overcome the contradiction between the core assumption of social science – that behavior is ultimately influenced by the behavior of other actors – and the core assumption of regression analysis – that observations are independent of each other.

Few empirical analyses control for or test theories of spatial dependence among cases. Social scientists should take spatial dependence more seriously. Where they test theories of spatial dependence, they should employ robustness tests and make plausible changes to the modelling of potentially confounding dynamics, common trends, common shocks, and spatial clustering. Given the over-riding importance of the weighting matrix, robustness tests which change the specification of **W** are even more important. Where researchers have no interest in testing theories of spatial dependence, they should nevertheless control for spatial effects in robustness tests. The lack of theoretical interest in spatial dependence will imply little knowledge about the various causes of spatial dependence. Nevertheless, spatial models can be estimated to explore whether estimated effects crucially depend on the baseline model assumption of no spatial dependence.

APPENDIX 14A: MODELS OF SPATIAL DEPENDENCE

There are three main types of spatial models that can be combined with each other, namely spatial-error, spatial-x, and spatial-lag (spatial autoregressive) models. Using a scalar notation, the spatial-lag model is:

$$y_{it} = \rho \sum_k w_{ikt} y_{kt} + \beta X_{it} + \varepsilon_{it} \qquad (14A.1)$$

where i, $k=1,2, \ldots, N$, $t=1,2, \ldots, T$, y_{it} is the value of the dependent variable in unit i at time t, estimated with a spatially lagged dependent variable $\sum_k w_{ikt} y_{kt}$ (with w_{ikt} the connectivity variable that connects senders of spatial stimulus k to receivers i and $\sum_k w_{ikt}$ therefore the weighting matrix $\mathbf{W}$), X_{it} is a vector of other explanatory variables and ε_{it} is an identically and independently distributed (i.i.d.) error process. Note that the spatial lag might enter the estimation model temporally lagged by one period instead of contemporaneously. The temporally lagged dependent variable as well as period and unit fixed effects might be added. The spatial-lag model is appropriate if and only if the dependent variable in one unit of interest is influenced by the dependent variable in other (but not necessarily all other) units of analysis. Take policies as an example. The policy choice of a jurisdiction (city, state, region or country) in part depends on policy choices taken by other jurisdictions. Spatial-lag variables are typically, though not always, endogenous. They are endogenous if spatial dependence is mutual, that is, if y_i depends on y_k and, vice versa, y_k depends on y_i. Hence, researchers use either spatial instrumental variable or spatial maximum likelihood techniques to estimate spatial models. There are other endogeneity and identification issues in models of spatial dependence that are discussed in detail in Gibbons et al. (2015).

Spatial-x models regress the dependent variable on the (weighted) values of one or more independent explanatory variables (other than the dependent variable) in other units:

$$y_{it} = \alpha + \rho \sum_k w_{ikt} x_{kt} + \beta X_{it} + \varepsilon_{it} \qquad (14A.2)$$

The spatial-x model is appropriate if and only if the dependent variable in one unit of interest is influenced by selected causes of the outcome (the dependent variable) in other units of analysis. For example, election results in one country may affect policy choices in another country. If a hard-liner government is elected in a rival country, another government may decide to increase military spending even though the rival nation does not increase her military spending. Likewise, a country's increase in active labor market spending may stimulate another government to increase interest rates.

Spatial-error models seek to identify spatial dependence in the error term, which is assumed to consist of two parts: the independent and identically distributed spatially uncorrelated component ε_{it}, and the spatial component $\sum_k w_{ikt} u_{kt}$. The model to be estimated is thus:

$$y_{it} = \alpha + \beta X_{it} + \varepsilon_{it} + \rho \sum_k w_{ikt} u_{kt} \qquad (14A.3)$$

Spatial-error models on their own are inappropriate for testing theories of spatial dependence since they relegate the spatial variation to the spatial residual variable instead of testing a specific hypothesis about spatial dependence in the dependent or one or more of the explanatory variables.

The spatial models can be combined with each other. For example, combining the spatial lag with spatial-x results in a model known as the spatial Durbin model. This model will be appropriate if the outcome (dependent variable) in the unit of analysis depends on both outcomes and outcome determinants in other units. Consider tax competition. If a country's capital tax rate is influenced both by capital tax rates in other countries and factors that influence another country's capital tax rate, a spatial Durbin model is appropriate.

Empirically, it is often impossible to identify the correct model of spatial dependence. For example, Gibbons and Overman (2012) show that the spatial-error model can be re-arranged to form a spatial Durbin model, which includes both a spatial-lag and a spatial-x component, and vice versa. The choice of spatial model should be driven by theory.

15 Conclusion

The validity of inferences that researchers make, whether in the natural or in the social sciences, has never been more contested. This has resulted in an outright crisis of science (Nosek et al. 2015). The fact that more and more published articles become retracted is the smallest of problems. There has always been fraud. Quite possibly, the scientific community simply becomes better at detecting it, which would signal progress rather than crisis. In any case, robustness testing cannot prevent fraud. It is no more difficult to blatantly invent or manipulate the results of a robustness test than it is to invent or manipulate the results from a baseline model.

The real problem lies elsewhere: researchers downplay, neglect or outright ignore uncertainty about their model specification, their estimation results, and the potentially imperfect validity of their inferences. The current crisis of science, particularly of the social sciences, results from incentives that force researchers to play a game and to present results, and the inferences based upon them, with greater certainty than could possibly exist given the complexity of social phenomena and the limits of the data we use. Social scientists follow a ritual in which they oversell their own research, but all other social scientists understand that the available evidence is weaker and the validity of the inferences much more uncertain than their proponents suggest. Accordingly, since everyone expects everyone to oversell their research, a more realistic and sincere discussion of findings is self-defeating.

This problem is most severe for those who believe that social science experiments and identification techniques provide a silver bullet for making valid inferences, entirely forgetting that their inferences too depend on a multitude of specification assumptions, many of which are arbitrary. The strength of robustness testing is its universality. There is no research design, method or technique that does not benefit from robustness testing. But failure to recognize or unwillingness to admit the imperfect validity of inferences plague regression analyses of observational data just as much. Robustness testing was invented by regression analysts to improve the validity of inferences based on observational data. If done well, robustness tests explore the stability of estimated effects in the presence of model uncertainty and thereby improve the imperfect validity of inferences.

Often, however, robustness tests are conducted with the intention of demonstrating the robustness of findings. The desired outcome – robustness – drives the robustness testing. The problem – model uncertainty – remains largely ignored. Yet, robustness testing only reduces the problem of model uncertainty if the selection of tests has been made with a serious intention to test and explore (rather than to demonstrate) the robustness of the baseline model's estimates.

What makes us optimistic is that robustness tests are not left to authors alone. The current system for publishing scientific articles and books consists of three groups of stakeholders: the author, who has an interest in publishing but also in gaining a good reputation for herself; the editor and reviewers, who have an interest in publishing interesting research with results and inferences which are valid with a high probability; and the readers and peers of the author who may not only cite (or not cite) a piece of research but who also may replicate the research findings and conduct additional robustness tests if they feel important tests have not been undertaken by the author.

We do not argue that the problem of cherry-picking results – a practice that verges on cheating – does not exist with robustness tests. But the severity of the problem should be reduced if reviewers and editors increasingly demand additional robustness tests from the authors or if it becomes more common in the social sciences to replicate and subject to further robustness testing the findings of important publications. In turn, reviewers, editors, and peers must depart from the silliness of interpreting lack of robustness in one or more dimensions as an indication of a fatal flaw in the research design or as conclusive evidence that a hypothesis has been falsified.

Social scientists should perceive lack of robustness predominantly as uncertainty about findings, and not as a reason to reject a hypothesis or a theory from which it is derived. Robustness tests can foster scientific progress because they provide information on remaining uncertainties of research findings that may help identify important questions, stimulate future research agendas, and pave the way for scientific progress. The most important conclusion that we draw from our book is therefore not that social scientists should conduct more and a greater variety of robustness tests – though this is certainly what we wish to happen. Rather, we hope that reading this book will change social scientists' perception of inconclusiveness and uncertainty. Social scientists should perceive lack of robustness predominantly as uncertainty about findings and inferences, and they should regard this uncertainty as an inevitable fact of a non-degenerate research area.

Moving away from a preference for finding only robust results requires a cultural change. We appreciate such change will not happen overnight. We would go even one step further and argue that the greatest promise for progress in the social sciences comes from analyses that are robust in most dimensions but lack robustness in a few important dimensions. Such analyses have the highest probability of opening up fruitful new research avenues. We are aware that this lack of robustness implies that, potentially, inferences are wrong and that other estimation models or other research designs eventually prove to be superior and arrive at different inferences. Yet, exactly this is scientific progress, while the uncritical concatenation of seemingly all-round robust empirical results is not.

No lunch is free. Robustness testing, carefully undertaken, increases the workload of empirical researchers. Some of the tests we have proposed in this book take a considerable amount of time to conduct. In some cases, additional data need to be selected. We strongly believe that the benefits are worth the costs. There is no better way of improving the validity of causal inferences based on regression analysis of observational data.

References

Achen, Christopher H. 2002. "Toward a new Political Methodology: Microfoundations and ART." *Annual Review of Political Science 5*, no. 1: 423–450.

Ai, Chunrong, and Edward C. Norton. 2003. "Interaction Terms in Logit and Probit Models." *Economics Letters* 80, no. 1: 123–129.

Alesina, Alberto, Silvia Ardagna, and Francesco Trebbi. 2006. *Who Adjusts and When? On the Political Economy of Reforms.* Working Paper no. 12049. National Bureau of Economic Research.

Alesina, Alberto, Arnaud Devleeschauwer, William Easterly, Sergio Kurlat, and Romain Wacziarg. 2003. "Fractionalization." *Journal of Economic Growth* 8, no. 2: 155–194.

Alesina, Alberto, and Allan Drazen. 1991. "Why Are Stabilizations Delayed?" *American Economic Review* 81, no. 5: 1170–1188.

Alesina, Alberto, and Howard Rosenthal. 1995. *Partisan Politics, Divided Government, and the Economy.* Cambridge: Cambridge University Press.

Altmann, Jeanne. 1974. "Observational Study of Behavior: Sampling Methods." *Behaviour* 49, no. 3: 227–266.

Angrist, Joshua D. 2004. "Treatment Effect Heterogeneity in Theory and Practice." *The Economic Journal* 114, no. 494: C52–C83.

Angrist, Joshua D., and Jörn-Steffen Pischke. 2009. *Mostly Harmless Econometrics: An Empiricist's Companion.* Princeton: Princeton University Press.

Arellano, Manuel. 1987. "Estimators." *Oxford Bulletin of Economics and Statistics* 49: 431–434.

Arellano, Manuel, and Stephen Bond. 1991. "Some Tests of Specification for Panel Data: Monte Carlo Evidence and an Application to Employment Equations." *The Review of Economic Studies* 58, no. 2: 277–297.

Bachrach, Peter, and Morton S. Baratz. 1962. "Two Faces of Power." *American Political Science Review* 56, no. 4: 947–952.

Bailey, Michael A. 2005. "Welfare and the Multifaceted Decision to Move." *American Political Science Review* 99, no. 1: 125–135.

Bailey, Michael A., and Forrest Maltzman. 2008. "Does Legal Doctrine Matter? Unpacking Law and Policy Preferences on the US Supreme Court." *American Political Science Review* 102, no. 3: 369–384.

Baldwin, David A. 1995. "Security Studies and the End of the Cold War." *World Politics* 48, no. 1: 117–141.

Baltagi, B., 2008. *Econometric Analysis of Panel Data*. Chichester: Wiley.

Banerjee, Abhijit V. 2007. *Making Aid Work*. Cambridge: MIT Press.

Barrett, Christopher B., and Michael R. Carter. 2010. "The Power and Pitfalls of Experiments in Development Economics: Some Non-random Reflections." *Applied Economic Perspectives and Policy* 32, no. 4: 515–548.

Bartels, Larry M. 1996. "Pooling Disparate Observations." *American Journal of Political Science* 40, no. 3: 905–942.

Baum, J. Robert, and Edwin A. Locke. 2004. "The Relationship of Entrepreneurial Traits, Skill, and Motivation to Subsequent Venture Growth." *Journal of Applied Psychology* 89, no. 4: 587.

Beardsley, Kyle, and Victor Asal. 2009. "Winning with the Bomb." *Journal of Conflict Resolution* 53, no. 2: 278–301.

Bechtel, M. M., and G. Schneider. 2010. "Eliciting Substance from 'Hot Air': Financial Market Responses to EU Summit Decisions on European Defense." *International Organization* 64, no. 2: 199–223.

Beck, Nathaniel, Kristian Skrede Gleditsch, and Kyle Beardsley. 2006. "Space is More than Geography: Using Spatial Econometrics in the Study of Political Economy." *International Studies Quarterly* 50, no. 1: 27–44.

Beck, Nathaniel, and Simon Jackman. 1998. "Beyond Linearity by Default: Generalized Additive Models." *American Journal of Political Science* 42, no. 2: 596.

Beck, Nathaniel, and Jonathan N. Katz. 1995. "What To Do (and Not To Do) with Time-series Cross-section Data." *American Political Science Review* 89, no. 3: 634–647.

Beck, Nathaniel, and Jonathan N. Katz. 1996. "Nuisance vs. Substance: Specifying and Estimating Time-Series-Cross-Section Models." *Political Analysis* 6: 1–36.

Beck, Nathaniel, and Jonathan N. Katz. 2007. "Random Coefficient Models for Time-Series – Cross-Section Data: Monte Carlo Experiments." *Political Analysis* 15, no. 2: 182–195.

Belsley, David A., Edwin Kuh, and Roy E. Welsch. 1980. *Regression Diagnostics: Identifying Influential Data and Sources of Collinearity*. Chichester: Wiley.

Ben-David, Dan, Robin L. Lumsdaine, and David H. Papell. 2003. "Unit Roots, Postwar Slowdowns and Long-run Growth: Evidence from Two Structural Breaks." *Empirical Economics* 28, no. 2: 303–319.

Berk, Richard A. 1983. "An Introduction to Sample Selection Bias in Sociological Data." *American Sociological Review* 48, no. 3: 386–398.

Berry, William D., Jacqueline H. R. DeMeritt, and Justin Esarey. 2010. "Testing for Interaction in Binary Logit and Probit Models: Is a Product Term Essential?" *American Journal of Political Science* 54, no. 1: 248–266.

Besley, Timothy, and Marta Reynal-Querol. 2011. "Do Democracies Select more Educated Leaders?" *American Political Science Review* 105, no. 3 (2011): 552–566.

Bigsten, Arne. 2013. *Globalization and Development: Rethinking Interventions and Governance*. London and New York: Routledge.

Blalock, H. M. 1964. *Causal Inferences in Nonexperimental Research*. Chapel Hill: University of North Carolina Press.

Boehmke, Frederick J. 2003. "Using Auxiliary Data to Estimate Selection Bias Models, with an Application to Interest Group Use of the Direct Initiative Process." *Political Analysis* 11, no. 3: 234–254.

Boehmke, Frederick J., Daniel S. Morey, and Megan Shannon. 2006. "Selection Bias and Continuous-Time Duration Models: Consequences and a Proposed Solution." *American Journal of Political Science* 50, no. 1: 192–207.

Boehmke, Frederick J., and Richard Witmer. 2004. "Disentangling Diffusion: The Effects of Social Learning and Economic Competition on State Policy Innovation and Expansion." *Political Research Quarterly* 57, no. 1: 39–51.

Böhm, K., A. Schmid, R. Götze, C. Landwehr, and H. Rothgang. 2013. "Five Types of OECD Healthcare Systems: Empirical Results of a Deductive Classification." *Health Policy* 113, no. 3: 258–269.

Boix, Carles. 2011. "Democracy, Development, and the International System." *American Political Science Review* 105, no. 4: 809–828.

Bollen, Kenneth A. 1989. *Introduction to Structural Equation Models with Latent Variables*. New York: Wiley.

Bound, John, Charles Brown, and Nancy Mathiowetz. 2001. "Measurement Error in Survey Data." *Handbook of Econometrics* 5: 3705–3843.

Box, George E. P. 1976. "Science and Statistics." *Journal of the American Statistical Association* 71, no. 356: 791–799.

Box, George E. P., and Norman Richard Draper. 1987. *Empirical Model-building and Response Surfaces*. New York: Wiley.

Bracht, Glenn H., and Gene V. Glass. 1968. "The External Validity of Experiments." *American Educational Research Journal* 5, no. 4: 437–474.

Brambor, Thomas, William Roberts Clark, and Matt Golder. 2006. "Understanding Interaction Models: Improving Empirical Analyses." *Political Analysis* 14, no. 1: 63–82.

Brand, Jennie E., and Juli Simon Thomas. 2013. "Causal Effect Heterogeneity." In Stephen L. Morgan (ed.), *Handbook of Causal Analysis for Social Research*, pp. 189–213. Dordrecht: Springer Netherlands.

Braumoeller, Bear F. 2008. "Systemic Politics and the Origins of Great Power Conflict." *American Political Science Review* 102, no. 1: 77–93.

Breen, R. 1996. *Regression Models: Censored, Sample Selected, or Truncated Data*. Vancouver: Sage.

Breitung, J., and M. H. Pesaran. 2008. "Unit Roots and Cointegration in Panels." In László Mátyás and Patrick Sevestre (eds.), *The Econometrics of Panel Data*, pp. 279–322. Berlin: Springer.

Brillinger, David R. 2002. "John W. Tukey's Work on Time Series and Spectrum Analysis". *The Annals of Statistics* 30, no. 6: 1535–1575.

Budge, Ian. 2001. *Mapping Policy Preferences: Estimates for Parties, Electors, and Governments, 1945–1998*. Oxford: Oxford University Press.

Bueno de Mesquita, Bruce, and Alastair Smith. 2005. *The Logic of Political Survival*. Cambridge: MIT Press.

Caliendo, Marco, and Reinhard Hujer. 2006. "The Microeconometric Estimation of Treatment Effects – An Overview." *Allgemeines Statistisches Archiv* 90, no. 1: 199–215.

Calmfors, Lars, and John Driffill. 1988. "Centralization of Wage Bargaining." *Economic Policy* 6, no. 1: 14–61.

Cameron, A. Colin, and Pravin K. Trivedi. 2010. *Microeconometrics Using Stata*. College Station: Stata.

Campos, Julia, Neil R. Ericsson, and David F. Hendry. 2005. *General-to-specific Modeling: An Overview and Selected Bibliography*. International Finance Discussion Papers No. 838. Board of Governors of the Federal Reserve System.

Carey, John M., and Simon Hix. 2011. "The Electoral Sweet Spot: Low-Magnitude Proportional Electoral Systems." *American Journal of Political Science* 55, no. 2: 383–397.

Carroll, R. J., D. Ruppert, and L. A. Stefanski. 1995. *Nonlinear Measurement Error Models. Monographs on Statistics and Applied Probability*. New York: Chapman and Hall.

Cartwright, Nancy. 2010. "What are Randomised Controlled Trials Good for?" *Philosophical Studies* 147, no. 1: 59–70.

Cartwright, Nancy, and Jeremy Hardie. 2012. *Evidence-based Policy: A Practical Guide to Doing it Better*. Oxford: Oxford University Press.

Castles, Francis G., and Peter Mair. 1984. "Left–right Political Scales: Some 'Expert' Judgements." *European Journal of Political Research* 12, no. 1: 73–88.

Cederman, Lars-Erik, Halvard Buhaug, and Jan Ketil Rød. 2009. "Ethno-nationalist Dyads and Civil War: A GIS-based Analysis." *Journal of Conflict Resolution* 53, no. 4: 496–525.

Cheibub, José Antonio, Jennifer Gandhi, and James Raymond Vreeland. 2010. "Democracy and Dictatorship Revisited." *Public Choice* 143, no. 1–2: 67–101.

Chow, Gregory C. 1960. "Tests of Equality between Sets of Coefficients in Two Linear Regressions." *Econometrica* 28: 591–605.

Claeskens, Gerda, and Nils Lid Hjort. 2008. *Model Selection and Model Averaging.* Cambridge: Cambridge University Press.

Clarke, Kevin A. 2005. "The Phantom Menace: Omitted Variable Bias in Econometric Research." *Conflict Management and Peace Science* 22, no. 4: 341–352.

Clarke, Kevin A., and David M. Primo. 2012. *A Model Discipline. Political Science and the Logic of Representations.* Oxford: Oxford University Press.

Cobb-Clark, Deborah A., and Thomas Crossley. 2003. "Econometrics for Evaluations: An Introduction to Recent Developments." *Economic Record* 79, no. 247: 491–511.

Cornfield, J., W. Haenszel, E. C. Hammond, A. M. Lilienfeld, M. B. Shimkin, and E. L. Wynder. 1959. "Smoking and Lung Cancer: Recent Evidence and a Discussion of Some Questions." *Journal of the National Cancer Institute* 22: 173–203.

Cronbach, Lee J. 1982. "In Praise of Uncertainty." *New Directions for Evaluation* 15: 49–58.

Cronbach, Lee J., and Karen Shapiro. 1982. *Designing Evaluations of Educational and Social Programs.* San Francisco: Jossey-Bass.

Cumming, Geoff. 2012. *Understanding the New Statistics: Effect Sizes, Confidence Intervals, and Meta-Analysis.* New York: Routledge.

Darmofal, David. 2006. *Spatial Econometrics and Political Science.* Society for Political Methodology Working Paper Archive: http://localgov.fsu.edu/readings_papers/Research%20Methods/Darmofal_Spatial%20Econometrics%2013%20ps.Pdf (last access 3 April 2017).

Darmofal, David. 2015. *Spatial Analysis for the Social Sciences.* Cambridge: Cambridge University Press.

Davidov, Eldad, Bart Meuleman, Jan Cieciuch, Peter Schmidt, and Jaak Billiet. 2014. "Measurement Equivalence in Cross-national Research." *Annual Review of Sociology* 40: 55–75.

Davidson, R., and J. G. MacKinnon, 2004. *Econometric Theory and Methods.* New York: Oxford University Press.

Davidsson, Per, and Frederic Delmar. 2012. "Dealing with Heterogeneity Problems and Causal Effect Estimation in Entrepreneurship Research." Unpublished working paper.

Davies, James C. 1962. "Toward a Theory of Revolution." *American Sociological Review* 27, no. 1: 5–19.

De Boef, Suzanna, and Luke Keele. 2008. "Taking Time Seriously." *American Journal of Political Science* 52, no. 1: 184–200.

Deaton, Angus. 2010, "Instruments, Randomization, and Learning about Development." *Journal of Economic Literature* 48, no. 2: 424–455.

DeBell, Matthew. 2013. "Harder than it Looks: Coding Political Knowledge on the ANES." *Political Analysis* 21, no. 4: 393–406.

Doering, Holger. 1995. *Parliaments and Majority Rule in Western Europe.* Frankfurt: Campus.

Duhem, P. M. M. 1954 [1906]. *La Théorie physique: son objet, sa structure. The Aim and Structure of Physical Theory.* Translated by Philip P. Wiener. Princeton: Princeton University Press.

Duncan, Otis Dudley. 1975. *Introduction to Structural Equation Models.* New York: Academic Press.

Editors. 2015. "Editorial Statement on Negative Findings." *Health Economics* 24: 505.

Efron, Bradley. 1979. "Bootstrap Methods: Another Look at the Jackknife." *The Annals of Statistics* 7, no. 1: 1–26.

Efron, Bradley, and Gail Gong. 1983. "A Leisurely Look at the Bootstrap, the Jackknife, and Cross-validation." *The American Statistician* 37, no. 1: 36–48.

Egorov, Georgy, Sergei Guriev, and Konstantin Sonin. 2009. "Why Resource-poor Dictators Allow Freer Media: A Theory and Evidence from Panel Data." *American Political Science Review* 103, no. 4: 645–668.

Enders, Walter, and Todd Sandler. 2005. "After 9/11 Is It All Different Now?" *Journal of Conflict Resolution* 49, no. 2: 259–277.

Enders, Walter. 2008. *Applied Econometric Time Series.* Chichester: Wiley.

Esarey, J., and N. Danneman. 2015. "A Quantitative Method for Substantive Robustness Assessment." *Political Science Research and Methods* 3, no. 1: 95–111.

Evans, Geoffrey. 1998. "On Tests of Validity and Social Class: Why Prandy and Blackburn are Wrong." *Sociology* 32, no. 1: 189–202.

Falbo, Toni. 1977. "Multidimensional Scaling of Power Strategies." *Journal of Personality and Social Psychology* 35, no. 8: 537–547.

Falk, Armin, and James J. Heckman. 2009. "Lab Experiments are a Major Source of Knowledge in the Social Sciences." *Science* 326, no. 5952: 535–538.

Fearon, James D. 2003. "Ethnic and Cultural Diversity by Country." *Journal of Economic Growth* 8, no. 2: 195–222.

Fearon, James D., and David D. Laitin. 2003. "Ethnicity, Insurgency, and Civil War." *American Political Science Review* 97, no. 1: 75–90.

Feld, Lars P., and Marcel R. Savioz. 1997. "Direct Democracy Matters for Economic Performance: An Empirical Investigation." *Kyklos* 50, no. 4: 507–538.

Feldstein, Martin. 1982. "Inflation, Tax Rules and Investment: Some Econometric Evidence." *Econometrica* 41: 825–862.

Fernandez, Raquel, and Dani Rodrik. 1991. "Resistance to Reform: Status Quo Bias in the Presence of Individual-Specific Uncertainty". *American Economic Review* 81, no. 5: 1146–1155.

Fisher, Irving. 1973. "I Discovered the Phillips Curve: 'A Statistical Relation between Unemployment and Price Changes'". *Journal of Political Economy* 81, no. 2, Part 1: 496–502.

Fisher, Ronald A. 1925. *Statistical Methods for Research Workers.* Edinburgh: Oliver and Boyd.

Fisher, Ronald A. 1958. "Cancer and Smoking." *Nature* 182, no. 4635: 596.

Fisher, Ronald A. 1966. *The Design of Experiments.* New York: Hafner.

Folke, Olle, Shigeo Hirano, and James M. Snyder. 2011. "Patronage and Elections in US States." *American Political Science Review* 105, no. 3: 567–585.

Fox, John. 1991. *Regression Diagnostics: An Introduction.* London: Sage.

Frank, Kenneth A. 2000. "Impact of a Confounding Variable on a Regression Coefficient." *Sociological Methods and Research* 29, no. 2: 147–194.

Frank, Kenneth, and Kyung-Seok Min. 2007. "Indices of Robustness for Sample Representation." *Sociological Methodology* 37, no. 1: 349–392.

Franzese, Robert J. 1999. "Partially Independent Central Banks, Politically Responsive Governments, and Inflation." *American Journal of Political Science* 43: 681–706.

Franzese, Robert J. 2003. "Multiple Hands on the Wheel: Empirically Modeling Partial Delegation and Shared Policy Control in the Open and Institutionalized Economy." *Political Analysis* 11, no. 4: 445–474.

Freedman, David A. 1991. "Statistical Models and Shoe Leather." *Sociological Methodology* 21, no. 2: 291–313.

Freedman, David A. 2009. "Diagnostics Cannot have Much Power against General Alternatives." *International Journal of Forecasting* 25, no. 4: 833–839.

Freedom House. 2013. *Freedom in the World 2013.* https://freedomhouse.org/

Galton, Francis. 1889. "Personal Identification and Description." *Journal of Anthropological Institute of Great Britain and Ireland* 18: 177–191.

Ganzach, Yoav. 1997. "Misleading Interaction and Curvilinear Terms." *Psychological Methods* 2, no. 3: 235.

Ganzach, Yoav. 1998. "Nonlinearity, Multicollinearity and the Probability of Type II Error in Detecting Interaction." *Journal of Management* 24, no. 5: 615–622.

Garrett, Geoffrey, and Deborah Mitchell. 2001. "Globalization, Government Spending and Taxation in the OECD." *European Journal of Political Research* 39, no. 2: 145–177.

Gehlbach, Scott, Konstantin Sonin, and Ekaterina Zhuravskaya. 2010. "Businessman Candidates." *American Journal of Political Science* 54, no. 3: 718–736.

Gelman, A., and H. Stern. 2006. "The Difference between 'Significant' and 'Not Significant' is Not Itself Statistically Significant." *The American Statistician* 60, no. 4: 328–331.

Gerber, Alan S., and Gregory A. Huber. 2009. "Partisanship and Economic Behavior: Do Partisan Differences in Economic Forecasts Predict Real Economic Behavior?" *American Political Science Review* 103, no. 3: 407–426.

Gerber, Alan S., and Gregory A. Huber. 2010. "Partisanship, Political Control, and Economic Assessments." *American Journal of Political Science* 54, no. 1: 153–173.

Gibbons, Stephen, Eric Neumayer, and Richard Perkins. 2015. "Student Satisfaction, League Tables and University Applications: Evidence from Britain." *Economics of Education Review* 48: 148–164.

Gibbons, Stephen, and Henry G. Overman. 2012. "Mostly Pointless Spatial Econometrics?" *Journal of Regional Science* 52, no. 2: 172–191.

Gibler, Douglas M., and Jaroslav Tir. 2010. "Settled Borders and Regime Type: Democratic Transitions as Consequences of Peaceful Territorial Transfers." *American Journal of Political Science* 54, no. 4: 951–968.

Gill, Jeff. 1999. "The Insignificance of Null Hypothesis Significance Testing." *Political Research Quarterly* 52, no. 3: 647–674.

Gleditsch, Kristian S., and Michael D. Ward. 1997. "Double Take a Reexamination of Democracy and Autocracy in Modern Polities." *Journal of Conflict Resolution* 41, no. 3: 361–383.

Goodman, S. N. 1992. "A Comment on Replication, p-values and Evidence." *Statistics in Medicine* 11, no. 7: 875–879.

Granger, Clive W. J. 1996. "Can we Improve the Perceived Quality of Economic Forecasts?" *Journal of Applied Econometrics* 11, no. 5: 455–473.

Granovetter, Mark. 1978. "Threshold Models of Collective Behavior." *American Journal of Sociology* 83, no. 6: 1420–1443.

Griliches, Z., and W. M. Mason. 1972. "Education, Income, and Ability." *Journal of Political Economy* 80, no. 3: S74–S103.

Gross, J. H. 2015. "Testing What Matters (If You Must Test at All): A Context-Driven Approach to Substantive and Statistical Significance." *American Journal of Political Science* 59, no. 3: 775–788.

Grossman, G., and A. Krueger. 1995. "Economic Environment and the Economic Growth." *Quarterly Journal of Economics* 110, no. 2: 353–377.

Hafner-Burton, Emilie M., Laurence R. Helfer, and Christopher J. Fariss. 2011. "Emergency and Escape: Explaining Derogations from Human Rights Treaties." *International Organization* 65, no. 4: 673–707.

Hainmueller, Jens, and Dominik Hangartner. 2013. "Who gets a Swiss Passport? A Natural Experiment in Immigrant Discrimination." *American Political Science Review* 107, no. 1: 159–187.

Hamilton, James D. 1994. *Time Series Analysis*. Princeton: Princeton University Press.

Hamilton, James D. 2003. "What is an Oil Shock?" *Journal of Econometrics* 113, no. 2: 363–398.

Hammond, E. C., 1964. "Smoking in Relation to Mortality and Morbidity. Findings in First Thirty-four Months of Follow-up in a Prospective Study Started in 1959." *Journal of the National Cancer Institute* 32, no. 5: 1161–1188.

Hanmer, Michael J., and Kerem Ozan Kalkan. 2013. "Behind the Curve: Clarifying the Best Approach to Calculating Predicted Probabilities and Marginal Effects from Limited Dependent Variable Models." *American Journal of Political Science* 57, no. 1: 263–277.

Hansen, Bruce E. 1996. "Methodology: Alchemy or Science: Review Article." *Economic Journal* 106, no. 438: 1398–1413.

Hays, Jude C., and Robert J. Franzese. 2009. "A Comparison of the Small-sample Properties of Several Estimators for Spatial-lag Count Models." Unpublished working paper, University of Illinois Champaign-Urbana.

Heckman, James J. 1979. "Sample Selection Bias as a Specification Error." *Econometrica* 47, no. 1: 153–161.

Heckman, James J. 1990. "Varieties of Selection Bias." *American Economic Review* 80, no. 2: 313–318.

Heckman, James J. 2005. "The Scientific Model of Causality." *Sociological Methodology* 35, no. 1: 1–97.

Heckman, James J., Jeffrey Smith, and Nancy Clements. 1997. "Making the Most out of Programme Evaluations and Social Experiments:

Accounting for Heterogeneity in Programme Impacts." *The Review of Economic Studies* 64, no. 4: 487–535.

Heckman, James J., Sergio Urzua, and Edward Vytlacil. 2006. "Understanding Instrumental Variables in Models with Essential Heterogeneity." *The Review of Economics and Statistics* 88, no. 3: 389–432.

Heckman, James, and Edward Vytlacil. 2005. "Structural Equations, Treatment, Effects and Econometric Policy Evaluation." *Econometrica* 73, no. 3: 669–738.

Helm, David T. 2000. "The Measurement of Happiness." *American Journal on Mental Retardation* 105, no. 5: 326–335.

Hendry, David F. 2002. "Applied Econometrics without Sinning." *Journal of Economic Surveys* 16, no. 4: 591–604.

Hendry, David F., and Hans-Martin Krolzig. 2005. "The Properties of Automatic GETS Modelling." *The Economic Journal* 115, no. 502: C32–C61.

Hendry, David F., A. R. Pagan, and J. D. Sargan. 1984. "Dynamic specification." *Handbook of Econometrics* 2: 1023–1100.

Hilbe, Joseph M. 2011. *Negative Binomial Regression.* Cambridge: Cambridge University Press.

Hills, Peter, and Michael Argyle. 2002. "The Oxford Happiness Questionnaire: A Compact Scale for the Measurement of Psychological Well-being." *Personality and Individual Differences* 33, no. 7: 1073–1082.

Ho, D. E., K. Imai, G. King, and E. A. Stuart. 2007. "Matching as Nonparametric Preprocessing for Reducing Model Dependence in Parametric Causal Inference." *Political Analysis* 15, no. 3: 199–236.

Hoeting, Jennifer A., David Madigan, Adrian E. Raftery, and Chris T. Volinsky. 1999. "Bayesian Model Averaging: A Tutorial." *Statistical Science* 14, no. 4: 382–401.

Hogan, Michael J. 1992. *The End of the Cold War: Its Meaning and Implications.* Cambridge: Cambridge University Press.

Holland, Paul W. 1986. "Statistics and Causal Inference." *Journal of the American Statistical Association* 81, no. 396: 945–960.

Honaker, James, and Gary King. 2010. "What to do about Missing Values in Time-series Cross-section Data." *American Journal of Political Science* 54, no. 2: 561–581.

Hoover, Kevin D., and Stephen J. Perez. 1999. "Data Mining Reconsidered: Encompassing and the General-to-specific Approach to Specification Search." *The Econometrics Journal* 2, no. 2: 167–191.

Hoover, Kevin D., and Stephen J. Perez. 2004. "Truth and Robustness in Cross-country Growth Regressions." *Oxford Bulletin of Economics and Statistics* 66, no. 5: 765–798.

Høyland, Bjørn, Karl Moene, and Fredrik Willumsen. 2012. "The Tyranny of International Index Rankings." *Journal of Development Economics* 97, no. 1: 1–14.

Hsee, Christopher K., and Judy Ningyu Tang. 2007. "Sun and Water: On a Modulus-based Measurement of Happiness." *Emotion* 7, no. 1: 213–218.

Hsiao, Cheng. 2003. *Analysis of Panel Data*. Cambridge: Cambridge University Press.

Hsiao, Cheng, Dean C. Mountain, M. W. Luke Chan, and Kai Y. Tsui. 1989. "Modeling Ontario Regional Electricity System Demand Using a Mixed Fixed and Random Coefficients Approach." *Regional Science and Urban Economics* 19, no. 4: 565–587.

Hsiao, Cheng, and M. Hashem Pesaran. 2004. *Random Coefficient Panel Data Models*. Paper No. 4.2. Institute of Economic Policy Research (IEPR).

Hsiao, Cheng, and M. Hashem Pesaran. 2008. "Random Coefficient Models." In László Mátyás and Patrick Sevestre (eds.), *The Econometrics of Panel Data*, pp. 185–213. Berlin: Springer.

Hug, Simon. 2003. "Selection Bias in Comparative Research: The Case of Incomplete Data Sets." *Political Analysis* 11, no. 3: 255–274.

Huntington, Samuel P. 1996. *The Clash of Civilizations and the Remaking of World Order*. New York: Simon and Schuster.

Imai, Kosuke, Luke Keele, Dustin Tingley, and Teppei Yamamoto. 2011. "Unpacking the Black Box of Causality: Learning about Causal Mechanisms from Experimental and Observational Studies." *American Political Science Review* 105, no. 4: 765–789.

Imai, Kosuke, Gary King, and Elizabeth A. Stuart. 2008. "Misunderstandings between Experimentalists and Observationalists about Causal Inference." *Journal of the Royal Statistical Society: Series A (Statistics in Society)* 171, no. 2: 481–502.

Imbens, Guido W. 2010. "Better LATE than Nothing." *Journal of Economic Literature* 48: 399–423.

Jaccard, James, and Robert Turrisi. 2003. *Interaction Effects in Multiple Regression*. Thousand Oaks, London, New Delhi: Sage.

Jackman, Simon. 1999. "Correcting Surveys for Non-response and Measurement Error using Auxiliary Information." *Electoral Studies* 18, no. 1: 7–27.

Jaggers, Keith, and Monty Marshall. 2007. *Polity IV Project: Political Regime Characteristics and Transitions, 1800–2007. Database Codebook*. Center for Systemic Peace. http://www.systemicpeace.org/ (last access 3 April 2017).

Kam, Cindy, and Robert J. Franzese. 2009. *Modeling and Interpreting Interactive Hypotheses in Regression Analysis*. Ann Arbor: University of Michigan Press.

Kammann, Richard, Marcelle Farry, and Peter Herbison. 1984. "The Analysis and Measurement of Happiness as a Sense of Well-being." *Social Indicators Research* 15, no. 2: 91–115.

Katz, Michael L., and Carl Shapiro. 1985. "Network Externalities, Competition, and Compatibility." *American Economic Review* 75, no. 3: 424–440.

Kaufman, D., A. Kraay, and M. Mastruzzi. 2010. *The Worldwide Governance Indicators: Methodology and Analysis*. Working Paper no. 5430. World Bank Policy Research.

Keane, M. P. 2010. "Structural vs. Atheoretic Approaches to Econometrics." *Journal of Econometrics* 156, no. 1: 3–20.

Keefer, Philip, Eric Neumayer, and Thomas Plümper. 2011. "Earthquake Propensity and the Politics of Mortality Prevention." *World Development* 39, no. 9: 1530–1541.

Keefer, Philip, and David Stasavage. 2002. "Checks and Balances, Private Information, and the Credibility of Monetary Commitments." *International Organization* 56, no. 4: 751–774.

Keele, Luke John. 2008. *Semiparametric Regression for the Social Sciences*. Chichester: Wiley.

Kennedy, Peter. 2008. *A Guide to Econometrics*. Malden: Blackwell Publishing.

King, Gary, James Honaker, Anne Joseph, and Kenneth Scheve. 2001. "Analyzing Incomplete Political Science Data: An Alternative Algorithm for Multiple Imputation." *American Political Science Association* 95, no. 1: 49–69.

King, Gary, Robert O. Keohane, and Sidney Verba. 1994. *Designing Social Inquiry: Scientific Inference in Qualitative Research*. Princeton: Princeton University Press.

King, Gary, and Langche Zeng. 2001a. "Explaining Rare Events in International Relations." *International Organization* 55, no. 3: 693–715.

King, Gary, and Langche Zeng. 2001b. "Logistic Regression in Rare Events Data." *Political Analysis* 9, no. 2: 137–163.

Kozma, Albert, and M. J. Stones. 1980. "The Measurement of Happiness: Development of the Memorial University of Newfoundland Scale of Happiness (MUNSH)." *Journal of Gerontology* 35, no. 6: 906–912.

Krolzig, Hans-Martin, and David F. Hendry. 2001. "Computer Automation of General-to-specific Model Selection Procedures." *Journal of Economic Dynamics and Control* 25, no. 6: 831–866.

Kuha, Jouni, and Jonathan Temple. 2003. "Covariate Measurement Error in Quadratic Regression." *International Statistical Review* 71, no. 1: 131–150.

Kuznets, Simon. 1955. "Economic Growth and Income Inequality." *American Economic Review* 45, no. 1: 1–28.

Kyung, Minjung, Jeff Gill, and George Casella. 2010. "Estimation in Dirichlet Random Effects Models." *The Annals of Statistics* 38, no. 2: 979–1009.

Langbein, Laura, and Stephen Knack. 2010. "The Worldwide Governance Indicators: Six, One, or None?" *Journal of Development Studies* 46, no. 2: 350–370.

Lassen, David Dreyer, and Søren Serritzlew. 2011. "Jurisdiction Size and Local Democracy: Evidence on Internal Political Efficacy from Large-scale Municipal Reform." *American Political Science Review* 105, no. 2: 238–258.

Lau, Lawrence J. 1986. "Functional Forms in Econometric Model Building." *Handbook of Econometrics* 3: 1515–1566.

Leamer, Edward E. 1978. *Specification Searches: Ad hoc Inference with Nonexperimental Data.* Chichester: Wiley.

Leamer, Edward E. 1983. "Let's Take the Con out of Econometrics." *American Economic Review* 73, no. 1: 31–43.

Leamer, Edward E. 1985. "Sensitivity Analyses Would Help." *American Economic Review* 75, no. 3: 308–313.

Lemons, John, Kristin Shrader-Frechette, and Carl Cranor. 1997. "The Precautionary Principle: Scientific Uncertainty and Type I and Type II Errors." *Foundations of Science* 2, no. 2: 207–236.

Leung, Siu Fai, and Shihti Yu. 1996. "On the Choice between Sample Selection and Two-part Models." *Journal of Econometrics* 72, no. 1: 197–229.

Levine, Ross, and David Renelt. 1992. "A Sensitivity Analysis of Cross-country Growth Regressions." *American Economic Review* 82, no. 4: 942–963.

Lewis, Brian N., and Jenny A. Cook. 1968. "Some Comments and Recommendations Concerning Inter-coder Reliability." *Psychological Reports* 22, no. 3c: 1213–1225.

Lipsmeyer, Christine S., and Ling Zhu. 2011. "Immigration, Globalization, and Unemployment Benefits in Developed EU States." *American Journal of Political Science* 55, no. 3: 647–664.

Lohr, Sharon. 2009. *Sampling: Design and Analysis.* Boston: Cengage Learning.

Lukes, Steven. 1974. *Power: A Radical View.* London: Macmillan.

Maddala, Gangadharrao S. 1998. "Recent Developments in Dynamic Econometric Modelling: A Personal Viewpoint." *Political Analysis* 7: 59–87.

Magnus, Jan R. 1999. "The Success of Econometrics." *De Economist* 147, no. 1: 55–71.

Manski, Charles F. 1990. "Nonparametric Bounds on Treatment Effects." *American Economic Review* 80, no. 2: 319–323.

Manski, Charles F. 1995. *Identification Problems in the Social Sciences.* Cambridge: Harvard University Press.

Martin, Cathie Jo, and Duane Swank. 2004. "Does the Organization of Capital Matter? Employers and Active Labor Market Policy at the National and Firm Levels." *American Political Science Review* 98, no. 4: 593–611.

Martin, Cathie Jo, and Duane Swank. 2008. "The political origins of coordinated capitalism: Business organizations, party systems, and state structure in the age of innocence." *American Political Science Review* 102, no. 2: 181–198.

McAleer, Michael. 1994. "Sherlock Holmes and the Search for Truth: A Diagnostic Tale." *Journal of Economic Surveys* 8, no. 4: 317–370.

Montgomery, J. M., and B. Nyhan. 2010. "Bayesian model averaging: Theoretical developments and practical applications." *Political Analysis* 18, no. 2: 245–270.

Morgan, Stephen L., and Jennifer J. Todd. 2008. "A Diagnostic Routine for the Detection of Consequential Heterogeneity of Causal Effects." *Sociological Methodology* 38, no. 1: 231–281.

Morgan, Stephen L., and Christopher Winship. 2015. *Counterfactuals and Causal Inference*, 2nd edn. Cambridge: Cambridge University Press.

Mukherjee, Bumba, and David Andrew Singer. 2010. "International Institutions and Domestic Compensation: The IMF and the Politics of Capital Account Liberalization." *American Journal of Political Science* 54, no. 1: 45–60.

Munck, Gerardo L., and Jay Verkuilen. 2002. "Conceptualizing and Measuring Democracy Evaluating Alternative Indices." *Comparative Political Studies* 35, no. 1: 5–34.

Neumayer, Eric. 2002. "Do Democracies Exhibit Stronger International Environmental Commitment? A Cross-country Analysis." *Journal of Peace Research* 39, no. 2: 139–164.

Neumayer, Eric, and Thomas Plümper. 2010. "Spatial Effects in Dyadic Data." *International Organization* 64, no. 1: 145–166.

Neumayer, Eric, and Thomas Plümper. 2011. "Foreign Terror on Americans." *Journal of Peace Research* 48, no. 1: 3–17.

Neumayer, Eric, and Thomas Plümper. 2012. "Conditional Spatial Policy Dependence: Theory and Model Specification." *Comparative Political Studies* 45, no. 7: 819–849.

Neumayer, Eric, and Thomas Plümper. 2016a. "W." *Political Science Research and Methods* 4, no. 1: 175–193.

Neumayer, Eric, and Thomas Plümper. 2016b. "Inequalities of Income and Inequalities of Longevity: A Cross-country Study." *American Journal of Public Health* 106, no. 1: 160–165.

Neumayer, Eric, Thomas Plümper, and Fabian Barthel. 2014. "The Political Economy of Natural Disaster Damage." *Global Environmental Change* 24: 8–19.

Neumayer, Eric, Thomas Plümper, and Mariaelisa Epifanio. 2014. "The 'Peer-effect' in Counterterrorist Policies." *International Organization* 68, no. 1: 211–234.

Nickell, S. 1981. Biases in Dynamic Models with Fixed Effects. *Econometrica* 49, no. 6: 1417–1426.

Nielsen, Richard A., Michael G. Findley, Zachary S. Davis, Tara Candland, and Daniel L. Nielson. 2011. "Foreign Aid Shocks as a Cause of Violent Armed Conflict." *American Journal of Political Science* 55, no. 2: 219–232.

Nordås, R., and C. Davenport. 2013. "Fight the Youth: Youth Bulges and State Repression." *American Journal of Political Science* 57, no. 4: 926–940.

Nordhaus, William D. 1975. "The Political Business Cycle." *Review of Economic Studies* 42, no. 2: 169–190.

Nosek, B. A., et al. 2015. "Estimating the Reproducibility of Psychological Science." *Science* 349, no. 6251: aac4716-1-aac4716-8.

Pan, Wei, and Kenneth A. Frank. 2003. "A Probability Index of the Robustness of a Causal Inference." *Journal of Educational and Behavioral Statistics* 28, no. 4: 315–337.

Peach, J. T., and J. L. Webb. 1983. "Randomly specified macroeconomic models: Some implications for model selection." *Journal of Economic Issues* 17, no. 3: 697–720.

Pearl, Judea. 2000. "Causal Inference without Counterfactuals: Comment." *Journal of the American Statistical Association* 94, no. 450: 428–431.

Pearl, Judea. 2015. "Detecting Latent Heterogeneity." *Sociological Methods and Research* (published online; forthcoming in print). doi: 10.1177/0049124115600597.

Pemstein, Daniel, Stephen A. Meserve, and James Melton. 2010. "Democratic Compromise: A Latent Variable Analysis of Ten Measures of Regime Type." *Political Analysis* 18, no. 4: 426–449.

Perkins, Richard, and Eric Neumayer. 2013. "The Ties that Bind: The Role of Migrants in the Uneven Geography of International Telephone Traffic." *Global Networks* 13, no. 1: 79–100.

Pesaran, M. Hashem, Davide Pettenuzzo, and Allan Timmermann. 2006. "Forecasting Time Series Subject to Multiple Structural Breaks." *The Review of Economic Studies* 73, no. 4: 1057–1084.

Pietryka, Matthew T., and Randall C. MacIntosh. 2013. "An Analysis of ANES Items and Their Use in the Construction of Political Knowledge Scales." *Political Analysis* 21, no. 4: 407–429.

Plümper, Thomas, and Eric Neumayer. 2009. "Famine Mortality, Rational Political Inactivity, and International Food Aid." *World Development* 37, no. 1: 50–61.

Plümper, Thomas, and Eric Neumayer. 2010a. "The Level of Democracy during Interregnum Periods: Recoding the Polity2 Score." *Political Analysis* 18, no. 2: 206–226.

Plümper, Thomas, and Eric Neumayer. 2010b. "Model Specification in the Analysis of Spatial Dependence." *European Journal of Political Research* 49, no. 3: 418–442.

Plümper, Thomas, and Eric Neumayer. 2013. "Health Spending, Out-of-pocket Contributions, and Mortality Rates." *Public Administration* 91, no. 2: 403–418.

Plümper, Thomas, Christina J. Schneider, and Vera E. Troeger. 2006. "The Politics of EU Eastern Enlargement: Evidence from a Heckman Selection Model." *British Journal of Political Science* 36, no. 1: 17–38.

Plümper, Thomas, and Richard Traunmüller. 2016. "The Sensitivity of Sensitivity Tests." Unpublished manuscript, Vienna and Frankfurt.

Plümper, Thomas, and Vera E. Troeger. 2007. "Efficient Estimation of Time-invariant and Rarely Changing Variables in Finite Sample Panel Analyses with Unit Fixed Effects." *Political Analysis* 15, no. 2: 124–139.

Plümper, Thomas, and Vera E. Troeger. 2011. "Fixed-effects Vector Decomposition: Properties, Reliability, and Instruments." *Political Analysis* 19, no. 2: 147–164.

Plümper, Thomas, and Vera E. Troeger. 2016. "Fixed Effects Models and Dynamic Model Misspecification." Unpublished manuscript, Warwick and Vienna.

Plümper, Thomas, Vera E. Troeger, and Philip Manow. 2005. "Panel Data Analysis in Comparative Politics: Linking Method to Theory." *European Journal of Political Research* 44, no. 2: 327–354.

Plümper, Thomas, Vera E. Troeger, and Hannes Winner. 2009. "Why is There no Race to the Bottom in Capital Taxation?" *International Studies Quarterly* 53, no. 3: 761–786.

Przeworski, Adam, M. Alvarez, J. A. Cheibub, and F. Limongi. 2000. *Democracy and Development: Political Institutions and Well-being in the World, 1950–1990.* Cambridge: Cambridge University Press.

Puhani, Patrick. 2000. "The Heckman Correction for Sample Selection and its Critique." *Journal of Economic Surveys* 14, no. 1: 53–68.

Quine, Willard van Orman. 1951. *Mathematical Logic.* Cambridge: Harvard University Press.

Rainey, C. 2014. "Arguing for a Negligible Effect." *American Journal of Political Science* 58, no. 4: 1083–1091.

Ravallion, Martin. 2012. "Fighting Poverty One Experiment at a Time: A Review of Abhijit Banerjee and Esther Duflo's Poor Economics: A Radical Rethinking of the Way to Fight Global Poverty." *Journal of Economic Literature* 50, no. 1: 103–114.

Rivera-Batiz, F. L. 1999. "Undocumented Workers in the Labor Market: An Analysis of the Earnings of Legal and Illegal Mexican Immigrants in the United States." *Journal of Population Economics* 12, no. 1: 91–116.

Rodrik, Dani. 1996. "Understanding Economic Policy Reform." *Journal of Economic Literature* 34, no. 1: 9–41.

Rosenbaum, Paul R. 1991. "A Characterization of Optimal Designs for Observational Studies." *Journal of the Royal Statistical Society, Series B* 53, no. 3: 597–610.

Rosenbaum, Paul R. 2002. *Observational Studies.* New York: Springer.

Rosenbaum, Paul R. 2010. *Design of Observational Studies.* New York: Springer.

Royston, Patrick, and Douglas G. Altman. 1994. "Regression using Fractional Polynomials of Continuous Covariates: Parsimonious Parametric Modelling." *Applied Statistics* 43, no. 3: 429–467.

Rubin, Donald B. 1974. "Estimating Causal Effects of Treatments in Randomized and Nonrandomized Studies." *Journal of Educational Psychology* 66, no. 5: 688.

Rubin, Donald B. 1976. "Inference and Missing Data." *Biometrika* 63, no. 3: 581–592.

Rubin, Donald B. 2008. "For Objective Causal Inference, Design Trumps Analysis." *The Annals of Applied Statistics* 2, no. 3: 808–840.

Ruggeri, Andrea, Theodora-Ismene Gizelis, and Han Dorussen. 2011. "Events Data as Bismarck's Sausages? Intercoder Reliability, Coders' Selection, and Data Quality." *International Interactions* 37, no. 3: 340–361.

Ryder, Norman B. 1964. "Notes on the Concept of a Population." *American Journal of Sociology* 69, no. 5: 447–463.

Sala-i-Martin, Xavier X. 1997. "I just ran Two Million Regressions." *American Economic Review* 82, no. 2: 178–183.

Sala-i-Martin, Xavier X., Gernot Doppelhofer, and Ronald I. Miller. 2004. "Determinants of Long-Term Growth: A Bayesian Averaging of Classical Estimates (BACE) Approach." *American Economic Review* 94, no. 4: 813–835.

Salganik, Matthew J., and Douglas D. Heckathorn. 2004. "Sampling and Estimation in Hidden Populations Using Respondent-driven Sampling." *Sociological Methodology* 34, no. 1: 193–240.

Sartori, Anne E. 2003. "An Estimator for Some Binary-Outcome Selection Models without Exclusion Restrictions." *Political Analysis* 11, no. 2: 111–138.

Schafer, Joseph L., and John W. Graham. 2002. "Missing Data: Our View of the State of the Art." *Psychological Methods* 7, no. 2: 147–177.

Scheve, Kenneth, and Matthew J. Slaughter. 2004. "Economic Insecurity and the Globalization of Production." *American Journal of Political Science* 48, no. 4: 662–674.

Schindler, Kati, and Tilman Brück. 2011. *The Effects of Conflict on Fertility in Rwanda.* Discussion paper no. 1143. German Institute for Economic Research.

Schleiter, Petra, and Edward Morgan-Jones. 2009. "Constitutional Power and Competing Risks: Monarchs, Presidents, Prime Ministers, and the Termination of East and West European Cabinets." *American Political Science Review* 103, no. 3: 496–512.

Schmitt, Carina. 2016. "Panel Data Analysis and Partisan Variables: How Periodization Does Influence Partisan Effects." *Journal of European Public Policy* 23, no. 10: 1442–1459.

Sekhon, Jasjeet S. 2007. *Alternative Balance Metrics for Bias Reduction in Matching Methods for Causal Inference.* Survey Research Center, University of California, Berkeley.

Sekhon, Jasjeet S. 2009. "Opiates for the Matches: Matching Methods for Causal Inference." *Annual Review of Political Science* 12: 487–508.

Shadish, William R., Thomas D. Cook, and Donald Thomas Campbell. 2002. *Experimental and Quasi-experimental Designs for Generalized Causal Inference.* Belmont: Wadsworth Cengage Learning.

Sieberer, Ulrich. 2011. "The Institutional Power of Western European Parliaments: A Multidimensional Analysis." *West European Politics* 34, no. 4: 731–754.

Sigelman, Lee, and Langche Zeng. 1999. "Analyzing Censored and Sample-selected Data with Tobit and Heckit models." *Political Analysis* 8, no. 2: 167–182.

Simmons, J. P., L. D. Nelson, and U. Simonsohn. 2011. "False-Positive Psychology: Undisclosed Flexibility in Data Collection and Analysis

Allows Presenting Anything as Significant." *Psychological Science* 22, no. 11: 1359–1366.

Solow, R. M. 1956. "A Contribution to the Theory of Economic Growth." *The Quarterly Journal of Economics* 70, no. 1: 65–94.

Steenbergen, Marco, and Bradford Jones. 2002. "Modeling Multilevel Data Structures." *American Journal of Political Science* 46: 218–237.

Stegmüller, Daniel. 2011. "Apples and Oranges? The Problem of Equivalence in Comparative Research." *Political Analysis* 19: 471–487.

Stevens, Stanley Smith. 1946. "On the Theory of Scales of Measurement." *Science* 103: 677–680.

Strijbis, Oliver. 2013. "Prototypical Weighting toward a Solution for Macrosociological Comparisons of Fuzzy Cases." *Sociological Methods and Research* 42, no. 4: 458–482.

Swamy, Paravastu A. V. B. 1970. "Efficient Inference in a Random Coefficient Regression Model." *Econometrica* 38, no. 2: 311–323.

Temple, Jonathan R. W. 1998. "Robustness Tests of the Augmented Solow Model." *Journal of Applied Econometrics* 13, no. 4: 361–375.

Thomas, Melissa A. 2010. "What Do the Worldwide Governance Indicators Measure?" *European Journal of Development Research* 22, no. 1: 31–54.

Tobler, Waldo R. 1970. "A Computer Movie Simulating Urban Growth in the Detroit Region." *Economic Geography* 46: 234–240.

Treier, Shawn, and Simon Jackman. 2008. "Democracy as a Latent Variable." *American Journal of Political Science* 52, no. 1: 201–217.

Tsebelis, George. 1995. "Decision Making in Political Systems: Veto Players in Presidentialism, Parliamentarism, Multicameralism and Multipartyism." *British Journal of Political Science* 25, no. 3: 289–325.

Tsebelis, George. 1999. "Veto Players and Law Production in Parliamentary Democracies: An Empirical Analysis." *American Political Science Review* 93, no. 3: 591–608.

Tucker, Joshua A., Alexander C. Pacek, and Adam J. Berinsky. 2002. "Transitional Winners and Losers: Attitudes toward EU Membership in Post-Communist Countries." *American Journal of Political Science* 46, no. 3: 557–571.

Valliant, Richard, Alan H. Dorfman, and Richard M. Royall. 2000. *Finite Population Sampling and Inference: A Prediction Approach.* Chichester: Wiley.

Vanhanen, Tatu. 2000. "A New Dataset for Measuring Democracy, 1810–1998." *Journal of Peace Research* 37, no. 2: 251–265.

Vella, Francis. 1998. "Estimating Models with Sample Selection Bias: A Survey." *Journal of Human Resources* 33, no. 1: 127–169.

Vreeland, James Raymond. 2008. "The Effect of Political Regime on Civil War." *Journal of Conflict Resolution* 52, no. 3: 401–425.

Wansbeek, Tom, and Erik Meijer. 2000. *Measurement Error and Latent Variables in Econometrics*. Amsterdam: Elsevier.

Ward, J. H., Jr. 1963. "Hierarchical Grouping to Optimize an Objective Function." *Journal of the American Statistical Association* 58: 236–244.

Watters, John K., and Patrick Biernacki. 1989. "Targeted Sampling: Options for the Study of Hidden Populations." *Social Problems* 36, no. 4: 416–430.

Western, Bruce. 1998. "Causal Heterogeneity in Comparative Research: A Bayesian Hierarchical Modelling Approach." *American Journal of Political Science* 42, no. 4: 1233.

Wilson, Sven E., and Daniel M. Butler. 2007. "A Lot More to Do: The Sensitivity of Time-series Cross-section Analyses to Simple Alternative Specifications." *Political Analysis* 15, no. 2: 101–123.

Winship, Christopher, and Stephen L. Morgan. 1999. "The Estimation of Causal Effects from Observational Data." *Annual Review of Sociology* 25: 659–706.

Wooldridge, Jeffrey M. 2000. *Introductory Econometrics: A Modern Approach*, 1st edn. Cincinnati: South-Western Educational Publishing.

Wooldridge, Jeffrey M. 2010. *Econometric Analysis of Cross Section and Panel Data*. Cambridge: MIT Press.

Ziliak, S. T., and D. N. McCloskey. 2008. *The Cult of Statistical Significance: How the Standard Error Costs us Jobs, Justice, and Lives*. Ann Arbor: University of Michigan Press.

Index